Europe's Last Frontier?

Europe's Last Frontier?
Belarus, Moldova, and Ukraine between Russia and the European Union

Edited by
Oliver Schmidtke and
Serhy Yekelchyk

palgrave
macmillan

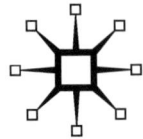
First published in 2008 by
PALGRAVE MACMILLAN™
175 Fifth Avenue, New York, N.Y. 10010 and
Houndmills, Basingstoke, Hampshire, England RG21 6XS.
Companies and representatives throughout the world.

PALGRAVE MACMILLAN is the global academic imprint of the Palgrave Macmillan division of St. Martin's Press, LLC and of Palgrave Macmillan Ltd. Macmillan® is a registered trademark in the United States, United Kingdom and other countries. Palgrave is a registered trademark in the European Union and other countries.

ISBN-13: 978-0-230-60372-1
ISBN-10: 0-230-60372-6

Library of Congress Cataloging-in-Publication Data

Europe's last frontier? : Belarus, Moldova, and Ukraine between Russia and the European Union / edited by Oliver Schmidtke and Serhy Yekelchyk.
    p. cm.
    Includes bibliographical references and index.
    ISBN 0-230-60372-6 (alk. paper)
    1. Belarus—Foreign relations—1991- 2. Moldova—Foreign relations—1991- 3. Ukraine—Foreign relations—1991- 4. European Union—Europe, Eastern. 5. Russia (Federation)—Foreign relations. I. Schmidtke, Oliver. II. Yekelchyk, Serhy.
DK507.8175.E95 2008
341.242'20947—dc22   2007023316

A catalogue record of the book is available from the British Library.

Design by Scribe Inc.

First edition: January 2008

10 9 8 7 6 5 4 3 2 1

Permissions
Yurii Andrukhovych's poem "Atlas. Medytatsii" courtesy *Krytyka*, nos. 1–2 (2006). The English translation is by Hiroaki Kuromiya.

Transferred to Digital Printing 2009

Contents

Acknowledgments   vii

Contributors   ix

Introduction   1
Oliver Schmidtke and Serhy Yekelchyk

1   Out of Russia's Long Shadow: The Making of
        Modern Ukraine, Belarus, and Moldova   9
        Serhy Yekelchyk

2   From Soviet Ukraine to the Orange
        Revolution: European Security Relations
        and the Ukrainian Identity   31
        Natalie Mychajlyszyn

3   Belarus in the Lukashenka Era: National
        Identity and Relations with Russia   55
        Per Anders Rudling

4   Post-Soviet Moldova's National
        Identity and Foreign Policy   79
        Steven D. Roper

5   The Donbas—The Last Frontier of Europe?   97
        Hiroaki Kuromiya

6   In the Minority in Moldova:
        (Dis)Empowerment through
        Territorial Conflict   115
        Hülya Demirdirek

7   The Promise of Europe: Moldova and
        the Process of Europeanization   133
        *Oliver Schmidtke and
        Constantin Chira-Pascanut*

8   Taking Ukraine Seriously:
           Western and Russian Responses
           to the Orange Revolution   157
           Derek Fraser

9   The Failed Revolution: Reflections on
           the 2006 Elections in Belarus   175
           David R. Marples

10   EU-Russia Relations and the
           Repercussions on the "In-Betweens"   195
           Stefan Gänzle

Selected Bibliography   231
Index   245

Acknowledgments

This book is the result of an eponymous conference, held at the University of Victoria on March 3–4, 2006. Most chapters in their present form differ substantially from the original papers presented there, yet the conference and the volume share both the conception and the list of participants. With this in view, we would like to begin by thanking the entities that made the conference possible in the first place. The University of Victoria EU Initiative, funded by the European Commission through the Centers of Excellence program, was the single largest contributor. We have also received generous financial support from the Office of the Vice-President Academic, the Office of the Vice-President Research, the Faculty of Humanities, the Department of Germanic and Slavic Studies, the Department of History, and the World History Caucus—all at the University of Victoria.

As editors, it has been our great pleasure to work with an unusually conscientious and well-organized group of contributors, whose ability to submit great texts on time and revise them speedily was beyond the norm for today's academia. But neither the volume nor the conference would have been possible without the dedicated support staff at the European Studies Program. Dr. Gabriela Chira, assistant to the director, handled the most difficult logistical problems efficiently and cheerfully. Beate Schmidtke dispensed invaluable advice during the preparation of the budget and also counseled us on financial and reporting issues. Constantin and Monaliza Chira-Pascanut helped greatly with the conference; Constantin also assisted with bibliographic research during the preparation of this collection. Ole J. Heggen, a cartographer with the Department of Geography, expertly designed the map of Belarus, Moldova, and Ukraine. Katherine Gilks was extremely helpful in the preparation of the bibliography and in finding answers to the many puzzles that surfaced when we started bringing the articles together. But it was our good fortune in securing the assistance of Jillian G. Shoichet that made possible the publication of this volume only one and a half years after the conference. A doctoral student at UVic and a freelance copy-editor working on contracts for many academic publishers, Jillian did an outstanding job joining the chapters together logically, stylistically, and grammatically. She has set for others at UVic working on this project, the editors included, a formidable example of efficiency and professionalism. We particularly appreciate Jillian's help during the last month before the text's submission to the publisher, when both of us were out of the country and relied heavily on her organizational skills.

At Palgrave Macmillan USA, we would like to thank Toby Wahl for taking an early interest in this manuscript and offering us a contract, and Kate Ankofski for answering a multitude of minute questions and shepherding the manuscript through copy-editing and production stages. We appreciate the time and effort of the anonymous reviewer, who looked at our material twice and made valuable suggestions.

We also appreciate the time and effort of all our colleagues at the University of Victoria who attended the sessions and commented on the presentations, but especially of Greg Blue, who read all the papers in advance, attended all sessions, and made numerous helpful suggestions for improvements.

Last but not least, we are grateful to our families for tolerating our hectic lifestyles and long workdays, which make conferences and collections happen. Oliver is grateful to Beate, Sophie, and Alissa for their patience with his irregular working hours, and Serhy thanks Olga and Yulia for putting up with him for far too long.

Contributors

Constantin Chira-Pascanut is a PhD candidate at the University of Victoria. He holds an MA in history from the University of Victoria, as well as a BA in history and a degree in law. He completed an internship at the European Commission in Brussels in 2002. His research interests include historical perspectives of European integration, the EU Neighbourhood Policy, the enlargement of the European Union, EU immigration policy, and European law.

Hülya Demirdirek is an assistant professor of anthropology at the University of Victoria. Recently she has researched the flow of sexual and domestic labor between Moldova and Turkey; she coedited a special issue of *Focaal—European Journal of Anthropology*, "Sexual Encounters, Migration and Desire in Post-socialist Context(s)." Her main research interests include aspects of postsocialist transformation, in particular ethnicity and nationalism, history-memory, and transnationalism.

Derek Fraser is a former ambassador of Canada to Kiev, Athens, and Budapest. He is now a senior research associate at the Centre for Global Studies at the University of Victoria, where he has specialized in Ukraine and "failed states." He has supported democratization in Ukraine, contributed to and organized academic and foreign policy conferences, and commented in the media.

Stefan Gänzle is a visiting assistant professor (DAAD) at the Institute for European Studies and the Department of Political Science at the University of British Columbia. His research interests include European integration, EU foreign policy, and the EU's impact on third countries. He is the editor (with Allen Sens) of *The Changing Politics of European Security: Europe Alone?* (2007).

Hiroaki Kuromiya is a professor of history at Indiana University (Bloomington) and the author of *Stalin: Profiles in Power* (2005), *Freedom and Terror in the Donbas: A Ukrainian-Russian Borderland, 1870s–1990s* (1998), and other works.

David R. Marples is a professor in the Department of History and Classics at the University of Alberta. He is the author of books on Belarus, contemporary Ukraine, and the consequences of the Chernobyl disaster. His latest book, *Heroes and Villains: Constructing National History in Contemporary Ukraine*, will be published by Central European University Press (2007).

Natalie Mychajlyszyn is director of professional training and development at the Norman Paterson School of International Affairs. Her research interests and areas of publication include international relations in the post-Soviet region and Ukrainian foreign policy, European security institutions, civil-military relations, conflict prevention and resolution, and nationalism and ethnic politics.

Steven D. Roper is a visiting associate professor at the School of Foreign Service in Qatar at Georgetown University and an associate professor of political science at Eastern Illinois University. He is the author of *Romania: The Unfinished Revolution* and co-author of *Designing Criminal Tribunals: Sovereignty and International Concerns in the Protection of Human Rights*. He is currently completing a coedited volume entitled *The Effect of Party and Campaign Finance on Post-Communist Party Development*.

Per Anders Rudling is a doctoral candidate in history at the University of Alberta. His dissertation focuses on the construction of a Belarusian national identity. Research interests include nationalism, diaspora, and identity politics. Educated in Uppsala and San Diego, he teaches history and is the editor of *Past Imperfect* (University of Alberta).

Oliver Schmidtke is an associate professor in the Department of Political Science and the Department of History at the University of Victoria, where he also holds a Jean Monnet Chair in European History and Politics.

Serhy Yekelchyk is an associate professor of Slavic studies and history and chair of the Department of Germanic and Slavic Studies at the University of Victoria. His recent books include *Stalin's Empire of Memory: Russian-Ukrainian Relations in the Soviet Historical Imagination* (2004) and *Ukraine: Birth of a Modern Nation* (2007).

Map of Belarus, Moldova, and Ukraine

Introduction

Oliver Schmidtke and Serhy Yekelchyk

Since the collapse of Communism, the European continent has witnessed rapidly shifting political boundaries and a profound geopolitical transformation in the former Soviet Union's sphere of influence. For the countries in Central and Eastern Europe, the division of the continent at the end of the Cold War ushered in an often dramatic reshaping of their political and national identity. In political debates, this reorientation in the post-Communist area has often been framed as the choice between adopting a pro-Western course and staying loyal to the traditional alliance with Russia. One critical expression of these competing loyalties has been the search for a new collective security system in Europe and the gradual expansion of NATO as a Western military alliance toward Russia's borders. Yet the tension between the Communist legacy and the historical attachment to Russia on the one hand and the growing attraction of Western Europe and the EU on the other has also shaped the path to domestic socio-political reform in formerly Communist countries. Western ideas and institutions of liberal democracy and market economy have become major vehicles, promoting and directing the course of transformation. They have provided a blueprint for modernization and change.

The European Union's impressive eastward enlargement has shaken the traditional political and cultural notions of "Europe." With the accession of the Czech Republic, Estonia, Hungary, Latvia, Lithuania, Poland, and Slovakia in 2004, and that of Bulgaria and Romania in 2007, the EU's eastern neighbors are now Russia, Belarus, Ukraine, and Moldova—none of which is likely to join the EU any time soon. With the Cold War division of Europe finally undone, a new fault line has appeared much farther to the east of where the Iron Curtain used to be. Countries previously included in the concept of "Eastern Europe" now prefer to identify their location as Central or East-Central Europe. Given the recent geopolitical changes, it is not surprising how contested the East-West geographical designation is. It creates new symbolic boundaries and, with it, forms of inclusion and exclusion. This dividing line is disputed and invested with various meanings: it can refer to the wide gap among levels of prosperity in Western and Eastern Europe, forms of membership in international organizations, the performance of democracy, or, as put dramatically by Samuel Huntington, a "Velvet Curtain of cultural difference" replacing the Iron Curtain as the most significant dividing line in Europe. Membership in the European Union is only one criterion, albeit an important one, employed in the construction of a new political and cultural divide.

A new "Eastern Europe" seems to have shrunk to a small group of countries, even though some of them are geographically very large—Russia, Ukraine, Belarus, and Moldova. Of these four, Russia has not expressed interest in joining the EU, but the three other states that remain torn between it and the EU still struggle to find their place in the new Europe. Ukraine, Belarus, and Moldova have much in common, but their trajectories increasingly diverge. The Orange Revolution in 2004 thrust Ukraine to the front pages of the world press and transformed it into a genuine democracy, although the new president's pro-Western orientation is now balanced by the pro-Russian tendencies of the anti-Orange government coalition. Belarus is labeled by the United States and the EU as "Europe's last dictatorship." And while Moldova is the only state in Europe ruled by the Communist Party, this republic increasingly orients itself toward the West.

Now torn in loyalty and in the vision of their political future between Russia and the EU, Belarus, Moldova, and Ukraine until recently firmly belonged to Russia's sphere of influence, a reality that the West did not question. The three former Soviet republics were also ruled by regimes with questionable democratic credentials. The Orange Revolution in Ukraine in 2004 has challenged this legacy in the largest of the three states by bringing to power the reformist, pro-Western presidential candidate, although in 2006, his pro-Russian opponent became prime minister, symbolizing the uncertainty of Ukraine's strategic choice. A recent westward turn in Moldova's geopolitical orientation was more gradual, and Belarus remains firmly within Russia's orbit. But the "return to Europe" now discussed freely by Ukrainian and Moldovan commentators (probably to the envy of their Belarusian colleagues, who do not exactly enjoy freedom of speech) will involve more than political changes at the top. In all three states, ethnic Russians constitute the largest national minority, and a significant share of the non-Russian population uses Russian as the language of convenience. (In Moldova, ethnic Ukrainians are technically more numerous, but most of them speak Russian and identify as part of a single East Slavic minority that sees Russia as its chief protector.) Moreover, the modern notion of what it means to be a Belarusian, a Moldovan, or a Ukrainian has been shaped by these lands' historical interaction with the Russian Empire and the Soviet Union.

Other components of the Soviet legacy in the region include the importance of economic ties with Russia (often underwritten by energy dependency on Russian oil and gas), a shared post-Communist political culture, and compactly settled national minorities pushing for regional autonomy. In other words, historical legacy is no less important than present-day political realities in determining how these states will redefine their domestic and external identity and whether these states will one day become members of a united Europe. The Soviet legacy contributes to a volatile political system and deep political cleavages in the region, which are often articulated in terms of an allegiance to Russia or Western Europe, respectively.

Domestically and internationally, Europe's "last frontier" is subject to a power struggle between the increasingly assertive Russia and the European Union. While the former can point to the history it shared with the three states throughout much of the twentieth century, the latter has been successful in initiating a process of "Europeanization" on its eastern frontier, setting benchmarks for legal-political reforms and promising lucrative access to the European markets and financial assistance from the EU. Providing a political vision for the future of these post-Communist countries, the EU and the "West" present themselves as an attractive model for political and socio-economic development with the promises of liberal democracy and prosperity. In the same vein, the EU and its member states have become increasingly more attractive economic partners, providing opportunities to challenge dependency on economic relations with Russia.

This collection brings together historians specializing in Belarus, Moldova, and Ukraine with political scientists who work on the EU's enlargement and Russia's policy toward former Soviet republics. In the ten chapters that follow, the contributors analyze the three states' historical relationships with Russia, the resulting peculiarities of their political and cultural development, the potential for ethnic strife, and the prospects for political change and possible future integration in a united Europe. The transformation of these former Soviet republics is examined against the backdrop of a changing geopolitical reality in Europe: While the border between the West and the East was firmly entrenched in the Cold War, it became a matter of political and symbolic redefinition after 1989 and is now a major reference in these countries' attempts to shape their post-Soviet future.

The collection provides an up-to-date analysis of historical development and recent events in Belarus, Moldova, and Ukraine, as well as the EU's and Russia's policies in the region. On a more theoretical level, the collection advances our understanding of identity-shaping processes, the persistence and transformation of nationalism, the dynamics of imperial disintegration and nation-building processes in the post-Soviet political space, and international political influences as a factor in post-Communist transition. The authors of this volume seek to understand and conceptualize how the new geopolitical reality in Europe, the rivalry between Russia and the West, has shaped the domestic transformation of the three post-Communist countries under investigation. At the same time, they are interested in how these competing loyalties are shaped by nationally specific historical legacies, narratives of national identities, and contemporary political struggles.

There is no shortage of works analyzing individual Eastern European countries' relations with the West and prospects for joining the EU. What sets this collection apart, however, is its emphasis on Russia as the third—and often decisive—component in this geopolitical equation, and on the lasting legacy of the Russian and Soviet rule in the region as this component's historical dimension. In one way or another, all contributions to this volume address the complex interplay between the historical legacy, changing geopolitical reality, and domestic political transformations in Belarus, Ukraine, and Moldova.

In his introductory chapter, Serhy Yekelchyk surveys the history of Belarus, Moldova, and Ukraine before their emergence as independent states in 1991, focusing on nation building within modern multinational empires. The author argues that the widely accepted models of nationalism's progression from cultural interest to mass political mobilization to independence ignore the imperial context; the most impressive achievements of nation building in the three countries were actually consequences of state intervention—particularly Soviet affirmative-action policies during the interwar period. As this chapter traces the three nations' historical relations with Russia, it introduces the reader to the main junctures of Belarusian, Moldovan, and Ukrainian histories, and to legacies of history as reflected in the region's permeable national identities.

Natalie Mychajlyszyn's chapter examines the European dimension of Ukraine's post-Soviet identity. It re-examines the process by which the idea of "Europe" has come to be incorporated into the idea of "Ukraine," and Ukraine's fluctuations through the presidential administrations of Leonid Kravchuk, Leonid Kuchma, and Viktor Yushchenko. The author achieves her purpose by considering Ukraine's relations with Europe's leading institutions—the OSCE, NATO, and the European Union—consistent with the argument that a state's identity is influenced by interactions with institutions that are themselves manifestations of a particular identity and set of values. The chapter highlights the most fundamental element of Ukraine's post-Soviet identity where Europe is concerned: security. Indeed, Ukraine's relationship with the European security institutions is representative of the extent to which its identity has changed—from that of an adversary of Europe to that of a security partner.

Per A. Rudling argues that Belarus is the country with the weakest national identity in Europe. Torn between the long-hegemonic Polish and Russian cultures and languages, Belarus did not develop a modern Belarusian identity until the end of the nineteenth century. Dominance by far stronger neighbors contributed to the country's weak civil society, still in its infancy at the time of President Lukashenka's ascent to power. Since 1994, the civil society has been under siege as Lukashenka has established an increasingly authoritarian political system. Belarusian neo-authoritarianism maintains symbolic attributes of the Belarusian Soviet Socialist Republic, while its political fabric is a new phenomenon: a mix of statism, nostalgia, and authoritarianism based upon a national identification with the legacy of the "Soviet people." The chapter stresses the link between denationalization and the present-day authoritarianism in Belarus.

As Steven Roper demonstrates in his chapter on post-Soviet Moldova, the alignment of Moldovan foreign policy toward European institutions has occurred as Moldovan identity has evolved over the past decade. Due to Russia's role in the ongoing crisis in Transnistria and westward reorientation of Moldovan trade, there has been an important change in the manner in which Moldovans view themselves and Europe. Ironically, this change in policy and attitude has occurred at a time when the Moldovan Communist Party controls all government institutions. Under the leadership of President Voronin, the country increased diplomatic and economic links with the EU and EU member states, which ultimately resulted in the signing of the EU-Moldova Action Plan in February 2005.

Hiroaki Kuromiya focuses on the Donbas, Ukraine's eastern industrial region, where Russian culture remains predominant, and nostalgia for Soviet times runs high. The Orange Revolution elevated the Donbas to international notoriety as the alleged bulwark of reaction, where massive electoral fraud was engineered by the presidential candidate Viktor Yanukovych, the province's former governor. Yet the Donbas' identity is more complex. Historically situated in the "wild field," the Donbas functioned as a frontier region, an "exit" for people of many nationalities who sought freedom. It is often portrayed as the last frontier of cultural "Europe" and the region least amenable to European civilization and democracy. Paradoxically, however, Kuromiya argues that the Donbas may have the potential to break through narrowly nationalistic, regionalist, or pro-Russia politics to push Ukraine decisively toward Europe.

Focusing on a different aspect of redefined forms of nationalism in post-Communist Eastern Europe, Hülya Demirdirek examines the status of minorities in the Republic of Moldova during and after Soviet rule. In her interpretation, the legacy of Soviet rule lingers on and, with its legacy of strategically nurturing ethno-nationalist movements, shapes the role of the ethnic minority in the newly formed Republic of Moldova. Comparing the formation of Gagauzia and Transnistria as autonomous (if not state-like) regions, Demirdirek sheds light on how ethnic-territorial conflicts reflect historically deeply enshrined perceptions of ethnic consciousness, forms of social memory, and structures of political power. Of critical importance in Demirdirek's interpretation are the heritage of the Soviet (ethnic) classification system and the persistence of local elites from the Soviet era. These minorities then use images of the competing loyalties between Russia and the West to boost their political cause against the backdrop of post-Communist Moldovan nationalism. The conflict between the "East" and the "West" becomes a strategic resource and a reference point in redefining nationalism and the claims of ethnic-territorial minorities.

Oliver Schmidtke and Constantin Chira-Pascanut look at the influence of the "West" in Moldova from the perspective of the European

Union: They analyze the process of Europeanization of this eastern frontier of the European Union and the growing influence of the EU as a driving force in promoting political and economic reforms. They show that, with its European Neighbourhood Policy and incentives for compliance with EU principles of governance, the EU as a soft power has gradually extended its influence in the Central and Eastern European states. This process is illustrated with reference to Moldova and the recent decision of its Communist leadership to seek close collaboration with the EU at the expense of its formerly very strong partnership with Russia. While there is no realistic prospect of full membership in the EU for this country at the moment, the "promise of Europe" has shaped the political agenda domestically and internationally. The case of Moldova illustrates how the "West" is present as an ideological and material force, providing critical support for a certain agenda of political and market reform.

Ukraine likewise needs the EU's political and financial support because this country's strategic choice between the East and the West is no longer as certain as it had appeared immediately after the Orange Revolution. Ambassador Derek Fraser argues that Ukraine has a long way to go before becoming a stable democracy with a prosperous market economy. It is held back by its history and the obstruction of Russia, which seeks to recover its power and to block the eastward expansion of the EU and NATO. Analyzing the achievements and challenges of the Orange Revolution, Fraser points to the critical importance of Ukraine's relationship with Russia—an interpretation confirmed by the events of the first postrevolutionary years. In his view, the West needs to reconsider its approach toward Ukraine by showing more patience, developing more diplomatic flexibility, and devoting greater resources to the transformation of the country. In the end, the relationship between Russia and the West will be of decisive importance in determining Ukraine's political course. With this in mind, the EU—rather than NATO, which is still widely perceived as anti-Russian—should lead the way among the Western organizations in working closely with Ukraine.

Unlike Moldova and Ukraine, Belarus has not embarked on a pro-Western course. David R. Marples analyzes why Belarus has failed to follow the path of neighboring states, away from Moscow's sphere of interest and toward democratization. His focus is on the domestic debate in this country and its resistance to pro-Western ideas. On the surface, the 2006 presidential election seems to have cemented the power of President Lukashenka. Yet Marples shows how this grip on power is far more fragile, considering the role of the united opposition and tendencies in civil society. Beyond the domestic debate and power struggle, he illustrates the considerable influence that Russia and, in a far more limited way, Western European countries have on the Lukashenka regime. The economic stability of the country, one of the key factors in Lukashenka's electoral success, is highly dependent on the development of the Russia-Belarus Union and the attitude of the Putin government toward Belarus. In terms of popular support, the Belarusian population, torn between the open invitation to join the Russian federation and the distant prospect of EU membership, seems to support the country's independent status.

In his longer, concluding chapter, Stefan Gänzle systematically addresses the question raised by most of the collection's authors: He analyzes how the evolution of EU-Russian relations has impacted the three-country region. Gänzle discusses Russia's policies toward its "near abroad" and demonstrates how the EU has gradually moved away from treating the former Soviet states as a bloc and, most notably with its Partnership and Cooperation Agreements and Neighbourhood Policy, has developed individual strategies for all countries. The move away from an uncritical "Russia first" approach and toward the EU's strategic interests in the region has created some tension in the EU's relations with Russia. Gänzle argues that the EU's influence on the three countries under investigation depends on whether an increasingly alarmed Russia continues to perceive the EU as a menace to its own authority in the region.

Out of Russia's Long Shadow: The Making of Modern Ukraine, Belarus, and Moldova

Serhy Yekelchyk

Ukraine, Belarus, and Moldova are among the world's youngest states, having claimed their independence in the wake of the Soviet collapse in 1991. The peoples that gave their name to these polities have histories just as ancient and epic as those of other European nations, yet they lack a continuous state tradition. When modern nation-states developed in Europe during the nineteenth century, Ukrainians, Belarusians, and Moldovans lived in the corner of this continent still ruled by multinational dynastic empires: the Ottoman, the Russian, and the Austrian. Because of prolonged foreign domination, the three peoples no longer retained their indigenous political institutions, ruling elites, or native literary traditions. But in the age of nationalism, beginning in the late eighteenth century, patriotic intellectuals all over Eastern Europe began reinventing their nationalities based on the new notions of popular sovereignty and "nation" as a cultural community rooted in peasant culture.

The prominent Czech scholar Miroslav Hroch concluded in his study of Europe's non-dominant ethnic groups that these nationalities usually undergo three consecutive stages in their national movement: initial academic interest in the nation's history and culture; elite creation and propagation of modern high culture; and the national elite's political mobilization of society on a mass level.[1] While the general trends in the Ukrainian, Belarusian, and Moldovan national movements correspond to this scheme, the policies of their imperial masters, or regional geopolitical factors (external to Hroch's sociological portrait of the national movement), frequently threaten to skew this model beyond recognition.[2]

The three-phase model is also teleological in that it assumes a natural progression of national movements, from cultural interest to mass political mobilization—and by implication, to victory over imperial oppressors. Yet the Ukrainian, Belarusian, and Moldovan historical experience demonstrates that it was imperial collapse that provoked the popular movement toward sovereignty and not the other way around. The collapse of multinational empires in Eastern Europe at the end of World War I and the disintegration of the Soviet Union in 1991 provided the nationalities with two chances to obtain independent statehood, but these geopolitical shifts were largely not of their making. These two occasions were only the most recent examples of decisive external influences in the history of an Eastern European borderland that for centuries had seen its fortunes shaped by conflicts between the great powers of the day.

In addition, the most impressive achievements of nation building in Ukraine, Belarus, and Moldova were not natural outcomes of local national movements, but consequences of state intervention—particularly Soviet nationalizing policies during the interwar period. One scholar even proposes to view this period when a state uses its power to complete nation building as a fourth phase to complement Hroch's three initial ones.[3] Finally, present-day students of nationalism are wary of seeing nation building as a process with clear start and end dates, and indeed, the three independent republics that emerged after the USSR's dissolution demonstrate that independence was only a starting point for new debates about national identity and nation-building programs. (In the Belarusian case, one can also speak of "denationalization" after independence.[4]) At the start of the new millennium, national identity issues in the three countries are inseparable from foreign policy issues, particularly in defining the countries' place between the expanding European Union (EU) and Russia. But the larger point is that identity and geopolitics have always been intertwined in this part of Europe, as elsewhere, even before the modern idea of nationhood developed.

Imperial Rule and Nation Building in a Borderland

Ukrainian and Belarusian are East Slavic languages closely related to the third language of this subgroup, Russian. This cultural affinity to the dominant nationality of the Russian Empire and the Soviet Union in modern times has been a mixed blessing for the Ukrainians and Belarusians. As individuals, they were best positioned to make careers by passing themselves off as Russians, but as ethnic communities, they were the easiest targets for assimilation. For modern nationalists, sharing historical origins with the Russians also meant the need to rewrite their national histories, for by the time nineteenth-century patriotic intellectuals envisioned nations based on peasant cultures, the Russian imperial narrative had already claimed many glorious pages of the common East Slavic past.

This was particularly true of Kyivan Rus, the mighty East Slavic state that existed from the ninth to the thirteenth centuries. The early Russian tsars were descended from the Kyivan princes, and subsequent chroniclers developed theories about the transfer of power from Kyiv to the northeastern city of Vladimir and then to Moscow. The uninterrupted development of the Russian state proved a convenient narrative framework at a time when national histories were being written, resulting in Kyivan Rus becoming the recognized starting point of Russian history. Many textbooks still treat it as the "first Russian state," although the core principalities of medieval Rus were in what is now Ukraine, and present-day Ukrainians and Belarusians have just as legitimate (or better) a claim to its legacy than Russians. It was only in the early twentieth century that the Ukrainian historian Mykhailo Hrushevsky openly claimed Kyivan Rus for Ukrainian history. He famously compared the relations between the capital of Kyiv and the principalities of Vladimir and Moscow, from which the Russian Empire developed, to those between Rome and its Gallic provinces.[5] Belarusian historians, meanwhile, began emphasizing the de facto autonomy from Kyiv of Polatsk (Polotsk) Principality in the northwest, which they saw as the nucleus of the Belarusian lands.

An increasingly loose federation of principalities, Kyivan Rus was dealt a final blow by the Mongol invasions of 1237–42. Among the lands that fell under Mongol suzerainty, the Vladimir-Moscow principality eventually became the new center of gravity—and the pivot of the future Russian state. In the west, however, the Grand Duchy of Lithuania emerged as a major regional power, absorbing by the end of the fourteenth century all of today's Belarus and much of what is now

Ukraine. Although ruled by pagan Lithuanian princes (whose language belonged to the Baltic branch), the East Slavs, who had been Orthodox Christians since the ninth century, constituted a large majority of the Grand Duchy's population. Descendants of the Rus princes and boyars played a leading role in politics, and their language, a bookish Church Slavonic with strong traces of Belarusian and Ukrainian dialects, was the official language of the state. Lacking any other episodes of statehood until the twentieth century, modern Belarusian patriots in particular have claimed the Grand Duchy of Lithuania for their national history. Present-day historians of Belarus speak of the fifteenth and sixteenth centuries as the "golden age of Belarusian culture."[6]

The Lithuanian princes, however, converted to Roman Catholicism after the Duchy's union with Poland in the late fourteenth century. In 1569, Lithuania and Poland united into a single state, the Polish-Lithuanian Commonwealth, with Catholicism as the dominant religion. The Ukrainian and Belarusian nobilities initially fought for their rights, but eventually began converting to Catholicism and assimilating into Polish culture. In 1596, the majority of Orthodox bishops, encouraged by the Polish authorities, created the Uniate Church, which recognized the supremacy of the pope while preserving Eastern rites. The peasantry, however, remained Orthodox and spoke the Ukrainian and Belarusian dialects. As the sense of religious oppression mounted, so did social tensions. Most of the Ukrainian lands had been transferred to direct Polish rule, resulting in the enserfment of the peasantry by Polish nobles, most of whom did not live on their Ukrainian estates. These nobles leased their right to collect taxes to local managers, usually Jews, who then became targets of popular anger.

A social, national, and religious conflict exploded in 1648, when the Ukrainian officer Bohdan Khmelnytsky started a rebellion against Polish rule. Led by the Cossacks (originally guards of the southern steppe frontier employed by Polish governors), the revolt quickly grew into a peasant war against landlords and their managers and a religious war of Orthodox against Catholics, Uniates, and Jews. Following a string of defeats, the Polish king was forced to recognize Cossack administration in three Ukrainian palatinates, thus allowing for the creation of a Cossack state under *Hetman* Khmelnytsky—the focal point of Ukrainian historical narratives ever since.[7] An exhaustive war with Poland resumed, however, and in 1654, Khmelnytsky placed his Cossack state under the protection of the Russian tsar. The meaning of the 1654 Pereiaslav Treaty remains the subject of controversy. In contrast to the official Russian and Soviet position that Pereiaslav "reunited" Ukraine and Russia, Ukrainian historians have presented the treaty as merely a military alliance, dynastic union, or protectorate. In any case, in the long run, the Russian authorities began curtailing Cossack autonomy while establishing their direct rule over Ukraine east of the Dnieper. (The lands to the west, except for Kyiv, remained under Poland.) In the battle of Poltava in 1709, Tsar Peter the Great extinguished the last Ukrainian attempt to separate from Russia by defeating the united forces of the Cossack leader Ivan Mazepa and King Charles XII of Sweden. The Ukrainian Cossack officer class then began its slow descent into assimilation.

The Belarusian lands and Ukraine west of the Dnieper remained under Polish rule until the late eighteenth century, when Russia, Prussia, and Austria undertook the so-called "three partitions" of this state, eliminating Poland from the map of Europe during the period of 1772–95. As a result, the Russian Empire acquired all of Belarus and most of the Ukrainian ethnolinguistic territories, except for the westernmost region of Galicia, which fell to the Austrian Empire. (The Habsburg emperors also acquired from the declining Ottoman Empire another Ukrainian-populated region, Bukovyna, and, as kings of Hungary, were masters of a third region, Transcarpathia.)

During the late eighteenth and early nineteenth centuries, the Russian Empire also conquered the territories now constituting Moldova. They consisted of two historical regions with different historical traditions. The larger of the two, Bessarabia, lay between the Prut and Dniester Rivers and was an integral part of the Romanian Principality of Moldavia. The Romanian language and culture (belonging to the Romance family of languages) can be traced back to the Roman occupation of the Balkans during the second and third centuries, but the proto-Romanian principalities of Moldavia and Wallachia developed much later, during the fourteenth and fifteenth centuries. Bessarabia constituted only the eastern half of the Principality of Moldavia, but inherited its historical name in the twentieth century. Although Bessarabia shared history and culture with the other Romanian lands, it became separated from them in 1812, when Russia took this region from the Ottoman Empire, which had been a suzerain of the Romanian principalities since the early sixteenth century. Thus, Bessarabia was deprived of a chance to participate in the later unification of Romanian principalities in 1859, resulting in the creation of the independent Kingdom of Romania in 1881. The Russian authorities at first granted considerable autonomy to the Bessarabian boyars and clergy, but within decades began dismantling it.

The second and much smaller historical region was Transnistria, a narrow strip of land east of the Dniester. Once part of Kyivan Rus and then the Galician-Volhynian Principality, it had a mixed East Slavic and Romanian population and was never part of historical Moldavia. The Russian Empire wrested it from the Ottoman Empire in 1792 but did not consider this land to be connected to nearby Bessarabia.

In fact, the imperial bureaucrats initially gave little thought to the ethnic make-up of their newly incorporated territories. (One exception was the issue of whether to absorb or segregate the Jews—until the late eighteenth century there was no significant Jewish presence in the Russian Empire—but even this issue was more religious than it was political.)[8] They worried more about the religious uniformity of the East Slavs, who were officially considered "tribes" of the Russian people—hence the forced liquidation in 1839 of the Uniate Church in Belarus, as well as the earlier subordination of the Orthodox faithful in Ukraine to the Russian Orthodox Church. The authorities realized that the population of Bessarabia belonged to a different, Romanian, culture—in fact, the "Moldovan" (Romanian) language was used in administration until the middle of the century—but being Orthodox Christians and loyal subjects of the tsar remained a more important marker of political allegiance.[9]

Paradoxically, it was the fear of a nationalist spillover from abroad that awakened tsarist officials to the nationality problem in the western borderlands. This alarm was more justifiable in the case of Bessarabia, which was always a candidate for unification with the other Romanian lands. An anti-Turkish rebellion in Moldavia and Wallachia in 1821 influenced the curbing of Bessarabian autonomy in 1829. The development abroad of a movement for pan-Romanian union led to a purge of the "Moldovan" language from Bessarabian schools and administration in the 1850s.[10] In contrast, the tsarist authorities had a flawed rationale for banning publications in the Ukrainian and Belarusian languages after the 1863 rebellion of Polish nobles in the empire's western provinces. The Ukrainian and Belarusian peasants did not support the Polish rebels; neither did the early Ukrainian and Belarusian intelligentsia whom the bureaucrats erroneously suspected of being Polish agents. The celebrated example of Kastus Kalinowski (Kalinouski), a Polish rebel of Belarusian background who had tried in vain to appeal to the indigenous peasantry, is a case in point.

Far from establishing a deeper connection with the Poles, the subsequent development of Ukrainian and Belarusian nationalism involved the affirmation of their peoples' separateness from the Poles as well as from the Russians. The first, academic, stage of the national movement began in Ukraine during the late eighteenth century and in Belarus during the mid-nineteenth. The work of early writers, ethnographers, and researchers paved the way for the emergence of great literary figures—such as the Ukrainian poet Taras Shevchenko (1814–61) and the Belarusian poet Francishak Bahushevich (1840–1900)—who would develop the peasant vernacular into a medium of modern high culture. Beginning in the 1860s, Ukrainian patriots went further than their Belarusian counterparts in organizing small, clandestine circles of intellectual *hromady* (societies), which pursued cultural work. Time and again, however, tsarist crackdowns on publishing and performances in the Ukrainian and Belarusian languages hindered the attempts of the national intelligentsia, which could not complete what Hroch calls a cultural phase, let alone advance to the political stage of the national movement. Ukrainians in the Austro-Hungarian Empire were much better off, since that "patchwork empire" allowed the cultural development of its many nationalities and, after the Revolution of 1848, also gradually introduced public political participation.

Romanian speakers in Bessarabia and Transnistria are a special case, as they did not have to go through the stages of defining their national identity and initiating cultural work. Their weaker national intelligentsia (the boyars having been assimilated into the Russian culture) could borrow nationalist concepts that had been developed in the core Romanian lands to the west. More often than not, however, Bessarabian proponents of Romanian unification were forced to voice their opinions from abroad, deprived of access to their peasant constituency.

For all the nationalities on the Russian Empire's western fringes, a qualitative leap in the development of national identity came with the turbulent events of the early twentieth century, none of which originated in the region: the Revolution of 1905, World War I, and the Revolution of 1917.

Revolutionary Reassertion

At the turn of the twentieth century, Belarusians, numbering some 5.5 million in 1897, lagged behind the empire's other nationalities in the development of national consciousness. With their cities dominated by Poles, Jews, and Russians, the overwhelming majority of Belarusians were illiterate peasants unfamiliar with the modern notion of national identity. Although the Russian government distrusted the Polish gentry in this region, it did not encourage the development of Belarusian culture. On the contrary, the authorities repressed Belarusian culture, and if they provided the peasants with any education at all, it was in Russian. With less than 3 percent of the Belarusian population residing in cities and towns, Belarusians were quite possibly the least urbanized people in Europe. Their national awakening began late, the idea of a separate Belarusian nationality emerging only in the 1890s in the poems of Bahushevich. As other peoples in this part of Europe were entering the stage of mass mobilization, from 1906 to 1915, Belarusians were undergoing a belated literary revival enabled by the temporary softening of restrictions on the use of the Belarusian language after the Revolution of 1905. Belarusian cultural life of this period centered around the socialist-leaning weekly *Nasha niva* (Our Field).[11]

World War I brought destruction and population dislocation. By the time the Russian monarchy collapsed during the February Revolution (1917), half of Belarusian territory was occupied by the Germans. In the other half, patriotic activists managed to convene the All-Belarusian Congress in December of that year, only to have it disbanded by the Bolsheviks. According to the terms of the Brest-Litovsk Treaty that took Russia out of the war, Belarus was divided between Germany and Soviet Russia. The former allowed local nationalists to proclaim the Belarusian Democratic Republic (March 1918), while the latter created the Belarusian Soviet Republic (January 1919). Both were essentially puppet states masking, respectively, German and Bolshevik control behind the scenes. Subsequently, Belarus became a prize in the Soviet-Polish War, which ended with the final incorporation of western Belarus into Poland and the re-establishment of the Belarusian Soviet Socialist Republic in the east.

Belarus' neighbor to the south, Ukraine, presents a more complex case. Eastern, or Dnieper Ukraine, which was part of the Russian Empire, shared many characteristics with Belarus. A large nation of approximately 22 million in 1897, most ethnic Ukrainians were illiterate peasants. By the early twentieth century, however, a small Ukrainian intelligentsia boasted literary, theatrical, and musical traditions—maintained in spite of tsarist restrictions. Still, patriotic agitators did not have free access to the peasant masses. Major cities, including Kyiv, changed their Polish cultural character to Russian because the peasants who had moved there or joined the industrial workforce adopted Russian identity. The new working class (which grew quickly during the industrial boom of the 1890s) responded better to agitation by Russian socialists, and, indeed, all-Russian underground socialist parties had an impressive following in eastern Ukraine. Only the Revolution of 1905 enabled Ukrainian activists to publish their first daily newspaper, *Rada* (Council), and to start popular education societies in the countryside—concessions that the government would revoke by the beginning of World War I. Except for a brief period after 1905, political parties could operate only underground, and only socialist Ukrainian parties could muster any significant support.

Western Ukraine, which was part of the Austro-Hungarian Empire, had a very different historical experience. Numbering 3.5 million in 1910, Ukrainians in eastern Galicia (with its center in Lviv) suffered from Polish domination in the crown land of Galicia but benefited from education in their native tongue, freedom of cultural development, and—however limited—experience of political participation. The national movement began in the mid-nineteenth century, and in time benefited greatly from Ukrainian identification with the Greek Catholic (Uniate) Church, which clearly placed Ukrainians apart from (Roman Catholic) Poles. By the turn of the century, a massive network of Ukrainian print media, cooperatives, reading rooms, and cultural societies produced a generation of nationally conscious peasants.[12] Intellectuals, meanwhile, established that their people were not just *Rusyny* (Rus people, a self-designation dating back to Kyivan Rus) but a part of the greater Ukrainian nation. With political parties operating legally, the moderately nationalistic National Democrats dominated western Ukrainian politics.

In the northern part of the neighboring Austrian province of Bukovyna, where the ruling class was Romanian and most Ukrainians belonged to the Orthodox Church, the growth of the national movement largely followed the Galician model. This was not the case in Transcarpathia beyond the Carpathian Mountains, which belonged to the Hungarian part of the dual monarchy. There, the Hungarian upper classes encouraged assimilation and hindered the development of Ukrainian culture.

Of Ukraine's historical regions, western Ukraine felt the greatest impact of World War I. As the Russian army occupied Galicia and Bukovyna early in the war, it sought to "reunite" these lands with Russia. In the spring of 1915, Tsar Nicholas II paid a triumphant visit to Lviv, where his civil administration was actively suppressing organized Ukrainian life. The Austro-Hungarian Empire, in the meantime, had authorized the creation of a Ukrainian legion within its army. When the tsarist regime collapsed in February 1917, Ukrainian activists in Kyiv promptly established the Central Rada, headed by the respected historian Mykhailo Hrushevsky. In December, the nationalists proved unable to organize effective resistance to the Bolshevik army, which had invaded from Soviet Russia. Just before abandoning Kyiv in January 1918, the Central Rada proclaimed the independent Ukrainian People's Republic. But soon it was back in the capital, taking advantage of the German advance. Because the German high command disliked the socialist views of the Rada's leading ministers, it installed the conservative General Pavlo Skoropadsky as Ukraine's monarch, or *hetman* (April–December 1918). Following the German withdrawal after the end of World War I, the re-established Ukrainian People's Republic saw its authority collapse amid the chaos and violence of the Civil War, during which the (Bolshevik) Reds, the (Russian, anti-Bolshevik) Whites, Ukrainian forces, and bands of looters fought each other until, by the end of 1920, the better-organized Reds established control.

In western Ukraine, the revolution started later and had a national rather than social coloring. In November 1918, as the Austro-Hungarian Empire began disintegrating, Ukrainian activists proclaimed the creation of the Western Ukrainian People's Republic. In January 1919, the republic entered into a union with its eastern Ukrainian counterpart, but the unification was never implemented because western Ukrainians had to fight their own civil war against the new Polish state, which had the Allies' support. They lost this war in July. Subsequently, the Allies approved Polish control over all of Galicia, as well as the inclusion of Bukovyna in greater Romania, and Transcarpathia in the new state of Czechoslovakia.

Bordering Dnieper Ukraine in the southwest was Bessarabia, the most backward agricultural region on the empire's western fringes, with a literacy rate among Romanian-speakers there of a meager 6 percent (1897). After the Revolution of 1905, a national awakening manifested itself primarily in the discovery of the common pan-Romanian cultural heritage. Nationalists in Romania proper also sought to establish contacts with Moldovan intellectuals, hoping for eventual reunification; before the war and the revolution, however, this aim looked more like a pipe dream.

The February Revolution gave Moldovans an unexpected chance to organize. By October 1917, various civic and military groups managed to convene a national assembly in Chişinău, which declared Bessarabia autonomous. The election of a national council, *Sfatul Ţării*, followed, but in January 1918, before this body could establish its authority, the Romanian army arrived in force—ostensibly by invitation of the Moldovan authorities, with the aim of protecting the country from the Bolshevik peril. The *Sfatul Ţării* first proclaimed the independent Moldovan Democratic Republic of Bessarabia (January) and then its union with Romania (March).[13] The Soviet Union never recognized the Romanian annexation of Bessarabia, however, and the Romanians failed to win full international recognition of this act.

One productive way to analyze the revolutionary events in the non-Russian borderlands is to look at the complex interaction of "class" and "nation" as two principal identity markers that competed in contemporary political discourse and influenced the nationalities differently.[14] But given that the western borderlands were positioned strategically between Russia proper and Western Europe, their internal ideological struggles and nation-building projects were overridden time and again by the intervention of the great powers, which reshaped states and nations based on their own global interests.[15]

Meeting the Challenge of Nationalism

Rogers Brubaker has suggested that the new nation-states that replaced the multinational empires after World War I were essentially "nationalizing" states, protecting and promoting the political domination, economic welfare, and culture of their "core" nations.[16] This is, of course, an ideal model, useful in comparative analysis but too general to be sustained in most case studies. Nevertheless, the notion of a "nationalizing state" captures a significant feature of the interwar period, when states were interfering aggressively in nation-building processes.

Western Belarus and the largest part of western Ukraine found themselves within the new Polish state. In the Belarusian lands, where modern national consciousness was slow to develop, the population's grievances found expression in the popularity of socialism. Following a brief interlude in the early 1920s, when minority rights had been well protected, Poland (which became an authoritarian dictatorship after 1926) adopted a policy of assimilating Belarusians by closing their schools and encouraging the spread of Roman Catholicism. In addition, Poland handled the redistribution of large landed estates in such a way that the primary beneficiaries were not local Belarusian peasants but Polish colonists. The Polish government repeatedly manipulated census results to play down the domination of Polish colonists in an area that was ethnically Belarusian. As a result of such policies and an unsatiated peasant appetite for land, the Communist Party of Western Belarus and its legal arm, the Belarusian Union of Peasants and Workers, grew in popularity until they were suppressed in 1927. The 1930s saw further government repression of Belarusian cultural institutions and the forcible closure of Orthodox churches.

In Galicia, the Polish government attempted to enforce similar policies against the local Ukrainian population, but the response was different—namely, the birth of Ukrainian radical nationalism. With civic discipline and a highly developed national consciousness, Ukrainians were frustrated by the defeat of the Western Ukrainian People's Republic and the ensuing Polish domination. Assimilatory pressures only added to their sense of injustice. By the mid-1930s, it had become clear that a decade of political participation—including several attempts at compromise amongst the leading Ukrainian party, the Ukrainian National Democratic Alliance, and the authorities—had failed to stop national oppression. A new generation of disaffected young men and women became increasingly disappointed with the fruitless "collaborationism" of their elders. At a conference in Vienna in 1929, veterans of the Ukrainian-Polish war, students, and nationalist intellectuals created the Organization of Ukrainian Nationalists. The ideology of the new group emphasized the willpower of a strong minority as a way to restore the nation to greatness. The radical right soon grew into a mass movement.

Ukrainians in interwar Romania also experienced the effects of a policy of assimilation, which was formulated more clearly and enforced more strictly than in Poland. In contrast, the position of Ukrainians in Transcarpathia improved greatly. The Czechoslovak Republic, the only new state in Eastern Europe that remained a liberal democracy during the entire interwar period, provided government support for minority education and culture and allowed the use of minority languages in local administration. When Hitler began his dismemberment of Czechoslovakia in the fall of 1938, Transcarpathians took advantage of the situation to press for autonomy (October) and even proclaimed a short-lived independent Republic of Carpatho-Ukraine under President Avhustyn Voloshyn (March 15, 1939). Nazi Germany, however, handed Transcarpathia over to its Hungarian ally.

Finally, Romania spent much of the interwar period trying to integrate Bessarabia. This effort involved agrarian reform, the construction of roads and railroads, and the promotion of literacy. In the process, the government sought to promote a sense of Romanian patriotism in this province, which, all modernizing efforts notwithstanding, remained an impoverished periphery. Sales of Bessarabia's only significant export, wine, diminished when the province was separated from the Russian regions. Large minorities, such as Russians, Ukrainians, and Jews, complained about their treatment during the Romanian cultural offensive, and even many Moldovans found it difficult to switch from the Cyrillic alphabet to the Latin script. (In addition, the modern Romanian language borrowed most of its new political, technical, and scientific terminology from French, while Moldovans were accustomed to using Russian words.)[17] All in all, not only minorities but also the Moldovans themselves made it difficult for Romania to "nationalize" the region.

The Soviet Union, meanwhile, offered its own answer to the challenge of modern nationalism. The Bolshevik state attempted to disarm nationalism by promoting forms of minority nationhood—national territories, languages, cultures, and elites.[18] During the 1920s and early 1930s, the policy of *korenizatsiia* (indigenization) resulted in the creation of national republics or autonomous units, as well as the state's major investment in the development of non-Russian cultures. The Ukrainian and Belarusian Soviet Socialist Republics were among the beneficiaries of these policies. Between 1924 and 1933, the Ukrainians' share among Communist Party members in the republic increased from 33 to 60 percent. Literacy increased markedly, and by 1929, an impressive 97 percent of elementary school students were receiving instruction in Ukrainian. In contrast to 1922, when only one Ukrainian newspaper was in existence, in 1931, 89 percent of the republic's newspapers were published in Ukrainian.[19]

Like the rest of the USSR, however, in the late 1920s, Soviet Ukraine began to experience a violent transition to rapid industrialization and forced collectivization of agriculture. Stalinist social transformations went hand in hand with repressions against the national intelligentsia—including Mykola Skrypnyk, a prominent Ukrainian Bolshevik and chief architect of "Ukrainization," who shot himself in 1933. Parallel to this attack on Ukrainian culture, the state's murderous grain collection policies in the republic resulted in the catastrophic Famine of 1932–33, which took an estimated four to six million lives. By the late 1930s, the authorities had reverted to the promotion of the Russian language and Russian culture in Ukraine.

In the Belarusian SSR, a similar policy of Belarusization was implemented during the 1920s. Commissar of Education and later president of the Belarusian Academy of Sciences, Usevalad Ihnatouski initiated the Belarusization drive, but he was also among the first victims of the subsequent hunt for Belarusian nationalists. (Ihnatouski committed suicide in 1930.)[20] Like Ukraine, the Belarusian SSR in the 1930s saw an official effort to bring the national language closer to Russian. The Great Terror of the late 1930s completed the elimination of the generation of radical activists for whom socialism and non-Russian nation building were two potentially compatible projects.

Unlike Ukraine and Belarus, Soviet Moldova was not created as a union republic, becoming an autonomous republic only within the Ukrainian SSR (1924). From the very beginning, a Moldovan autonomy on the eastern bank of the Dniester, in Transnistria, was designed as a political magnet for Moldovans across the river in Bessarabia. Ethnic Moldovans constituted only 30 percent of the republic's population (Ukrainians were in the majority, at 48.5 percent), but the republic's existence was important for supporting the Soviet claim on Bessarabia. Following the high point of Moldovanization under Commissar for Education Pavel Chior (1928–30), this policy suffered setbacks. In a puzzling turn of events specific to Moldova, the authorities first ordered the switch from the traditional Cyrillic script to the Latin (1932) to stress the unity of the Moldovan and Romanian languages, and then ordered the return to the Cyrillic alphabet (1938), as it was closer to Russian.

Before the dust settled after the reversal of these indigenization policies, the Soviet nationalities policy changed again with the annexation of new territories in the west. Just as mature Stalinism established the Russians' priority status in the Soviet family of nations, Stalinist ideologues came to need an ethnic argument in their defense of the new conquests. The secret protocol attached to the August 1939 Molotov-Ribbentrop Pact assigned the eastern part of Poland and Bessarabia to the Soviet sphere of influence. The Soviet occupation of western Ukraine and Belarus in September 1939 was staged as the historic reunification of the Ukrainian and Belarusian nations, respectively.[21] Stalinist ideologues used the same argument to wrest Bukovyna from Romania in June 1940 and Transcarpathia from Czechoslovakia in 1945. Ironically, in view of all previous and subsequent efforts at establishing a Soviet Moldovan nationality, the annexation of Bessarabia in June 1940 was likewise justified by this land's allegedly Ukrainian character.[22] Still, Bessarabia became part of the Moldovan autonomous republic, while western Ukraine and western Belarus joined the existing Ukrainian and Belarusian republics.

All three republics, but in particular Belarus and Ukraine, became major battlefields during the Nazi-Soviet War that began in June 1941. The Nazis' racial ideology presented East Slavs as subhuman, and the invaders' brutality soon provoked popular resistance in Belarus and Ukraine. (Bessarabia, Bukovyna, and Transnistria were under Romanian control.) The Germans suppressed or ignored several nationalist attempts to proclaim state independence and, until the desperate times that came in 1943, were generally wary of working with the nationalists. Only late in the war, in a frantic effort to use the non-Russians' manpower, the Nazis established a national SS unit composed of Galician Ukrainians and allowed the creation of the Belarusian Land Defence. But by then the Red Army was unstoppable and, between the fall of 1943 and the summer of 1944, essentially reestablished its control over the three republics. The Ukrainian nationalist guerrillas, however, continued their resistance in western Ukraine's forests until the early 1950s, when the brutal Soviet counter-measures succeeded in achieving Soviet domination of the countryside. This was accompanied by a wave of mass deportations. Still, the armed resistance in the west profoundly traumatized Soviet ideologues, who subsequently always treated the region as nationalism prone.

The Late Soviet Period and Beyond

Postwar reconstruction involved quick industrial expansion in eastern Ukraine, but such formerly agricultural areas as Belarus, western Ukraine, and Moldova (primarily in Transnistria, with workers recruited from Russia and Ukraine) also acquired some modern industries. Politically and culturally, life in the western republics stabilized following de-Stalinization. Except for a brief period during the late 1950s and the early 1960s, the central authorities did not openly encourage assimilation into Russian culture, although they were clearly pleased when social processes pushed in this direction. Soviet ideologues and the KGB remained ever watchful for manifestations of "bourgeois nationalism" in the western borderlands, suppressing every potential source of resentment.[23] But the perpetual threat of "nationalism" was built into the Soviet system, which had institutionalized ethnic differences. There were administrators who, like the Ukrainian party boss Petro Shelest during the late 1960s, developed too strong an identification with their countries and cultures.[24] More important, the functioning of full-fledged national cultures, even Soviet-style ones, required the continued existence of a national intelligentsia.

Publicly, only small groups of intellectuals dared to express their discontent with the Soviet nationalities policy. Although much lionized in post-Soviet nationalist historiographies, the dissident movement did not and could not have brought down the Soviet empire. Until its rebirth under Gorbachev, the dissident movement remained the cause of hundreds of (at most a couple of thousand) activists. The dissident movement in fact began with attempts to show that Stalin and his successors had forsaken Leninist notions of national equality. This was the principal message of *Internationalism or Russification?* by the prominent Ukrainian dissident Ivan Dziuba.[25] Subsequently, dissidents began openly advocating national rights and self-determination, as well as the advancement of civil rights. In Ukraine, by far the largest western republic, the 1960s generation first explored the limits of artistic expression but soon established an opposition to the regime on the issues of civil rights and cultural freedoms. The underground *Ukrainian Herald* began appearing in 1970, and a large Ukrainian Helsinki Watch group emerged in Kyiv in 1976.

In contrast, dissent in Belarus was unorganized and limited to statements by intellectuals in defense of the national language. In Moldova, even such sporadic expressions of discontent were rare.

By the early 1980s, the general population in the western parts of the Soviet Union was reasonably informed about living standards in Eastern Europe and the so-called capitalist countries, and in its majority was cynical about Soviet ideology. Yet in those years the authorities almost succeeded in rooting out organized dissent. Mass expression of discontent did not emerge until Gorbachev's glasnost began creating a genuine public sphere. Only the reforms originating in Moscow allowed the non-Russian national movements to resume their interrupted (or frozen) nation-building projects by returning to what Hroch designates as the stage of mass mobilization. In all the western republics, the national cause acquired a truly mass following only after long-suppressed economic frustrations and social tensions had been relegated to the default channel of nationalist discourse.

Gorbachev's early glasnost policies, combined with the 1986 Chernobyl catastrophe (which, though originating in Ukraine, caused massive radioactive contamination in Belarus), gave rise to the first public protests against the Kremlin's environmental and cultural policies in the western Soviet Union. In Belarus, national awakening began in 1987, with cultural figures petitioning the government for the protection of Belarusian culture against assimilation. It escalated into open discontent in 1988, after the discovery of mass graves of the victims of Stalinist terror in Kurapaty Forest. Led by the archaeologist Zianon Pazniak, national activists began organizing the Belarusian Popular Front (BPF), modeled after similar fronts in the neighboring Baltic republics, but they met with fierce resistance from the authorities. The BPF's founding congress consequently took place in Vilnius, the capital of Soviet Lithuania, in June 1989.[26] Still, the republic's authorities effectively prevented the BPF from reaching out to the countryside.

In western Ukraine, a mass movement for the restoration of the Greek Catholic (Uniate) Church developed in 1987, while in eastern Ukraine, Chernobyl became the earliest unifying factor for the opposition. The civic ecological association Green World was founded in 1987, while the organization in defense of the national language, the Taras Shevchenko Ukrainian Language Society, was not established until February 1989. That same month, a more important political organization was born, namely, the Popular Movement for Restructuring. Better known simply as *Rukh* (Movement), it was similar in structure and political aims to the Baltic popular fronts in the early stages of their development.

In Moldova, the party managed to keep the forces of change at bay until mid-1988. But when the political control over the public sphere was released somewhat in the summer of that year, the republic's intellectuals promptly established both cultural organizations and the more politically oriented Democratic Movement in Support of Restructuring. (In May 1989, these and other pro-reform groups joined forces as the Moldovan Popular Front.) Like the Ukrainian opposition, the Moldovan opposition united around the issue of language, which in the Moldovan case entailed not just the status and protection of Moldovan as a state language, but also recognition of its unity with Romanian and its "return" to the Latin script. But in all the republics of the western belt, the language issue was a political one.

Although all the non-Russian popular fronts had been created ostensibly to assist Gorbachev in the implementation of his perestroika policies, they soon concentrated on issues that were specific to their nations. Originally limited to language, the environment, and Stalinist crimes, these issues already challenged the Soviet Union's legitimacy. Ultimately, Gorbachev's reforms gave nationalists the opportunity to go public, and the Kremlin proved unable to prevent them from launching mass mobilizations. Initially, the popular fronts included reformist Communists and minorities, but the opposition that they encountered from the conservative party leaderships in most republics, as well as from the emerging minority movements, radicalized their ideology.

Still, the March 1990 elections to the Supreme Soviet of the Belarusian SSR demonstrated the extent of the authorities' control, with the Communist Party winning 86 percent of the seats. After years of prodding by the intelligentsia, party bureaucrats agreed in January 1990 to pass a law making Belarusian the official state language. (By then, similar laws had been passed in all the other western republics of the Soviet Union.) Yet in practice the population of Belarus remained the most Russified and least politically active in the region.

In Ukraine, support for Rukh was unevenly distributed geographically. In western Ukraine the national movement enjoyed mass support, while in the east it relied primarily on the humanitarian intelligentsia in the cities. Correspondingly, during the 1990 elections, Rukh captured most of the seats from the western provinces and some in large, urban centers, but its total was only 90 out of 450 seats. Hard-line Communists remained policy-makers in the republic, although they now had to face opposition in Parliament. Still, following the example of other republics, especially Russia, the majority felt it necessary to pass a declaration of sovereignty (July 1990), which was more an affirmation of the republic's rights than a separatist statement.

In Moldova, however, the Popular Front, together with reformist Communists, won the majority of seats in the 1990 elections. The majority pushed through a number of Romanian-oriented cultural reforms that alienated the minorities. (It is worth noting, nevertheless, that the idea of union with Romania had little support even among Moldovans.) In August 1990, the Turkic-speaking Gagauz population in the south declared a separate Gagauz Republic with its capital in Comrat, and in September, Russians and Russian-speaking Ukrainians in Transnistria created the Dniester Republic with its capital in Tiraspol. Some fifty thousand Moldovan nationalist volunteers immediately marched on the Dniester Republic, where fighting would continue intermittently for several years.

When the abortive coup in August 1991 destroyed the center's remaining power structures, the Baltic republics were the first to claim their full independence. In Ukraine and Belarus, Communist-dominated parliaments also issued declarations of independence, on August 24 and 25, respectively. In an ideological void caused by the Soviet collapse, many bureaucrats embraced the idea of national independence as a new ideological justification for their stay in power. The Ukrainian referendum on independence on December 1, 1991, with over 90 percent voting in favor of separate statehood, delivered the final blow to the idea of reviving the Soviet Union. The general population, including minority voters, was swept away by promises of economic prosperity that state-run media and nationalist agitators issued so easily. Moldova was the last to declare independence, on August 27, 1991, and the question of possible union with Romania, which acquired practical significance overnight, caused further splits within the Popular Front and among reformist Communists.

In the years since the demise of the Soviet Union, Ukraine, Belarus, and Moldova have gone their separate ways, although their paths have been determined to a significant degree by Russian policies in the region. All three have considerable Russian minorities and maintain close economic ties with Russia, which is eager to reassert its political and economic influence on its western frontier. But the legacy of twentieth-century nation building has been even more important. All three republics are still struggling to define their national identity by intermittently stressing their separateness from Russia and their common past with Russia. For better or worse, local identities continue to be defined in their relation to the Russian imperial and Soviet nationalizing projects.

* * *

Ukrainian and Moldovan historians, as well as Belarusian nationalists, who can speak freely only from abroad, now present these nations' independence as a natural outcome of their peoples' age-long struggle against imperialist oppression. But a survey of the region's history during the past two centuries demonstrates that imperial policies could be both repressive and constructive, and in both cases they were a principal force shaping modern ethnic identities. Rather than simply cracking down on the pre-existing and immutable national groups, the empires shaped them with both repression and encouragement—sometimes in passing, as a side-effect of a larger geopolitical game. Thus, Hroch's sociological model of how "national movements" developed in Eastern Europe is at once correct and misleading: correct as an ideal type of nationalist activism in a stateless nation, but misleading because the state—the imperial state—was in fact always involved in the nation-building process. When it was building nations, the Soviet Union arguably accomplished more than any national movement in the former Russian Empire, yet it was also the most efficient at destroying national cultures when it wanted to. This ambiguous legacy of nation building within multinational empires continues to mold present-day Ukraine, Belarus, and Moldova.

Notes

1. Miroslav Hroch, *Social Preconditions of National Revival in Europe*, trans. Ben Fowkes (Cambridge: Cambridge University Press, 1985).
2. Roman Szporluk has made this argument in relation to Ukraine's historical experience. See Szporluk, "Ukraine: From an Imperial Periphery to a Sovereign State," in his *Russia, Ukraine, and the Breakup of the Soviet Union* (Stanford, CA: Hoover Institution Press, 2000), 361–94.
3. Terry Martin, *The Affirmative Action Empire: Nations and Nationalism in the Soviet Union, 1923–1939* (Ithaca, NY: Cornell University Press, 2001), 15.
4. See David R. Marples, *Belarus: A Denationalized Nation* (Amsterdam: Harwood Academic, 1999).
5. Serhii Plokhy, *Unmaking Imperial Russia: Mykhailo Hrushevsky and the Writing of Ukrainian History* (Toronto: University of Toronto Press, 2005).
6. Jan Zaprudnik, *Belarus: At a Crossroads in History* (Boulder, CO: Westview, 1993), 35.
7. *Hetman* is the traditional title of an elected Cossack leader.
8. See John Doyle Klier, *Russia Gathers Her Jews: The Origins of the "Jewish Question" in Russia, 1772–1825* (DeKalb: Northern Illinois University Press, 1986).
9. On the absence in the Russian Empire of a modern "nationalities policy," see Andreas Kappeler, *The Russian Empire: A Multiethnic History*, trans. Alfred Clayton (Harlow, UK: Longman, 2001).
10. Charles King, *The Moldovans: Romania, Russia, and the Politics of Culture* (Stanford, CA: Hoover Institution Press, 2000), 22.
11. Zaprudnik, *Belarus*, 64.

12. John-Paul Himka, *Galician Villagers and the Ukrainian National Movement in the Nineteenth Century* (Edmonton: Canadian Institute of Ukrainian Studies Press, 1988).

13. King, *The Moldovans*, 33–35.

14. Ronald Grigor Suny, *The Revenge of the Past: Nationalism, Revolution, and the Collapse of the Soviet Union* (Stanford, CA: Stanford University Press, 1993), 1–83.

15. Geoff Eley, "Remapping the Nation: War, Revolutionary Upheaval, and State Formation in Eastern Europe, 1914–1923," in *Ukrainian-Jewish Relations in Historical Perspective*, ed. Howard Aster and Peter J. Potichnyj, 205–46 (Edmonton: Canadian Institute of Ukrainian Studies Press, 1988).

16. Rogers Brubaker, *Nationalism Reframed: Nationhood and the National Question in the New Europe* (New York: Cambridge University Press, 1996), 83–84, 103–4.

17. King, *The Moldovans*, 43–47.

18. Martin, *The Affirmative Action Empire*, 1–27.

19. Paul Robert Magocsi, *A History of Ukraine* (Toronto: University of Toronto Press, 1996), 538–45.

20. Ivan S. Lubachko, *Belorussia under Soviet Rule, 1917–1957* (Lexington: University Press of Kentucky, 1972), 109–11.

21. Serhy Yekelchyk, *Stalin's Empire of Memory: Russian-Ukrainian Relations in the Soviet Historical Imagination* (Toronto: University of Toronto Press, 2004).

22. King, *The Moldovans*, 92.

23. Amir Weiner, "The Empires Pay a Visit: When Gulag Returnees Encountered East European Rebellions on the Soviet Western Frontier," *Journal of Modern History* 78, no. 2 (June 2006): 333–76.

24. On Shelest, see Yaroslav Bilinsky, "Mykola Skrypnyk and Petro Shelest: An Essay on the Persistence and Limits of Ukrainian National Communism," in *Soviet Nationality Policies and Practices*, ed. Jeremy R. Azrael, 105–43 (New York: Praeger, 1978); Jaroslaw Pelenski, "Shelest and His Period in Soviet Ukraine (1963–1972): A Revival of Controlled Ukrainian Autonomism," in *Ukraine in the 1970s*, ed. Peter J. Potichnyj, 283–305 (Oakville, ON: Mosaic, 1975); and Lowell Tillett, "Ukrainian Nationalism and the Fall of Shelest," *Slavic Review* 34, no. 4 (1975): 752–68.

25. See Ivan Dziuba, *Internationalism or Russification?* trans. M. Davies (London: Weidenfeld and Nicolson, 1968).

26. Marples, *Belarus*, 47–48.

2

From Soviet Ukraine to the Orange Revolution: European Security Relations and the Ukrainian Identity

Natalie Mychajlyszyn

Ukraine has faced many dilemmas and experienced numerous struggles since achieving independence from the Soviet Union in August 1991. None, however, has been as profound and fundamental to its existence as establishing a post-Soviet identity. With the collapse of the Soviet Union and discrediting of the ideology that informed Ukraine's political, economic, and international institutions for seventy years, the immediate task was set to locate a new source of inspiration that would satisfy the young state's needs and interests for the foreseeable future.

In the process of this search, Europe has stood as a beacon. Indeed, over consecutive Ukrainian governments and leaderships, a consensus has been built around the idea of Europe as the fulfillment of Ukraine's post-Soviet aspirations: a strong market economy, domestic stability, regional peace and security, democratic values, social progress, and high standards of living.

Accordingly, Ukraine's policies toward Europe have featured in particular the establishment, to various degrees and formalities, of relations with Europe's leading institutions, such as the Organization for Security and Co-operation in Europe (OSCE),[1] NATO, and the European Union (EU).

The shaping of Ukraine's post-Soviet identity has not been so linear or straightforward, however. Indeed, the same consensus that has been built around the European idea also makes a strong case for Ukraine's Eurasian heritage. In other words, Ukraine's post-Soviet identity is just as easily informed by its relations and ties with its dominating neighbor, Russia, and the creation of such institutions as the Commonwealth of Independent States and the Common Economic Space, in acknowledgement of (what is to some) Ukraine's natural essence. Moreover, Europe's place in Ukraine's identity has fluctuated across different presidential administrations. As time passed and relations among the key actors evolved in the post-Soviet era (i.e., with Europe, Russia, the United States, and Ukraine), a discussion among policy-makers and analysts about Ukraine's post-Soviet identity has moved away from the divisive dichotomous nature of the "either Europe or Russia" perspective to one that acknowledges Ukraine's integration of Europe and Russia.

This chapter examines the European dimension in Ukraine's post-Soviet identity. Its aim is to enable a better understanding of the process by which the idea of "Europe" has come to be incorporated into the idea of "Ukraine." It achieves this purpose by considering Ukraine's relations with Europe's leading institutions, the OSCE, NATO, and the EU, consistent with the argument that a state's identity is influenced by interactions with institutions that themselves are manifestations of a particular identity and set of values. In looking at these European institutions, the chapter highlights the most fundamental element of Ukraine's post-Soviet identity where Europe is concerned: security. Indeed, Ukraine's relationship with the European security institutions[2] is representative of the extent to which its identity has changed, from that of an adversary of Europe to that of a security partner. Thus, Ukraine's security relationship with Europe and its embedded place in Europe's security institutions has changed to reflect the incorporation of "Europe" in its post-Soviet identity.

Given that identities are held by several referents, it is important to clarify that this chapter attends to Ukraine's identity as a *state*. Such referents as ethnic, linguistic, and national groups, among others, are equally valid for study and certainly have received attention in this way, especially where Ukraine is concerned. This chapter, however, deliberately restricts its focus to Ukraine's post-Soviet state identity because it is as a state, a legal entity with international personality, that Ukraine interacts with other states in the international system—

and this interaction influences its identity. Moreover, in the international system, the primary referent of security is the state. Thus, to better understand Ukraine's post-Soviet identity in security relations, addressing the question in terms of *state* identity is an auspicious place to begin.

The significance of this examination of Ukraine's state identity and its security relations with Europe rests on many points. First, Ukraine is uniquely and unenviably located at the crossroads of East and West, a position of tremendous geo-strategic importance to the stability of Europe and Eurasia. As a result, understanding its place and impact on European security is of particular strategic significance. Second, as a previous member of the Soviet Union, in which Ukraine had a privileged military role second only to that of Russia, Ukraine is expected to have harbored the most hardened adversarial views of Europe and might be suspected of being among the most resistant to incorporating a European dimension into its post-Soviet identity. Third, Ukraine is no Russia in terms of size. Nor does it carry the burdens of being the successor to one of the vanguards of the Cold War and (falsely or not) maintaining a sense of pride and a status commensurate with that of being a great power. Thus, Ukraine is less constrained by such aspects in changing its security relationship with Europe. Finally, while since 1992 the relationship between Ukraine and the European security institutions has grown and developed at a steady pace, the evolution has been neither linear nor consistent, and invites closer scrutiny.

The chapter is structured in the following way: the following section presents the framework applied to make the case of the positive impact (in the neutral sense) on Ukraine's post-Soviet identity of Ukraine's relations with Europe's security institutions (i.e., the mutually influential impact of interactions, institutions, and identity). The next section reviews the place of Europe for Ukraine during the Cold War and the Soviet Union's existence, in order to establish the non-European nature of Ukraine's Soviet identity as a baseline. This discussion is followed by a presentation and assessment of Ukraine's post-Soviet relations with the OSCE, NATO, and the EU. The chapter will then evaluate the impact of European security relations on Ukraine's post-Soviet identity, considering in particular the stated policies and actions of the presidential administrations of Leonid Kravchuk (1991–94), Leonid Kuchma (1994–2004), and Viktor Yushchenko (2004 to the present).

Framework: Identity and Institutions[3]

State identity and institutions are mutually influential. Specifically, the identity of a state is constructed by way of its interaction with other states and institutions, or regularized patterns of interaction and relations. Thus, a state's identity is derived from the meaning ascribed to the interactions of that state with institutions and other states: If the interaction is positive or beneficial, the other state or institution is considered a partner; if the interaction is negative or harmful, the other is an adversary. The more frequent the interactions and the more sustaining the practices and behavior, the more reinforced the state identities and the relations with the corresponding institutions: "A state understands others according to the identity it attributes to them, while simultaneously reproducing its own identity through daily social practice."[4] In this way, states are categorized subjectively as "us" and "them" in terms of self-identification and perception of others. Thus, boundaries are drawn between partners and adversaries, creating bonds between those who share a common identity (subjectively or objectively) and defining limits between those who do not (again, subjectively or objectively).

Most importantly, as the environment in which institutions operate changes, so do the interactions among the constituent states and, consequently, their identities. In other words, institutions and identities persist as long as they are reinforced by and reproduce each other. Changes to the context of an institution will inevitably change interstate interactions and state identity, thereby changing the institution as well, even to the point of its demise if it can no longer be sustained or cannot successfully adapt to the new environment and manage new forms of interaction. Changes to a state's identity and to an institution, however, are not immediate. Instead, they are gradual, due to the reinforced and inter-subjective nature of interactions, institutions, and state identities. Thus, "new" identities will not be immediately apparent, and the nature and duration of the identity change will likely be ambiguous, its boundaries unclear.

In this context, we can better appreciate Europe's collection of security institutions as the manifestation of a collective identity shared not only by formal members but also by non-members who interact with this collective identity and reinforce trends of other and self-identification. Those states that participate in the institutions and share an identity are less likely to consider each other adversaries because of the reinforcing impact on their interactions. They are more likely to see each other as partners.

Thus, Ukraine's post-Soviet identity is changing to incorporate a European dimension, in part by its evolving, more cooperative relationship with Europe's security institutions. The more interactive Ukraine has become with the OSCE, NATO, and the EU since 1992, the farther Ukraine has distanced itself from the Soviet assessment of Europe as an adversary. Increasingly, it identifies its relationship with Europe as one of partnership.

The Soviet Era, European Security Relations, and Ukraine's Identity

For forty years or so, the Cold War held the world and especially Europe captive, imposing ideological and political divisions through continents, countries, and populations as the West, (heralding the virtues of liberal democratic market societies) faced off against the East (which promoted the superiority of Communism and command economies). The identities of "us" and "them" among states belonging to one or the other camp were informed by institutions created in part to reinforce these identities. To the east were such institutions as the Soviet Union, reinforced by the Warsaw Pact and Comecon. To the west was Europe,[5] reinforced by NATO and the European Economic Community (one of several forerunners to the EU).

The security dimension of the identifications was without doubt: Europe was considered the potential battleground for a "hot war" between the two ideology-driven adversaries. As they faced each other across the Iron Curtain in defense of their political and economic systems, each alliance developed detailed military strategies in the event of an armed confrontation. Their successful application and the cohesiveness of the alliances rested on beliefs and values commonly held and nurtured among the members of each alliance about the use of force and the adversary against whom each was preparing to wage war. These shared values and beliefs subsequently informed (and were informed by) the institutional structures that took shape to realize and reinforce the mission of each side. Indeed, given the ideological intensity of the confrontation and the high stakes involved in a potential war between NATO and the Warsaw Pact—possibly involving nuclear weapons— the perceived threat posed by the other alliance grew. Ultimately, the perceptions held by each alliance of the other crystallized.

Against this backdrop, Ukraine's identity was shaped almost exclusively by its constituent and republic status in the Union of Soviet Socialist Republics and its associate institutions. Its identity was honed over seventy years by Soviet policies regarding Ukraine's place in the USSR, the reconfiguration of history and historical events to suit these policies, and a policy of Soviet nationalism that reaffirmed Ukraine's allegiance to Moscow and Russia, among many others. Moreover, Ukraine's Soviet identity was reinforced by its contribution to the military mission of the Warsaw Pact, the military alliance of the Eastern Bloc marshalled by the Soviet Union, to defend the members of this military alliance against military aggression from NATO. Specifically, given Ukraine's geographical position on the front lines of any potential battle with NATO, its privileged status in the hierarchy of ethnicities in the Soviet Union as a Slavic people, and its lengthy historical relationship with Russia, Ukraine hosted the most advanced and best-equipped and -trained military bases and units, disproportionately populated the officer corps (second to Russia), and, most notably, was one of four republics with nuclear bases and nuclear weapons within its territory.[6]

The Conference on Security and Co-operation in Europe bears consideration in this respect as an institution that reinforced Ukraine's identity during this period. The CSCE was initiated in the early 1970s during the brief warming period in the East-West confrontation known as the détente, in order to negotiate a document on common principles and decision-making procedures by which to regulate areas of concern, in particular politico-military, economic, and humanitarian issues.[7] Although thirty-five countries participated, the Cold War lines of division were in force and negotiations were essentially carried out between the two sides: the East represented by the Soviet Union and its Bloc, the West led by the NATO allies.[8] The conference concluded in 1975 with the signing of the Helsinki Final Act, which (according to some) was considered the peace settlement for World War II in terms of its recognition of the inviolability of frontiers and implied recognition of the division of Europe.[9]

Thus, Ukraine's identity as a constituent member of the Soviet Union was reinforced by the USSR's participation in the CSCE negotiations and the divisiveness of the process, notwithstanding the outcome of a consensus document. This continued in the aftermath of the CSCE process during the follow-up meetings and the return to the Cold War climate in the late 1970s, when the process was used by each side to accuse the other of violating the principles and not living up to the commitments of the Final Act.

In all respects and in particular concerning security, Ukraine's identity was very much embedded with the Soviet Union, and Europe with its associated institutions was considered an adversary. More directly, Europe did not figure as a positive force in Ukraine's identity during the Soviet period and instead was a negative force, defining for Ukraine what it was not.

The Post-Soviet Era

In 1989, the Iron Curtain—as firm a boundary between "us" and "them" as there ever was—was unexpectedly and dramatically torn down. In a matter of weeks, Communism and command economies were discredited in the countries that made up the Warsaw Pact. In some cases slowly, and in some cases quickly, the countries of the East began pursuing political and economic reforms that would transform them from Communist systems into democratic market-economy societies. Equally dramatic, the anti-Communist revolution spread to the Soviet Union, the center and vanguard of the Communist world, and joined the anti-Union sentiment building up at the time. In 1991, these processes together led to the demise of the Soviet Union as a country and as an idea as, one after another, the fifteen republics that it comprised declared their sovereignty and independence and sought to redirect their systems onto a democratic, market-economy path. On December 31, 1991, the Soviet Union ceased to exist. Thus, the basis for Ukraine's identity for the previous seventy years vanished.

As a result of these fundamental changes, the nature of the security relationship between the European and Soviet institutions began to change as well. In effect, the end of the Cold War, the demise of Communism, and the collapse of the Soviet Union removed the barriers that generated animosity and distrust, which in turn prevented the development of a partnership. In this way, the perception of the other as an adversary began to soften.

Nonetheless, a critical security vacuum appeared where the states of the former Warsaw Pact and Soviet Union were concerned, the significance of which escalated against the eruption of civil wars in Yugoslavia, Azerbaijan, and Georgia, and the increasing ethnic tensions in Latvia, Estonia, and even Ukraine. Thus, European security relations were in need of a structure to institutionalize state interactions and to propel them more positively toward partnerships. In the process, new identities would be constructed to correspond with the new environment.

Ukraine found itself at the heart of these dramatic developments. Not only is its declaration of independence from the Soviet Union on August 24, 1991, cited as the critical nail in the coffin of the

USSR, but also in those early years when independence at times corresponded with anti-Sovietism and anti-Eurasianism, the nascent state found itself adrift without the institutional anchors that it had relied on in the past and that had shaped its identity. Indeed, early statements saw the newly independent state assert neutrality and rejection of military blocs as an element in its security policy.[10]

As the security vacuum slowly began to fill with the transformation of Cold War institutions, Ukraine's security relationship with Europe was altered, and now shows a corresponding change in its post-Soviet identity. Ukraine's identity has come to be more informed (in a positive way) by its unprecedented interactions with Europe's security institutions. In other words, the European dimension in Ukraine's post-Soviet identity has emerged. Although there would be fluctuations in the degree of intensity, Ukraine's interactions with the OSCE, NATO, and the EU have cemented Europe's place in Ukraine's identity.

CSCE / OSCE

In response to the dramatic changes in the European security environment, the CSCE process and schedule of meetings came to be institutionalized into the OSCE.[11] The changes have been numerous, but most notably include changes to the CSCE's concepts, structures, size, and, ultimately, name. Indeed, as the largest regional security organization, with fifty-five participating states, it is also the only organization to offer an inclusive forum to discuss non-traditional security concerns. In particular, the OSCE has come to represent one of the most intrusive security institutions, establishing (albeit with the consent of the participating state) on-site missions to monitor and advise on ethnic relations, ceasefires, and negotiations on conflict prevention and settlement. In this way, the OSCE contributes to European security and has defined its place in the relevant architecture in terms of promoting cooperative security and focusing on non-military, non-traditional dimensions of security, such as ethnic conflict and human and minority rights. The tools it applies are also of a non-military nature: the OSCE is not a military alliance and does not have institutionalized means by which to use force.

Thus, in January 1992, Ukraine's post-Soviet identity took its first tentative steps toward Europe when Ukraine joined—on its own standing—what was then the CSCE. Through its interactions with this institution, participating in its meetings organized at different levels of political authority, the European dimension of Ukraine's identity was planted and nurtured. Indeed, by way of its interactions, Ukraine received a great deal of attention by the OSCE and its various conflict-prevention mechanisms as it attempted to address the political status of Crimea, as well as that of the Crimean Tatars. In November 1994, the OSCE set up a field mission in Ukraine with a mandate in part to monitor and advise on these issues. Moreover, the High Commissioner on National Minorities, one of the new mechanisms created by the OSCE in its post–Cold War incarnation, also monitored and advised on the status of the Crimean Tatars. With the conclusion of the field mission's mandate in 1999, a project coordinator office was established in order to advance the cause of common issues and interests where Ukraine's non-traditional security issues are concerned, including the re-integration of military officers and defense conversion, among others.

Most recently, the OSCE organized its largest-ever election-monitoring mission for the 2004 presidential elections in Ukraine. In the aftermath of its findings that the second-round results did not respect democratic standards (specifically OSCE election commitments and Council of Europe and other European standards) and did not reflect the will of the people, and the Supreme Court ruling that the second-round results were invalid, the OSCE launched another mission to monitor the mandated repeat second round.[12] Moreover, the post–second-round situation and the launch of the Orange Revolution were discussed at the OSCE Ministerial Council meeting, prompting the inclusion of a statement of support in the meeting's concluding document. As well, the OSCE's secretary-general participated in the round-table meetings of European political leaders, who negotiated a resolution to the post–second-round impasse.

In these ways, the adversarial nature of the Ukrainian-European relationship has eroded and has been replaced by a security partnership to the extent that in particular the OSCE as a European security institution has offered assistance to Ukraine to address its internal security concerns. In the process, this evolving partnership has served to reinforce Europe's place in Ukraine's post-Soviet identity.[13]

As much of a marker as the OSCE is in chronicling the evolution of the European dimension in Ukraine's post-Soviet identity, it is not a compelling case of the extent to which Ukraine's post-Soviet identity has changed given the CSCE's Cold War–era membership of both Western and Eastern Blocs, notwithstanding the divisive character the clash brought to the CSCE process. A more meaningful measure of how far Ukraine's post-Soviet identity has come is its relations with NATO.

NATO

In the changing environment of the post–Cold War era, NATO also stepped up to fill the vacuum, establishing various channels and institutions by which to anchor the former Warsaw Pact and Soviet states.[14] More specifically, these additional security institutions within the NATO framework were established either multilaterally or bilaterally in an effort not only to manage the new security relationship with former adversaries, but also to instruct them in the principles and norms of acceptable behavior regarding the threat or use of force in an effort to promote regional stability and security.

Since 1992, NATO's outreach to its former adversaries has been institutionalized in a variety of ways. For instance, the North Atlantic Cooperation Council (NACC)—re-named the Euro-Atlantic Partnership Council (EAPC) in May 1997—was established in 1991 as a forum for cooperation and dialogue between NATO and the countries of Central and Eastern Europe and the newly independent states of the Soviet Union. The NACC/EAPC process was instrumental in carrying out regular, monthly consultations with the former adversaries about security and political matters, as well as setting work plans on various topics: defense planning and defense reform, crisis management, transparency, and regional cooperation, among others.

In another respect, the Partnership for Peace program (PfP) ranks as among NATO's most successful initiatives in its changing relationships with former adversaries.[15] Initiated in 1994, PfP provides a bilateral forum in which former adversaries pursue targeted activities pertaining to defense and military cooperation with NATO, including set military exercises as well as training seminars about democratic civil-military relations and transparency in defense-planning. Most importantly, under the related Individual Partnership Program, specific activities are selected and carried out according to the interests and needs of the partner in question, while preserving the integrity of NATO's strategic culture. Further exposure and enculturation to NATO's strategic culture is promoted through the international coordination center at Supreme Headquarters Allied Powers Europe (SHAPE) that provides on-site coordination facilities for non-NATO countries participating in NATO operations, such as peacekeeping missions.

The Membership Action Plan (MAP) was initiated at the 1999 Washington Summit to respond to the growing need to prepare in a more directed fashion potential candidates for membership in NATO, beyond the preparations provided by PfP. Thus, unlike PfP, MAP targets potential NATO members to facilitate their transition to membership and their achievement of important goals to this effect, concerning political and economic issues as well as defense/military ones. Most importantly, MAP provides a vital feedback mechanism by which the MAP country's progress is monitored by NATO.[16]

Most notably, the transition states of the former Soviet Bloc have been abandoning their former, Soviet-defined strategic culture in favor of the Euro-Atlantic values and beliefs surrounding the use of force, as manifested formally in their applications to join NATO or informally by way of partnership arrangements with NATO. Although the degree to which these values and beliefs are embraced and espoused varies across individual states, ultimately this has resulted in significant changes to the identity of "us" and "them." In other words, by pursuing partnership arrangements with NATO, and in some cases even membership, former adversaries have been interacting in ways that have altered others' perceptions of them and how others responded to them (i.e., acting less as adversaries and more like partners or future allies), processes that were mutually reinforcing.

The post–Cold War environmental changes dramatically removed the adversarial characteristic of Ukraine's interactions with NATO.[17] As the interactions between NATO and Ukraine developed and intensified, they prompted corresponding changes in the security relationship, reinforcing the non-adversarial nature and leading to unprecedented institutional dynamics, with Ukraine joining several NATO institutions,[18] such as NACC/EAPC.[19] When Ukraine joined PfP in February 1994, it was among the first of the former Soviet republics to do so.

The highlight of the changed relationship is unquestionably the 1997 Ukraine-NATO Charter on a Distinctive Partnership. Indeed, one NATO official noted that the NATO-Ukraine relationship entered a promising new phase after these developments in 1997, which offered unprecedented opportunities to give substance to the relationship.[20] Significantly, the charter lays out the principles of the parties' interaction, including the peaceful settlement of disputes and democratic civilian control of the military. It also identifies areas of cooperation between NATO and Ukraine, such as consultations on a variety of common security concerns, and the means by which that

cooperation would be operationalized, such as by way of joint seminars and working groups, as well as by way of a new institution, the
NATO-Ukraine Commission. In addition, NATO opened a NATO
Information and Documentation Centre in Kyiv to serve as a distribution center for NATO-related information and to better inform the
Ukrainian public and policy makers about NATO. Moreover, in 1998,
a Joint Working Group on Defence Reform was established to provide more focused attention to defense-related issues in the NATO-
Ukraine partnership. Following on these themes and objectives, in
1999, a NATO liaison office in Ukraine was established to concentrate
on areas of direct military cooperation and to facilitate such activities
as peacekeeping operations. The liaison office serves essentially as
NATO's representation within the General Staff; its primary purpose
is to facilitate the NATO-Ukraine/military relationship and interop-
erability in the context of PfP, peacekeeping, and other matters such
as defense and security-sector reform. In this respect, the NATO liaison office has served as a critical indication of NATO's widening
activities with Ukraine.[21]

In May 2002, Ukraine indicated its interest in formally joining
NATO. While an accession process has not yet been agreed to, and
despite Ukraine's preference for a MAP, NATO and Ukraine instead
agreed to an Action Plan in November 2002 at the Prague Summit.[22]
Nonetheless, the Action Plan serves as another means by which
Ukraine interacts in a directed, purposeful way with NATO. Indeed,
by 2005, 65 percent of the Action Plan had been implemented.[23]

Since May 2002, NATO membership has remained a goal of
Ukraine, underlining not only the distance travelled in terms of the
adversarial attitudes of the Cold War but also the fact that a simple
partnership was no longer a satisfactory option.[24] In April 2005, in an
attempt to advance the process, NATO and Ukraine agreed to launch
an Intensified Dialogue on Ukraine's NATO membership, generally
considered to be the last step before Ukraine is invited to negotiate a
MAP as the final preparation before an invitation to membership is
issued. Subsequently, meetings were held to identify expectations on
the part of Ukraine regarding the membership process.

The strong bonds at the defense and military level of cooperation
between NATO and Ukraine testify to the extent to which the relationship has changed and have a reciprocal effect on reinforcing the
bonds of cooperation and Ukraine's identity.[25] According to one
NATO official, there is a degree of honesty and transparency at this level
of interaction that was not there in previous years.[26] In this respect,

the programs and activities organized under PfP on military reform and joint exercises (numbering as many as eight hundred in 2002) have had a 90-percent success rate in terms of implementation, a dramatic improvement from 50 percent in the early period of their post-Soviet relationship.[27] The substance of the NATO-Ukraine relationship on a military level is also evident in Ukraine's participation in peacekeeping operations in the Balkans and in Kosovo, as well as its support for the NATO-led mission in Afghanistan and deployment of troops to Iraq, among other activities (including anti-terrorism measures).[28] As noted by one NATO official, attitudes toward NATO were easier to change and were in stronger evidence at the military level because of the emphasis on interactions in such activities, whereby military personnel were able to work with NATO firsthand.[29] Indeed, another official noted that most interactions between Ukraine and NATO are carried out at the military level rather than at the political or economic level.[30] As a result, there is very strong support among the military for NATO membership, especially among the middle ranks, because of the exposure and experience gained from their participation in NATO peacekeeping operations and PfP and joint exercises.[31]

We can now better understand that, as Ukraine's post–Cold War relationship with NATO became institutionalized, the markers that defined Ukraine and NATO as adversaries fell away as the two interacted with each other. These markers were replaced by other markers that identified them as partners and potential formal allies. In the process, the European dimension of Ukraine's post-Soviet identity has been reinforced.

European Union

While NATO is without a doubt the premier European security institution due to its military nature, the architecture of European security is crowded with organizations with legitimate claims to their (implicit or explicit) contributions to European security. The EU is one such institution. Born of a commitment to prevent the recurrence of another World War (and founded on the argument that states with strong economic and trade ties are less likely to go to war with each other), the security aspect of what evolved into the EU is undeniable. Indeed, in this respect, the EU's precursors—the European Coal and Steel Community, the European Economic Community, and the European Community—were largely perceived as the economic arm of NATO's military operations, building and promoting stability among its members.

The end of the Cold War expanded the scope of the EU's security mandate in two ways. First, its target zone of stability extended to include non-members of the former command economies of the Warsaw Pact and Soviet Union. Specifically, the more successful their transition toward market economies, the more stable their domestic political situation, the greater the potential for economic opportunities, and the wider the zone of stability. The stability of such a zone would be highly unyielding to any domestic and regional tensions with the accession of the most advanced transition economies, and former adversaries, into the EU itself. Second, the mandate of the EU (as it concerned regional security and security policy as a legitimate area of activity by EU members) expanded. In this respect, the EU members have created the mechanism for launching an EU peace-keeping force, as well as other capabilities pertaining to crisis and conflict management and prevention, and peacemaking, the so-called "Petersberg Tasks." The EU also established the decision-making infrastructures to effect these mandates: a Political and Security Committee, an EU Military Committee, and an EU Military Staff.

While the focus of Ukraine's interactions has been primarily on the EU's most developed and strongest feature (i.e., its economic dimension), these interactions nonetheless reinforce the place of "Europe" in Ukraine's post-Soviet identity. Most importantly, these interactions have reinforced Ukraine's acceptance of market-economy values and its rejection of the command economy and the Communist ideology that were such dominant features of its Soviet identity. The primary instrument for managing Ukraine's interactions with the EU is the 1998 Partnership Cooperation Agreement, which outlines the principles and objectives of the Ukraine-EU relationship, including trade and investment obligations and promotion of democratic reforms and economic development. Most indicative of the importance of Ukraine's relationship with the EU are the trade statistics that indicate that the EU has emerged as Ukraine's largest trading partner, accounting for 35 percent of Ukraine's total trade.[32] As a member of the EU's Neighbourhood Policy launched in 2004, in February 2005, Ukraine concluded an Action Plan with the EU, providing a framework for future interactions and closer cooperation with Ukraine on such issues as support for Ukraine's democratization; possible areas for military and defense cooperation; common foreign policy positions; and facilitation of adaptation of the *acquis communitaire*, the set of legal rules and legislation to be implemented by all member states of the EU.

Ukraine's Identity and European Security Institutions: Kravchuk, Kuchma, and Yushchenko in Perspective

As influenced as Ukraine's identity is by its interactions with the primary European security institutions of the OSCE, NATO, and the EU, the fluctuations in the European dimension of Ukraine's identity can also be traced to the three presidential administrations Ukraine has had since achieving independence in 1991.

Leonid Kravchuk (1991–94)

During Leonid Kravchuk's tenure as president, Ukraine's interactions with European security institutions were characterized by policies that sought to establish basic access to these institutions for Ukraine as an independent, sovereign state stepping out of the long Soviet/Russian shadow. That it was a priority to establish Ukraine's international identity as an independent state in order to legitimize its credibility on the international stage, thereby diminishing its vulnerability, was not surprising. Thus, Kravchuk's presidency was marked by Ukraine joining the CSCE/OSCE and the NACC/EAPC in early 1992, and by its becoming the first post-Soviet country to sign on to the PfP program in February 1994. Thus, European security relations reinforced Ukraine's independent character, as well as promoted the European dimension of Ukraine's identity. But "Europe" in itself was not the priority and remained rather superficial in Ukraine's post-Soviet identity. Indeed, Ukraine's foreign relations under Kravchuk were dominated by the de-nuclearization issue; European security relations served as a means to replace the security value that the nuclear weapons on Ukrainian territory were perceived to have, rather than as a distinct policy objective that corresponded with a post-Soviet "Ukraine-belongs-in-Europe" identity. In this respect, the Kravchuk administration was notably consistent. Indeed, Ukraine's non-Russian orientation during these early years was reinforced by Kravchuk's persistence in seeking security guarantees from the European security institutions against any threat to its reclaimed independence originating from Moscow. Moreover, Ukraine refused to accede to the defense/military structure of the CIS. Thus, the adversarial transformation was complete: Europe became the security partner, and Russia became the potential threat. Nevertheless, a total identification with Europe based on acceptance of and adherence to European values was yet to come.

Leonid Kuchma (1994–2004)

Unlike in most election campaigns in Western democracies, Ukraine's foreign orientation and identity played an important role in the July 1994 presidential campaign between Leonid Kravchuk and Leonid Kuchma. More specifically, due to the necessary level of activism regarding Europe that he pursued during his tenure, Kravchuk was perceived as a "Western" candidate in contrast to his opponent, Leonid Kuchma, who was perceived to be oriented toward Russia and maintaining Ukraine's historic ties with its former imperial power. Indeed, it was under Kuchma's tenure that Ukraine concluded a Treaty of Friendship and Cooperation with Russia in May 1997. Nevertheless, as committed as the Kuchma administration was to affirming Ukraine's Eurasian ties and identity based on its interactions and institutions, the European dimension was never completely refuted. Indeed, it was during Kuchma's ten years as president that the strongest steps were taken to institutionalize Ukraine's interactions with Europe, thereby reinforcing the European dimension in its identity. Thus, the OSCE was invited to establish a mandate to assist in the resolution of Crimea's political status; the NATO-Ukraine Charter on a Distinctive Partnership was signed in 1997, and the NATO Information and Documentation Centre (in Kyiv) and the NATO-Ukraine Commission were established. The Partnership Cooperation Agreement with the EU was signed in 1998, and the NATO-Ukraine Action Plan was concluded in November 2002. Many of these accomplishments, and the reinforcement of the European dimension in Ukraine's post-Soviet identity, were due to the strong European orientation of Borys Tarasiuk, formerly Ukraine's ambassador to NATO under Kuchma and also one of his foreign ministers. Thus, through the persistent interactions with Europe's security institutions, a consensus on the transition from Europe as adversary to Europe as security partner had become irreversible under Kuchma.

Nevertheless, as much as Europe was viewed as Ukraine's security partner in its post-Soviet interactions, on another level the extent to which the Kuchma administration was committed to Europe's place in

Ukraine's identity was never doubted to be a function of Ukraine's relationship with Russia. In other words, the Europe-Ukraine relationship and the European dimension of Ukraine's identity were advanced only when the Russia-Ukraine relationship was stable, and when the Europe-Russia relationship also advanced. Thus, the 1997 NATO-Ukraine Charter was signed following the completion of the 1997 NATO-Russia Founding Act and the establishment of the NATO-Russia Permanent Joint Council, as well as the signing of the Ukraine-Russia Treaty on Friendship and Cooperation. Moreover, the 2002 statement of intention to join NATO and the conclusion of the 2002 NATO-Ukraine Action Plan followed the establishment of the more substantive NATO-Russia Council established in 2002 to replace the NATO-Russia Permanent Joint Council. In this way, security relations with European institutions and the subsequent impact on the European dimension in Ukraine's identity were pursued insofar as they did not disrupt or undermine the Ukraine-Russia relationship.

As a result, during the Kuchma decade, the place of Europe in Ukraine's post-Soviet identity had the appearance of fluctuating in intensity and commitment. And it was under these conditions that the debate over Ukraine's dichotomous "either/or" identity gained prominence. The doubts about Ukraine's sincerity regarding Europe increased when statements and policies were not matched by deeds and implementation. In addition, the ambiguity of Ukraine's intentions where NATO and the EU were concerned amplified the situation. Thus, the interactions suffered, and a sense of "Ukraine fatigue" set in among the European security institutions. As a result, relations with European security institutions could advance only so far, leaving the potential for realizing the European component in Ukraine's post-Soviet identity unfulfilled.

Viktor Yushchenko (2004 to the Present)

If Kuchma's administration was a period of either/or in Ukraine's post-Soviet identity, the election of Viktor Yushchenko in the controversial 2004 presidential election harkened an era of "Europe *and* Russia." Yushchenko indicated in his campaign and presidential pronouncements the wisdom and accuracy of maintaining *both* orientations in Ukraine's post-Soviet identity. Notwithstanding the duality in Ukraine's identity, of all Ukraine's post-Soviet presidents, Yushchenko stands out as the strongest and most definitive advocate for moving Ukraine into Europe to reclaim what he sees as its European heritage and to strengthen the European component in its identity. Indeed, this was a prominent feature of his campaign platform. Thus, Yushchenko has been clear about his intention for Ukraine to join NATO and to set policies that advance the process farther than previous administrations. In his frequent visits to EU institutions, Yushchenko has also been clear about his intention for Ukraine to join the EU, again more so than Kravchuk and Kuchma.

Notwithstanding Yushchenko's open commitment to Ukraine's political and economic reforms, key criteria in advancing the Europe-Ukraine relationship, his ability to make good on these intentions is complicated by the Kuchma legacy and the resilience of the "Ukraine fatigue" factor. Yushchenko's contribution to reinforcing and clarifying the European component in Ukraine's post-Soviet identity has been to strengthen the consensus established by his predecessors. Expectations are certainly high regarding membership in NATO and the EU, but to show his sincerity and correct Ukraine's image in the eyes of the Europeans, Yushchenko will need to match words with deeds. Only then will Ukraine's post-Soviet identity be secured.

Conclusion

Since 1991, Ukraine has made great strides in asserting a European dimension in its post-Soviet identity, a process that was greatly influenced by its interactions with the European security institutions of the OSCE, NATO, and the EU. Indeed, the greater Ukraine's interactions with these institutions, the stronger the European identification and the more distant the adversarial relationship with Europe of the past. In this respect, a mutually reinforcing relationship between institutions and state identities cannot be denied. In other words, a state's identity is derived from the meaning ascribed to interactions with other institutions and states. Where Ukraine and Europe are concerned, changes to the international context due to the end of the Cold War led to changed perceptions of Europe as a partner and interactions that reinforced this perception, leading to Ukraine becoming part of Europe's security institutions and taking on a European mantle in its post-Soviet identity.

However, the process for Ukraine has not been linear or independent of the context. Thus, as secure as Europe's place is in Ukraine's post-Soviet identity, there have been fluctuations in the degree of its intensity. The Yushchenko presidency holds great promise for ending these fluctuations, clarifying intentions where Ukraine's future relationship with Europe is concerned. If he is successful, and the Ukraine fatigue factor can be weakened, the formalization of Ukraine's interactions with the European security institutions will prompt changes in discussions about Ukraine's post-Soviet identity that are less informed by questions concerning the legitimacy of Europe's place and more concerned with the place of Russia and Eurasia.

Notes

1. Since 1994, this has been the name of the process previously known as the Conference on Security and Co-operation in Europe.
2. While the European Union is most prominently an economic institution, its own evolution to incorporate security issues among its own members, partners, and non-members qualifies it for inclusion in this chapter. See the section below on the European Union.
3. Among some scholars, the discussion about the relationship between identity and institutions has been linked *inter alia* with social constructivism, postmodernism, poststructuralism, critical theory, postmaterialism, antipositivism, relativism, and structuration theory.
4. Ted Hopf, "The Promise of Constructivism in International Relations Theory," *International Security* 23, no. 1 (Summer 1998): 174–75n10.
5. While it would be more accurate to label this the Euro-Atlantic camp in order to acknowledge the role and presence of two non-European countries, the United States and Canada, the focus of this chapter is the European component and proceeds accordingly.
6. These four republics were Russia, Ukraine, Belarus, and Kazakhstan. Operational control for any launch of these nuclear weapons was strictly administered by a small command in the Soviet Union's military and political bureaucracy that, in general, excluded members of any ethnic group other than Russian.
7. For an exceptional review and analysis of this period in the history of the CSCE, see John Maresca, *To Helsinki: The Conference on Security and Co-operation in Europe, 1973–1975* (Durham, NC: Duke University Press, 1987).
8. The participating states of the CSCE also included neutral, non-aligned countries and regions of Europe, such as Austria, Sweden, Finland, Cyprus, the Holy See, Switzerland, and Yugoslavia, among others. For

more information, see the official website of the Organization for Security and Co-operation in Europe, http://www.osce.org.

9. The key components of the Final Act are the ten principles, or "Decalogue," and the three "baskets" of commitments dealing with politico-military, economic, and humanitarian issues. See the 1975 Final Act for the complete text of these three baskets. A fourth basket committed the participating states to follow-up conferences to monitor the implementation of these commitments.

10. Interview with representative of the Mission of Ukraine to NATO, Brussels, June 13, 2002; interview with analyst, National Institute of Strategic Studies, Kyiv, June 18, 2002; interview with official in the Ministry of Defense, Kyiv, June 19, 2002; interview with official in the General Staff of the Ukrainian Armed Forces, Kyiv, June 19, 2002; interview with official of the Ministry of Foreign Affairs, Kyiv, June 20, 2002. This is not to say that in the early years of Ukrainian independence there did not remain a residual anti-NATO perception in Ukraine to a degree because of the Soviet legacy having been so entrenched and because of the continued presence of the old guard, which kept up such perceptions. Interview with NATO official, Kyiv, June 20, 2002.

11. The CSCE process was noted to have been influential in bringing about the end of the Cold War and the collapse of the Soviet Union. J. Liska, "The Human Dimension in the Helsinki Process," in *International Security and Humanitarian Co-operation in the ReUnited Europe*, ed. Wolfgang Kleinwachter and Kaarle Nordenstreng (Tampere, Finland: University of Tampere, 1991). CSCE documents such as those from the 1989 Vienna Follow-Up Meeting and the 1990 Meeting of the Conference on the Human Dimension of the CSCE also note the contribution of the CSCE to the historical changes in Europe. The *1990 Charter of Paris for a New Europe* states in its preamble: "The courage of men and women, the strength of the will of the peoples and the power of the ideas of the Helsinki Final Act have opened a new era of democracy, peace and unity in Europe."

12. The OSCE/ODIHR Election Observation Mission opened in Kyiv on August 31, 2004, with fifty-seven experts and long-term observers deployed in the capital and twenty regional centers. To observe the re-run of the second round of the election, the size of the mission was increased to include a core team of twenty-one international experts based in Kyiv and fifty-five long-term observers in all the regions of Ukraine. On election day, the mission deployed more than 1,300 short-term observers representing forty-four OSCE participating states, including ninety-two parliamentarians from the OSCE Parliamentary Assembly, thirty-seven from the Parliamentary Assembly of the Council of Europe, twenty-seven from the NATO

Parliamentary Assembly and sixteen from the European Parliament. Nine hundred and eighty-one observers were accredited as OSCE/ODIHR observers. *Statement of Preliminary Findings and Conclusions: Presidential Election (Repeat Second Round), Ukraine, 26 December 2004*, International Election Observation Mission, December 27, 2004, Kyiv.

13. Natalie Mychajlyszyn, "The OSCE and the Prevention of Ethnic Conflict: Lessons Learned from Field Missions and the HCNM," in *Conflict Prevention: Grand Illusion or Path to Peace?* ed. Albrecht Schnabel and David Carment (Tokyo: United Nations University Press, 2002); "The OSCE: The Impact of International Factors on Regionalism in the Former Soviet States," in *Regionalism in Post-Soviet States*, ed. James Hughes and Gwendolyn Sasse (London: Frank Cass, 2001); "The OSCE in Crimea," *Helsinki Monitor* 9, no. 4 (1998); "The OSCE and Conflict Prevention: The Case of Ukraine," in *Balancing Hegemony: The OSCE in the CIS*, ed. S. Neil MacFarlane and Oliver Thränert (Kingston, ON: Queen's Centre for International Relations, 1997).

14. One interlocutor noted that NATO and its changing relationship with its former adversaries benefited from the visionary leadership of Manfred Woerner, who initiated the process of reaching out and integrating the former Warsaw Pact countries, then institutionalized and normalized the processes. Interview with NATO official, NATO, Brussels, June 12, 2003.

15. The PfP program is largely considered to have substantiated the initial process of reaching out to the former adversaries by way of NACC in an attempt to throw a lifeline and link these countries to NATO, thereby making it more difficult for the process to reverse itself. In other words, the former adversaries were being given a stake in the institutions by being integrated into it. Thus, PfP helped to move the relationship with former adversaries much more decisively in a particular direction than had other early initiatives, although the earlier ones were not any less significant for their time. Interview with NATO official, NATO, Brussels, June 10, 2003.

16. The institutionalization process was noted to have served an important role in also reassuring both NATO and the countries of Eastern Europe and the former Soviet Union in the transformation of their changed relationship. It is also interesting to note that, according to one interlocutor, the idea of institutionalizing interactions with the former adversaries outside of NATO formally is rooted in the Cold War and arms control and disarmament negotiations with the USSR, which were impossible to hold within NATO's framework, even though NATO had a stake in these negotiations. Thus, this was not an

entirely new or original development. Interview with NATO official, NATO, Brussels, June 10, 2003. Even so, it is surprising to note that according to one view, NATO underwent an institutionalization process more profoundly and more quickly than the OSCE during the same period. Interview with NATO official, NATO, Brussels, June 12, 2003.

17. Interview with Volodymyr Belashov, Deputy Head, Mission of Ukraine to NATO, Brussels, June 13, 2002.
18. The change in perception of NATO as an enemy by way of the deepening and institutionalization of Ukraine's interactions with NATO was confirmed by several officials interviewed. Interview with representative of the Mission of Ukraine to NATO, Brussels, June 13, 2002; Interview with official in the National Security and Defence Council, Kyiv, June 20, 2002.
19. The EAPC superficially rivals the OSCE as the largest security institution, but each considers complementary security issues and with different political venues and heritage.
20. Interview with NATO official, NATO, Brussels, June 11, 2003.
21. Interviews with official of the General Staff of the Ukrainian Armed Forces, Kyiv, June 19, 2002; NATO official No. 7, Kyiv, June 20, 2002.
22. The significance of this signal concerning the commitment of both sides to move the relationship forward should not be underestimated given the scandals surrounding the Ukrainian presidency at the time, regarding Kuchma and his mistreatment of several journalists in Ukraine and his violating the norm of freedom of the press, in addition to the discovery of some possible links between the Ukrainian government and the illegal sale of a Kolchuga radar system to Iraq. Interview with NATO official, NATO, Brussels, June 11, 2003.
23. Radio Era, Kyiv, March 23, 2005.
24. Interview with representative of the Mission of Ukraine to NATO, Brussels, June 13, 2002.
25. Interview with official of the General Staff of the Ukrainian Armed Forces, Kyiv, June 19, 2002.
26. Interview with NATO official, NATO, Brussels, June 11, 2003.
27. Interview with representative of the Mission of Ukraine to NATO, Brussels, June 13, 2002; Interview with NATO official, NATO, Brussels, June 11, 2003; Interview with NATO official, Kyiv, June 3, 2003.
28. Interview with NATO official, Kyiv, June 3, 2003. In part, these activities also serve to signal rather strongly a shared commitment to peacekeeping and conflict management.
29. Interview with official of the General Staff of the Ukrainian Armed Forces, Kyiv, June 19, 2002; Interview with NATO official, Kyiv, June 20, 2002.

30. Interview with official in the Ministry of Defense, Kyiv, June 19, 2002.
31. Interview with analyst, National Institute of Strategic Studies, Kyiv, June 18, 2002.
32. http://www.europa.eu.

3

Belarus in the Lukashenka Era: National Identity and Relations with Russia

Per Anders Rudling

The political development in the Republic of Belarus differs sharply from that of Poland, Ukraine, Latvia, and Lithuania during the past decade. While her neighbors have ascended on a path toward democracy and greater transparency, Belarus has been descending into authoritarianism. Politically, Belarus shows more similarities with the republics of post-Soviet Central Asia than with its neighbors in Europe. In fewer than fifteen years, Belarus has gone from being a new and fragile democracy to a pariah state, which the United States refers to as an "outpost of tyranny" and the European Union (EU) calls "the last dictatorship in Europe."[1] Belarus' political evolution during the post-Communist period can be divided into three phases: independence, liberalization, and establishment of democratic national institutions (1991–94); conflict between president and parliament, strengthening of the presidential powers, and weakening of democratic institutions and independence (1994–96); and one-man authoritarian rule (since 1997).[2] Why and how did this happen in Belarus? This article seeks to find some of the answers in the absence of a strong national identity and in the public's weak identification with the national institutions.

Language and Nationality

In Eastern Europe, language and religion have generally been the ethnic denominators and the primary carriers of national identity. Belarus lacks defined borders, both in terms of geography and language. There are no clear borders where Belarusian dialects cease to be spoken and where Russian and Polish dialects start. Many people speak a mixed language or dialect, known as *transianka*, to the abhorrence of Belarusian nationalist intellectuals. In many ways, this fluid ethnolinguistic border is symbolic of the relations between Belarus and its far larger eastern neighbor, Russia. In contrast, the western borders of Belarus are somewhat clearer, as a result of massive population transfers from 1944 to 1948 and from 1956 to 1958, which relocated the most nationally conscious parts of the Polish population.

For the past two centuries, Russian and Polish have been the languages of the elites, as well as the languages of learning in Belarus. Belarusian has largely remained the language of the simple people, and as such has not enjoyed a very high status. Since the language has been codified and standardized only within the past century, speakers of Belarusian dialects have traditionally referred to their vernacular as *prosta mova*, or "simple language." The Belarusian peasantry long lacked a strong sense of separate identity and commonly considered its language to be less prestigious than the language of its Polish and Russian overlords. In fact, as language signified social status, well into the twentieth century it was considered inappropriate for a Belarusian peasant to speak in Polish, *pa-pansku*, or to speak "like a gentleman."[3] Imperial Russian authorities, however, considered the Belarusians to be Russians, corrupted by Polish influences. The wave of national awakening that swept much of Eastern Europe in the nineteenth century came late to Belarus. In the absence of a modern "national" identity, significant sections of society referred to themselves simply as *tuteishy* (locals) well into the twentieth century.

A Weak Identity

Since the Bolshevik Revolution, the brief periods of "national" development in Belarus were, as a rule, the result of policies initiated by Moscow. There were three periods of Belarusization, followed by periods of national repression and cultural Russification. The first and most significant wave of Belarusization took place during the period of 1919 to 1929. The Belarusians received their own Soviet

Republic, the Belarusian language was conferred the status of a national language, and serious attempts were made to replace the prior Russian and Polish elites with native Belarusians. Stalin's reversal of policy around 1930 led to a virtual extermination of the national elite and a period of Russification. A second, much briefer Belarusization, initiated by Deputy Premier Lavrentii Beria, took place in 1953, but ended as Beria lost the power struggle and was executed. The third wave of Belarusization followed upon Gorbachev's perestroika and the collapse of the Soviet Union, particularly in the years 1991–94. But this came to an end as Lukashenka established his authoritarian regime.

Apart from the above-mentioned exceptions, Soviet and Polish rule provided an unfavorable climate for the development of a strong Belarusian identity. Unlike in Ukraine, in the Belarusian Soviet Socialist Republic (BSSR), Stalin was able to effectively exterminate the national elite. Of the Belarusian "literary intelligentsia" who wrote in Belarusian (poets, writers, publicists, linguists, and historians), more than 370 were shot (roughly the same number as were executed in Ukraine and Russia, republics that had populations five and fifteen times the population of Belarus, respectively[4]). Ninety percent of the Soviet Belarusian writers were arrested. Most of them perished.

The sizable Belarusian community in interwar Poland was also subject to brutal repression. Unlike their Ukrainian neighbors in Galicia, Belarusian community members were too weak and poorly organized to play the role of a viable reserve of Belarusian culture. The Polish government implemented policy of systematic colonization of the Belarusian lands it had conquered in the Polish-Soviet war of 1919–20, while grossly and systematically manipulating the population censuses, inflating the number of ethnic Poles in western Belarus. All Belarusian schools in Poland were shut down, with the result that well into the 1940s, the vast majority of western Belarusians remained illiterate. The Polish authorities interpreted the possession of books in Belarusian as a dangerous sign of disloyalty. As Belarusian-language publications were systematically censored and banned, by 1939, there was not a single publication left in the Belarusian language in Poland. This combination of widespread illiteracy and political oppression effectively prevented the small elite of nationalist intellectuals from spreading its ideas to the masses.[5]

Belarus suffered more deaths per capita than any other state in Europe during the war, losing as much as one-third of its population.

The shared memories of wartime suffering and the liberation by the Red Army in 1944 served as powerful sources for a common Soviet identity. During World War II, Soviet partisan activities were particularly strong in Belarus. Many of the postwar political leaders had a background as partisan fighters, were seen as war heroes, and gained a great deal of popularity during the Brezhnev era. One of these was Piotr Masherau, leader of the Communist Party of Belarus from 1965 to 1980, who became a genuinely popular figure. In Belarus, perhaps more than anywhere else in the Soviet Union, the concept of *Homo Sovieticus* had an impact on the collective identity. Among many Belarusians, this identification with the Soviet Union has survived the Union itself.[6]

Industrialization and Assimilation

The geopolitical changes after World War II meant that the BSSR no longer bordered hostile states and decreased the immediate threat that Belarus would again become a theater of war. Following the wartime destruction, the Soviet government decided on massive industrialization of the republic. The postwar era, particularly the periods of the seven-year plan of 1959 to 1965 and the five-year plan of 1965 to 1970, saw a dramatic industrialization and urbanization that weakened the people's sense of ties to the land; Belarusian peasants moved en masse to Soviet-style apartment complexes and a largely Russophone city life. This process took place during the Brezhnev- and Khrushchev-era period during which the official nationalities policies emphasized the so-called *sblizhenie* (drawing together) and *sliianie* (merging) of the peoples, aimed at forging a new man, the *Homo Sovieticus,* and a single, indivisible Soviet nation, where particularistic national factors were to diminish and disappear. The main vehicles for this policy were the promotion of the Russian language and the Russification of culture. For the new urban dwellers, Russian became the language of higher education and administration and the path to a career.[7] At the same time, Belarus saw significant material improvements. From being one of the most underdeveloped areas in the Russian empire and the Soviet Union, it quickly became one of the most heavily industrialized. In the collective memory, the era of Masherau was Belarus' days of glory. By 1980, Belarus was politically stable and one of the leading growth regions in the Soviet Union. This prosperity had attracted many retired Soviet military men, and Belarus turned into something of the Soviet equivalent of "Florida," a republic that attracted large numbers of retired Soviet military personnel and their families.[8] This group constitutes some six hundred thousand people, a significant number in a republic with a population of 9.7 million (July 2007 estimate). The influence of this group on the political culture in the republic has been significant.[9] The legacies of terror, war, and urbanization have contributed to the appearance of a culture that was first and foremost Soviet, and where the national, Belarusian aspects of culture were less emphasized. Modernity and industrialization arrived late to the republic, with the result that national mobilization was carried out in Russian, within the context of a Soviet framework.

There was—and still exists—a competing, separate, and westward-looking Belarusian nationalism, but political repression and unfavorable social conditions have prevented it from becoming a mass movement. Belarusian nationalism has remained the preoccupation of small groups within the intelligentsia. After the repression of the 1930s, it was not until the Gorbachev era that a nationalist movement, the Belarusian Popular Front, was able to exercise any significant influence in Belarusian politics. For a couple of years, it was the leading oppositional organization. Initially, its focus was on the rebirth of language and culture. Since independence, the movement has desired European integration, a soft transition to market economy, and a radical break with the country's Communist past. The Belarusian Popular Front was led from 1988 to 1996 by the archaeologist Zianon Pazniak, who had made a name for himself by unearthing a mass grave in Kuropaty outside Minsk in 1988, where he claimed between 150,000–200,000 and 500,000 victims of the Great Terror were buried.[10] The Front's moment of glory was short, and its influence peaked during the turbulent years between 1990 and 1992. Its success was hampered by its aggressive anti-Russian rhetoric and demands for border revisions with four of its five neighbors. Pazniak has claimed Vilnius from Lithuania and Bialystok from Poland, as well as the Smolensk, Briansk, Pskov, and Viazma provinces from Russia.[11] Soon the nationalists lost their political initiative. Revelations of Stalinist terror were unpopular among people who largely identified with the heroism of the Great Patriotic War, and the Belarusian public met the anti-Stalinism of the opposition with silence and hostility.[12]

At the beginning of the Gorbachev era, the future of the Belarusian language seemed dire. Not only was its use rapidly declining, but most Russified Belarusians showed little or no interest in reviving or learning the language. Belarusian was often seen as "a relic of pre-industrial, rural existence."[13] Belarusian was used primarily by the elderly and rural population, as many urbanized Belarusians looked at the relationship between Belarusian and Russian as that between a dialect and a literary language rather than of two languages of equal value. According to the 1999 census, 36.7 percent of the respondents indicated that they speak Belarusian at home, while 62.8 percent used Russian. More importantly, less than 50 percent were willing to advance their knowledge of the Belarusian language, testifying to its low status.[14]

On January 26, 1990, in an attempt to elevate the status of its language, the BSSR Supreme Soviet voted to make Belarusian the official language of the republic, starting September 1, 1990.[15] This move was highly unpopular within the bureaucracy, and government officials at all levels openly resisted the law. Despite the legislation, the Belarusian language never entered the corridors of power. Many Belarusians continued to view linguistic Russification as a natural and progressive development and did not link it to the demise of Belarusian culture.

In the wake of Gorbachev's perestroika, political alternatives and oppositional movements sprang up across the Soviet Union. In the elections to the Belarusian Supreme Soviet in 1989, the non-Communist opposition captured approximately thirty seats. Nevertheless, 86 percent, or 296 of the 345 deputies elected, were Communists.[16] Despite popular attachment to the Soviet Union, the BSSR Supreme Soviet made a declaration of sovereignty of the BSSR in foreign relations on July 27, 1990. This development followed in the footsteps of the Russian republic, which had declared its sovereignty two weeks earlier.[17] The Belarusians' deep attachment to the Soviet Union was expressed in the union-wide referendum on March 17, 1991, in which 82.7 percent of the Belarusian voters voted in favor of keeping the Soviet Union as a renewed federation of equal, sovereign republics. This was higher than the USSR average, 76.4 percent, and the highest figure of any republic outside Central Asia.[18] The nationalist opposition had previously been toying with alternatives to a Russian-dominated union, but its proposed Baltic–Black Sea federation, consisting of the Baltic states, Belarus, Ukraine, and Moldova and oriented toward the West and the United States, met with little interest both in Belarus and among the elites of the intended partners.[19]

Unlike in the neighboring Baltic countries and Ukraine after the fall of Shcherbytsky, there simply was no national Communist faction within the Communist Party of Belarus (CPB). On the contrary, the CPB was thoroughly de-nationalized. Firmly rooted in the Soviet order, its leaders took orders from Moscow rather than catering to what they considered to be a group of isolated and subversive intellectuals.[20] Likewise, the majority of the Belarusian population also behaved differently from the peoples of the Baltics. The Belarusians neither acted nor responded as a nation, while the sections of society that could have been capable of such action were not in positions of authority.

Belarus was also the most militarized of the Soviet republics and was home to the most strategic and secret Soviet military bases. The republic is considered part of a pro-Communist so-called "Red Belt," along with eastern Ukraine and southwestern Russia (where Communist officials have managed to stay in power ever since the collapse of the Soviet Union), and identification with Belarus has remained relatively low. Belarus remained the least "nationalized" of the former Soviet republics: in 1992, only 35.9 percent of Belarusians agreed with the statement "My home is Belarus."[21] During the Soviet period, a different form of identity had taken root—a pan-Soviet identity, centered around the heroism of the Great Patriotic War and pride in the achievements of the Soviet Union. In the late 1980s, 69 percent of Belarusians identified themselves as "Soviet," the highest percentage of any Soviet Republic.[22] Belarusians and foreign observers alike often emphasize the "Soviet" atmosphere, which still lingers in Belarus. Former acting head of state Stanislau Shushkevich complains that the Soviet Belarusians became the most Soviet of all people in the former USSR, "more Soviet than the Russians themselves, and could not hide their pride in that fact."[23] A recent American travel guide suggests Belarus as a worthwhile destination for anyone who wonders what life in the Soviet Union was like:

> If you are looking for a true Soviet city, skip Moscow and go to Minsk, where the fall of communism has led to a reluctant shuffle, rather than an enthusiastic gallop, west. With imaginary political reforms and concrete construction everywhere, not to mention the omnipresent police, everyone is asking if the government is giving Minsk a new face or just a new façade.[24]

The achieving of full independence in 1991 was largely a result of external factors. There was little popular support for separation from the USSR. The Belarusian Communist leadership had been among the first to break open the champagne when hardliners attempted to oust Gorbachev in August 1991. Belarusian media, still firmly in the hands of the CPB, openly supported the coup.[25] In fact, the leading newspapers kept printing pro-coup articles even after the coup had failed.[26] The miscalculation in regards to the failed 1991 coup was a disaster for the Belarusian leadership, one that discredited them and bereaved them of the support from the center in Moscow. The CPB was outlawed, again a move that followed the lead of Moscow. Even though its party was gone, the Communist majority in the Belarusian Supreme Soviet kept dominating the political landscape. A main impetus behind the August 25, 1991, declaration of independence was the vain attempt by the old *nomenklatura* to ensure its political survival following the demise of the Soviet Union and the Soviet Communist Party. For almost a year, there was much political uncertainty. The old establishment was still very much in a state of shock and politically paralyzed. This began to change following an attempt by the Belarusian Popular Front (BPF) to assert its authority by pushing for pre-term elections in 1992. As this backfired, the old *nomenklatura* began the re-consolidation of its power base.[27]

Belarus was poorly prepared for the switch to a market economy. In opinion polls, only 20 percent supported the introduction of private property in industry and agriculture, while a majority was solidly opposed. The platforms of the various political parties varied, but in regards to economic reforms, those of the nationalist BPF differed little from those of the Communists.[28] The nationalists focused on symbolic issues such as language and culture. The old *nomenklatura* establishment did not want to break with the Soviet past and identified with the memories of the Soviet past. Neither side was prepared to undertake any serious reform programs—scared by the chaotic "shock therapy" in Russia. The leading Belarusian politicians vacillated between an emphasis on the need for a soft transition to a market economy and no transition at all.

Overall, the Soviet-era power structures in Belarus were able to withstand the wave of popular revolutions that swept Eastern Europe in 1989 and 1991. Much of this can be attributed to the weak sense of national identity and the weakness of the opposition.

Reluctant Independence

The struggle over national identity haunted Belarus after the collapse of socialism. It polarized the political landscape into pro-Russian Soviet nostalgic "isolationists" and an anti-Russian camp of nationalist "westernizers." This polarized political climate allowed for the successful establishment of a third political force. It allowed a relative outsider, Aliaksandr Lukashenka, to establish a new form of autocracy.[29] Until 1994, Belarus maintained the political structures of the BSSR. The speaker of the Supreme Soviet, Stanislau Shushkevich, filled the role of acting head of state. The government consisted almost exclusively of former Communists and was led by Viacheslau Kebich, who represented the old system and the *nomenklatura*. Before he entered politics in 1990, he had been the chair of the Belarusian planning agency, Gosplan.[30] Soon after Belarus became independent, a commission to write a new constitution was established. It was soon clear that Belarus would become a "presidential" republic, much like Russia and Ukraine. A new constitution was adopted on March 15, 1994, and presidential elections followed shortly thereafter. With the support of the *nomenklatura*, Kebich appeared to have an enormous advantage over his opponents. His campaign portrayed him as a "Masherau of today." Kebich declared that the 1991 Belovezha treaty, which had dissolved the Soviet Union, had been a great mistake and promised to restore the Soviet Union in a revised form.[31]

In terms of competing in Soviet nostalgia and class populism, however, Kebich was soon challenged by a somewhat unlikely candidate: a thirty-nine-year-old former *sovkhoz* (state farm) chairman by the name of Aliaksandr Lukashenka. Lukashenka was heading a parliamentary anti-corruption committee and conducted a skillful populist campaign under the slogan "Neither with the left, nor with the right, but with the people."[32] This strategy turned out to be quite successful in the midst of an economic crisis, as a majority of Belarusian voters were rather centrist and attracted to the message of Soviet nostalgia.[33] Lukashenka's claims to have had his car fired upon with machine guns during the election campaign gave him an aura of being an honest political outsider. Lukashenka described himself as a "Soviet Belarusian"; he had made a name for himself as an aggressive crusader against the Belovezha treaty, demanding the restoration of the USSR. He was able to exploit the issue of bilingualism to his advantage, appearing as the moderate candidate who desired societal harmony, and rejected the excesses of the BPF. His verbal attacks on the *nouveaux riches* and the "dirty swines" who had ruined the USSR were delivered in simple language that appealed to ordinary people, disillusioned with the political infighting.

Lukashenka established close relations with Russian anti-Western political forces, such as the Communist Party of the Russian Federation, the ultra-nationalist Vladimir Zhirinovskii, the Soviet restorationist Sergei Baburin, and others who had been successful in the December 1993 election to the Russian Duma. During his presidential campaign, Lukashenka appeared in the Russian Duma on invitation by Vladimir Zhirinovskii to argue for a new union between Russia and Belarus. The decline of the BPF and its strategic mistakes during the 1994 presidential elections facilitated Lukashenka's success. By 1994, the BPF had a narrow support base. In popular memory, the Front became associated with infighting, corruption, and the economic collapse of the early 1990s. Knowing that their candidate could not win, the BPF ran a campaign that encouraged people to vote for anyone but the official candidate, Kebich.[34]

The Lukashenka Era

In the presidential elections of 1994, widely perceived as free and fair, the nationalists did poorly. Zianon Pazniak received 12.9 percent of the votes cast, Shushkevich 9.9. Lukashenka, who ran as an independent candidate on a platform of anti-corruption and Soviet nostalgia, won 45.1 percent of the vote.[35] In the second round of the election, a run-off between Lukashenka and Kebich, the *nomenklatura* candidate, Lukashenka won a full 80.1 percent of all votes cast, with 14.2 percent for Kebich.[36] The rise of Lukashenka epitomized something new and unique in the post-Soviet political landscape. With the exception of nationalist dissident Zviad Gamsakhurdia's brief interregnum in Georgia, Lukashenka was the only leader in the Commonwealth of Independent States (CIS) who had not belonged to the *nomenklatura*. The old power apparatus restoration attempts were interrupted in 1994, while a new form of authoritarian order was established under Lukashenka. It promised to deliver what Kebich had not.

The authoritarian reconstruction began almost immediately after Lukashenka was sworn in, in June.[37] The new president envisioned a presidency with near-dictatorial powers and began a process of systematically undermining the parliament. This was by no means a unique development but followed a similar trend across the CIS. Locked in a conflict with the legislature, Russian president Boris Yeltsin had in 1993 used force to dissolve the democratically elected Russian Supreme Soviet and introduced a new power structure and new state symbols. While Yeltsin replaced Soviet-era symbols with imperial Russian symbolism, Lukashenka instead restored Soviet state symbols.

Following a tradition of populism, Lukashenka established a system of using referenda to achieve his goals. The issue of new state symbols was put to a vote, and official results indicated that 75 percent of the Belarusian voters approved the changes. To the new leader, the referendum may have mattered little. Even before the official results of the referendum had been released, the old flags and symbols had been removed from all official buildings in Minsk.[38]

The white-red-white flag and the coat of arms of the short-lived and ill-fated Belarusian People's Republic, which had once again become the coat of arms of the Republic of Belarus in 1991, were replaced by slightly modified Soviet Belarusian state symbols in 1995. The old flag that had flown above the Supreme Soviet was ritually disgraced and torn up, the pieces sold as souvenirs to symbolize the end of an old era and the beginning of a new, much as pieces of the Berlin wall were sold after the fall of the German Democratic Republic. At the same time, the Russian language (formally a minority language in the republic, although spoken by a majority of its population) was granted status equal with that of Belarusian.

In response to Lukashenka's provocative change of state symbols, Pazniak reacted with outrage and promised to ban all Communist organizations, and any organization opposing the Belarusian language and state symbols of 1991 to 1995. Shushkevich, a moderate, pro-Western nationalist, puts a considerable part of the blame for Lukashenka's ascent to power on the BPF: "The unrestrained maximalism of the Belarusian Popular Front was in fact bordering on extremism and made impossible the hope of finding even a minimal common ground between *nomenklatura* and opposition."[39]

In order to weaken the parliamentary system further, Lukashenka openly urged Belarusian voters to boycott the 1995 parliamentary elections, since a turnout of less than 50 percent would have given him a legitimate reason to disband the Supreme Soviet and rule alone.[40] When this strategy did not work, Lukashenka single-handedly rewrote the constitution. The changes extended his term in office by two years and created a second chamber of parliament, the National Assembly, whose members are handpicked by the president. The new constitution allows the parliament to discuss state expenditures only with the consent of the president. Lukashenka also fired the old Constitutional Court and replaced it with a new Court, appointed by the president and firmly under his control. The changes in the constitution give the president the right to issue decrees that have the force of law, circumventing the parliament. Lukashenka put these suggestions to the people in a referendum on November 24, 1996; the changes were approved by 70 percent of the voters.[41] The referendum was sharply criticized internationally, and the OSCE, the EU, the United States, and the Council of Europe have refused to accept its legitimacy. Following this, Lukashenka dissolved the parliament. By 1996, Lukashenka had established a semi-dictatorial system of government, where separation of power existed only on paper.

Like the dictators of the 1930s, Lukashenka put much emphasis on establishing the link between the leader and the people. His image is constantly present: in shop windows, on public buildings, in the press, and on television. On Belarusian television in June 2003, Lukashenka commented on his style of leadership: "Am I a dictator? My position and the state will never allow me to become a dictator.... But an authoritarian ruling style is characteristic of me, and I have always admitted it."[42]

In October 2004, a third referendum on the constitution was held, one that removed the presidential two-term limit, effectively allowing Lukashenka to become president for life. By now, no one was surprised when the chair of the election committee announced that the president had won "an elegant victory" with 77.3 percent of the votes in his favor and a turnout of 89.73 percent. The opposition and the OSCE condemned the election as rigged.[43] Four months before the scheduled presidential elections in 2006, Lukashenka appeared on national television and informed his people that they would simply elect him in the next election—"What can you do? You'll elect me"—adding that polls showed the president as having a 75 percent backing.[44]

Erratic Policies

Over time, Lukashenka's rule has become increasingly eccentric and erratic. He has made a point of building soccer stadiums and ice rinks across the country and likes to pose in front of cameras while roller-skating or skiing with his cabinet. He has described himself as an "atheist Orthodox," has praised Adolf Hitler, and has publicly stated a desire for Belarus to re-acquire its nuclear weapons, which were transferred to Russia after the collapse of the Soviet Union.[45] In terms of foreign policy, he has oriented Belarus toward fellow international pariahs such as Qaddafi's Libya, Milošević's Serbia, al-Assad's Syria,

Saddam Hussein's Iraq, and Ahmadinejad's Iran. He long identified with Serbia and Milošević personally. During the 1999 crisis, he traveled to Yugoslavia to propose that Serbia join his Belarusian-Russian union.[46] After Milošević's fall, Lukashenka offered him political asylum in Belarus. Lukashenka has also found a friend in Hugo Chavez's Venezuela.

At the same time, relations with the West have continually deteriorated due to a number of diplomatic crises. In September 1995, an American hot air balloon was shot down over Belarus, killing two crewmembers. Belarus has not apologized, nor offered compensation to the families.[47] In 1998, Lukashenka attempted to evict several Western embassies from Minsk. The official reason given was a need for sewage repairs, but the real reason seems to have been that Lukashenka, who himself lived in the exclusive Drozdy compound outside Minsk, did not want to share his living environment with foreigners.[48] Only after a coordinated protest and a seven-month diplomatic boycott by EU, U.S., and Japanese ambassadors in view of Lukashenka's violation of the Vienna Convention did Lukashenka allow the ambassadors to return to their residences. Relations with the EU—in particular Belarus' immediate neighbors to the west (Poland and the Baltic States) and the Czech Republic—have remained chilly. Lukashenka has accused Poland of having "become a bridgehead from which the invasion of the former Soviet Union advances" and has cracked down on the Polish community in Belarus, accusing it of disloyalty and causing Warsaw to recall its ambassador from Minsk.[49] During the November 2002 NATO meeting in Prague, the Atlantic organization made it clear that neither Lukashenka nor Ukrainian president Leonid Kuchma was welcome. Lukashenka erupted in a tirade against the Czechs, claiming that "the position of the Czechs in Belarus will be ruined for all future—and if not for all future so at least for a very long time," and threatened to have "drugs and illegal immigrants" invade Western Europe across the Belarusian border.[50] U.S. president George W. Bush included Belarus in his "Axis of Evil," while Secretary of State Condoleezza Rice, in her Senate hearings prior to her confirmation as Secretary of State in January 2005, included Belarus as the sole European country in a list of "outposts of tyranny" to be given particular attention by the U.S. government. Belarus got to share this dubious honor with Cuba, Myanmar, and Zimbabwe.[51] As a result of Lukashenka's confrontational foreign policy, Belarus has become increasingly isolated. Some of Lukashenka's allies, such as Slobodan Milošević and Saddam

Hussein, have been toppled, while the governments of Syria and Iran are increasingly isolated and discredited. Belarus remains the only European state that is not a member of the Council of Europe.

While Belarus' relations with the West are poor, perhaps what is more serious for Lukashenka is that relations with Russia have become more complicated since Putin's rise to power. Lukashenka has invested much of his political capital in the idea of a restored union with Russia, a project that is primarily his brainchild. The "union" between Russia and Belarus was formed on April 2, 1996, and an actual "Union Treaty" was signed on April 2, 1997. The idea was to create a union state with a joint currency, a revolving presidency and government, and a common parliament (with members delegated by the national parliaments).[52] But the union treaty has only ever had symbolic meaning, and the two countries still have their national currencies. It has become obvious that this is a union of increasingly unequal partners as the economy, influence, and power of Russia vastly exceeds that of Belarus. While Yeltsin always paid lip service to this union, Putin has shown little interest in this arrangement. It appears that in the mid-1990s, the unpopular Yeltsin treated this half-hearted union as an attempt to muster support for his policies. Since Putin does not carry the same historical baggage as Yeltsin, the union treaty is of less importance to him.

In fact, Putin has been able to use pro-integration sentiments to his advantage. At a meeting between the two presidents in August 2002, Putin suddenly announced a new policy vis-à-vis Belarus. At a joint press conference, Putin stunned Lukashenka with the suggestion that Belarus ought to be dissolved and the six Belarusian provinces added to the Russian Federation: "That would be a union state in the full meaning of the word," Putin declared. The official reaction from Minsk was one of shock. Suddenly, the conditions had changed. Putin had not only stolen Lukashenka's political platform; he could claim to outdo him in enthusiasm for reintegration. Putin's plan would eliminate Lukashenka as a political player in Russia, and dispense with a political rival. Lukashenka unexpectedly found himself on the same side as the nationalist opposition and quickly redefined himself as a Belarusian patriot, a staunch defender of Belarusian independence and sovereignty.[53] "What would be the reaction of the citizens of Belarus? Absolute dismissal, an absolute no," Lukashenka stated, and accused Putin of "having gone further than Lenin and Stalin" with his proposed annexation. Lukashenka has, perhaps correctly, perceived Putin's new plan as a provocation.

His responses have even contained not-so-subtle threats: Lukashenka has defiantly asked whether Russia wants "a second Chechnya on their western flank."[54]

For some time, the plans for a union seemed dead and Lukashenka's future uncertain. Some Russian papers openly speculated that his days in power were numbered.[55]

The Orange Revolution has left Belarus more isolated than before, as Lukashenka's relation to his southern neighbor is more strained now that Kuchma is no longer in office.

Following the Orange Revolution in Ukraine, Lukashenka insisted there would be no such revolution in Belarus, whether "rose, orange or banana," and that he would assure security "no matter what it costs."[56] Indeed, Lukashenka seems prepared to go to great lengths to preserve his power. Undeniably, there is order in Lukashenka's Belarus. The question is at what price this has been established. Lukashenka has increasingly shown ambitions to regulate everyday life through tight control of mass culture. He has ordered that 80 percent of the music played on Belarusian radio must be Belarusian and has expressed an ambition to triple the Belarusian population, calling on Belarusian families to have a minimum of three children, adding that "Belarus will be able to feed 30 million people."[57]

The intellectual climate in Belarus has grown more rigid, with Lukashenka's government taking an active part in rewriting the country's past. In time for the sixtieth-anniversary celebration of the victory over Nazi Germany, Belarusian state-run bookstores began stocking a 700-page book entitled *To Stalin Bow, Europe*, a collection of the dictator's speeches and articles glorifying Stalin and his era. In 2004, Lukashenka opened a memorial museum dedicated to the founder of the Cheka in Dzerzhinovo outside Minsk and referred to Feliks Dzerzhinskii as the kind of "great person" Belarus could use today.[58] This process of restoring the Soviet historical memory was started in 1995, when Lukashenka's government ordered the replacement of post-Soviet textbooks in high schools and universities with Soviet editions in Russian. "Stop cursing the country's past leaders, beginning with our main leader, Stalin, and ending with others!" Lukashenka demanded. "Just stop it! We were not around in those days, and we do not know what really happened. I can only suggest, since I am in roughly the same position [as Stalin], that they went about business the same way it has always been done."[59] An official investigation into the Kuropaty grave site where nationalist activist and Front founder Zianon Pazniak claimed to have uncovered the bodies of some 200,000 of Stalin's victims concluded that the number of victims was much smaller and that they were Jewish deportees from across Europe who had been murdered by the Nazis. A Belarusian historian, who preferred anonymity, stated that "[t]his regime is not quite Soviet, but it treats the Soviet period as though it were a lost paradise."[60]

The nostalgic component is indeed central to Lukashenka's ideology. In the absence of a clear sense of direction, in a government that is "neither right, nor left," Lukashenka has had little to offer but fear: fear of the West, fear of economic reforms, fear of change. The absence of radical reforms like those in neighboring Russia made the economic decline in Belarus less rapid than in Russia and Ukraine during the 1990s. "Many people feel that we have electricity and gas and are paid on time. People think that there are no other presidents [like Lukashenka]" is a typical response in Belarus to questions about why Lukashenka still enjoys relatively high approval ratings.[61] The fact that Belarus long had the highest ranking for the Human Development Index among the CIS states has been one of Lukashenka's strongest arguments. In 2000, Belarus was ranked as sixtieth in the world, while Russia was listed as seventy-first.[62] At the same time, many of the official economic statistics produced by the Belarusian government are misleading, and it is clear that the economic situation in Belarus is stagnant. In 2002, the Belarusian economy was 3 percent that of Russia, while its population was 7 percent that of Russia.[63]

Future Prospects for Belarusian Authoritarianism

History, symbolism, and ritual reminiscence of the glory days of Soviet power have been given a central place in the political life of Belarus. Other than in its use of symbols, Lukashenka's government is hard to position. Where does one place on a political scale a system described as "market socialism" by a self-proclaimed "atheist Orthodox"? It could be argued that Lukashenka is in fact an entirely new and unique political phenomenon. Until the recent color revolutions, Lukashenka was one of very few leaders in the CIS who did not have a *nomenklatura* background. His brand of populism and authoritarianism, combined with the pomp and public displays of Soviet-era political rituals, had some parallels during the 1990s in Milošević's Serbia and Meciar's Slovakia but is now largely confined to Belarus.

Stanislau Shushkevich has characterized Lukashenka's Belarus as a "neo-Communist" society. Shushkevich describes this "neo-Communism" as an ideology of Communist revenge, a system to mobilize the population in support of an anti-democratic, authoritarian regime. According to Shushkevich, the Lukashenka regime attempts to realize its goals through postponing the introduction of a market economy, minimizing individual freedom, and promoting propaganda of equality. This is accompanied by an aggressive anti-Western rhetoric and seclusion from liberal democratic impulses.[64]

It is uncertain what the future holds for Belarus. On one hand, Lukashenka's authoritarian system is fairly stable, if stagnant, and there are no serious contenders waiting in the background. At the same time, Belarus is isolated and at the mercy of Russia, on whose energy it is heavily dependent. Recently, Moscow has demonstrated its preparedness to use its energy monopoly to influence Belarusian politics. Increasingly, it appears that the Kremlin's preparedness to subsidize the Lukashenka regime stands in proportion to the influence it can exercise over Belarus. Lukashenka's circle of friends is small and shrinking. As it becomes increasingly clear that the current course does not solve Belarus' problems, Lukashenka's appeal is waning, even among his core supporters. Yet, in the absence of radical reforms and with the semblance of material well-being, maintained by an inexpensive energy supply from Russia, there has not been sufficient discontent to generate a revolt against the system. Politically, however, the support for Lukashenka is much weaker among city dwellers, the young, and the educated. Increased contact with the outside world through traveling, tourism, and the widespread use of the Internet is bound to make the younger generations, those not attracted to Soviet nostalgia, increasingly aware of their country's pariah status, isolation, and lack of opportunity.[65] This is also a generation that is growing up in an independent Belarus. Regardless of their limited symbolism, the Belarusian coat of arms, national hockey teams, anthem, flag, passport, stamps, and currency signify an independent country. It remains to be seen to what extent the veneration of past Soviet glories is sufficient to instill and maintain Soviet-era values in the younger generation. Support for independence is also stronger among the younger generation, which lacks memories of the Soviet Union. In fact, Lukashenka himself has found it opportune to use Belarusian patriotism in his rhetoric against Putin's assimilationist schemes. This seems to indicate the rise of a new, Belarusian identity that both Russian- and Belarusian-speaking Belarusians can identify with. Their identity is no longer that of *tuteishy* (locals), but that of a people involved in a process of constructing an identity separate from that of Russians and Poles. At the same time, this identity is weak and ambiguous, in search of references with which or against which it can identify. Nostalgia and confusion contributed to Lukashenka's success in establishing his authoritarian system, yet it is an authoritarianism based upon Luksahenka's personality rather than upon a coherent ideology. Unless the system changes significantly, it is unlikely to outlive its founder.

With the recent changes in the constitution, however, Lukashenka has made it possible to remain president for life. Since he is relatively young (having been born in 1954), this could theoretically mean another thirty years in office. In reality, the survival of dictators is linked to economic conditions, and seemingly well-established oligarchies are often highly vulnerable to mass protest if they are perceived to lack credibility. For now, it seems as if Lukashenka's hold on power is relatively strong, due in large part to economic stability (or rather the absence of rapid decline) and the government's provision of basic social services and benefits. A January 2006 poll conducted by the Lithuanian-based Gallup/Baltic Service shows that Lukashenka enjoyed a 55 percent support, which would have allowed him to win a free election. Official unemployment stands at 1.5 percent, while the country's GDP in U.S. dollar terms doubled from 2002 to 2005. The average Belarusian monthly wage in 2005 was $205 (an increase from $150 in 2004), while the average monthly pension in 2005 was $98 (compared to $63 the previous year). In a poll conducted by two Slovak non-governmental organizations in the same month, 24 percent of Belarusians assessed their economic situation as "very good," while another 59 percent described their situation as "fair." Only 13 percent described their situation as "bad" or "very bad."[66]

Given both genuine popular support for Lukashenka and his habit of rigging elections, nobody expected anything but a massive Lukashenka victory in the 2006 presidential elections. "He does not like figures below 75 percent," the leading opposition candidate Aliaksandr Milinkevich stated. The opposition predicted massive protests, and that some fifteen thousand to twenty-five thousand protesters would gather on the streets in Minsk.[67] However, after the election commission announced that Lukashenka had won with 83 percent of the votes (with only 6.1 percent for Milinkevich, his closest opponent), few people took to the streets. The estimates vary between two thousand and ten thousand people at the peak of the

protests on March 25, which coincided with the opposition commemorating the eighty-eighth anniversary of the Belarusian People's
Republic.[68] The morning before, the police had arrested some 300
people and had 274 protesters convicted for hooliganism and civil
disobedience. As the protests quickly subsided, Lukashenka seemed
poised for another five years as president. The Organization for
Security and Co-operation in Europe, represented by five hundred
observers from thirty-eight countries, declared that the election had
failed to meet democratic standards. The EU declared the election
"fundamentally flawed" and introduced sanctions against those
responsible for the fraud.[69]

Despite Moscow's irritation with Lukashenka, it is not clear
whether Russia is prepared to see an abrupt change of direction in
Belarusian politics. After seeing its influence eroded in Ukraine,
Georgia, and Moldova, it is unlikely that the Kremlin is prepared to
lose a strategic, if awkward, ally. Given Belarus' relative economic stability and Lukashenka's powerful backing by Russia, a Ukrainian-
style "color revolution" in Belarus seems unlikely in the immediate
future.

Notes

1. "EU Issues Condemnation of Belarus 'Dictatorship,'" *Radio Free Europe/Radio Liberty*, April 15, 2005; "UN Monitor Says Belarus Close to Dictatorship," *Radio Free Europe/Radio Liberty*, March 29, 2005.

2. Kjell-Albin Abrahamson, *Vitryssland—89 millimeter från Europa* (Stockholm: Fischer, 1999), 85.

3. Curt Woolhiser, "Constructing National Identities in the Polish-Belarusian Borderlands, Part 1," *Ab Imperio* 1 (April 2003).

4. Stanislau Shushkevich, *Neokommunizm v Belarusi: ideologiia, praktika, perspektivy* (Smolensk, Russia: Skif, 2002), 34, cites Leanid Marakou, *Vyniščenne* (Minsk: LFM Neman, 2000).

5. Stephen L. Guthier, *The Belorussians: National Identification and Assimilation, 1897–1970* (Ann Arbor: University of Michigan Press, 1977), 48.

6. David R. Marples, *Belarus: From Soviet Rule to Nuclear Catastrophe* (New York: St. Martin's, 1996), 120.

7. Marples, *Belarus*, 39.

8. Aleksandr Feduta, *Lukashenko: politicheskaia biografiia* (Moscow: Referendum, 2005): 107.

9. Nikolai Zenkovich, *Tajny ushedshego veka: Granitsy, spory, obidy* (Moscow: Olma, 2005), 17–18, 134.

10. David R. Marples, "Kuropaty: The Investigation of a Stalinist Historical Controversy," *Slavic Review* 53, no. 2 (1994): 514.

11. Tobias Ljungvall, *Kontroll: Rapport från Vitryssland* (Stockholm: Svenskt Internationellt Liberalt Centrums förlag, 2003), 29; Nikolai Zenkovich, *Tajny ushedshego veka*, 342.

12. Marples, *Belarus*, 135.

13. Steven M. Eke and Taras Kuzio, "Sultanism in Europe: The Socio-Political Roots of Authoritarian Populism in Belarus," *Europe-Asia Studies* 52, no. 3 (May 2000): 534.

14. Jan Zaprudnik, *Belarus: At a Crossroads in History* (Boulder, CO: Westview, 1993), quotes O. Gasparovich at 116–17: "Nam iavno ne khvataet svezhego vozdukha kul'tury," *Belaruskaia dumka* 10 (1993): 14; Ustina Markus, "The Bilingualism Question in Belarus and Ukraine," *Transition* 2 (November 29, 1996): 18.

15. Zaprudnik, *Belarus*, 138. This policy of making Belarusian the only language of the republic was unpopular with the majority of the population, and in a referendum in May 1995, 83.1 percent of the votes cast were in favor of conferring the Russian language status equal to that of Belarusian (Eke and Kuzio, "Sultanism in Europe," 534).

16. A. P. Vaitovich et al., eds., *Belarus': na miazhy tysyachahoddziau* (Minsk: Belaruskaia Entsyklapedyia, 2000), 265.

17. Helen Fedor, ed., *Belarus and Moldova: Country Studies* (Washington, DC: Federal Research Division, Library of Congress, 1995), 65.

18. I. I. Kovkel and E. S. Iarmusik, *Istoriia Belarusi: S drevneishikh vremen do nashego vremeni* (Minsk: Aversev, 2000), 576; Eke and Kuzio, "Sultanism in Europe," 527; Coit Blacker and Condoleezza Rice, "Belarus and the Flight from Sovereignty," in *Problematic Sovereignty: Contested Rules and Political Possibilities*, ed. Stephen D. Krasner (New York: Columbia University Press, 2001), 226, citing Kathleen J. Mihalisko, "Belarus: Retreat to Authoritarianism," in *Democratic Changes and Authoritarian Reactions in Russia, Ukraine, Belarus, and Moldova*, ed. Karen Dawisha and Bruce Parrott (Cambridge: Cambridge University Press, 1997), 242, erroneously claims that "83 percent of those casting ballots in Belarus voted affirmatively—the highest percentage of any republic in the Soviet Union."

19. Kovkel and Iarmusik, *Istoriia Belarusi*, 571.

20. Marples, *Belarus*, 127.

21. Ibid., 37.

22. As a comparison, in Russia the figure was 63 percent, in Ukraine, 42 percent. Astrid Sahm, "Belarus' Von der parlamentarischen Republik zum präsidentalen Regime," in *Die Ukraine und Belarus' in der Transformation: Eine Zwischenbilanz*, ed. Rainer Lindner and Boris Meissner (Köln, Germany: Wissenschaft und Politik, 2001), 125, cites Juri Lewada, *Die Sowjetmenschen* (Berlin: Broschiert, 1992), 25.

23. Stanislau Shushkevich, *Neokommunizm v Belarusi*, 35.

24. Amy McGoldrick, "Belarus," in *Let's Go, Eastern Europe: The World's Bestselling Budget Travel Series, completely Updated & Revised for 2002* (New York: St. Martin's, 2002), 67.

25. Blacker and Rice in "Belarus and the Flight from Sovereignty," 226; following Mihalisko, "Belarus," 241–42; and George Sanford, "Belarus on the Road to Nationhood," *Survival* 38, no. 1 (1996): 144; Zenkovich, *Tajny ushedshego veka*, 414–15.

26. Zenkovich, *Tajny ushedshego veka*, 418.

27. Sherman W. Garnett and Robert Legvold, eds., *Belarus at the Crossroads* (Washington, DC: Carnegie Endowment for International Peace, 1999), 3.

28. Feduta, *Lukashenko*, 51.

29. Grigory Ioffe, "Understanding Belarus: Belarusian Identity," Part 2, in *Europe-Asia Studies* 55, no. 8 (2003): 1255–56; but see also Jan Zaprudnik, "Misrepresentation of Belarus (Grigory Ioffe's spurious arguments)," unpublished notes, 2005, p. 5, on the use of the term "Westernizer" in a Belarusian context.

30. Ljungvall, *Kontroll*, 24.

31. Feduta, *Lukashenko*, 84–85, 123.

32. Ibid., 156.

33. An opinion poll from April 1994 showed 12 percent of Belarusians wanted a right-wing president and 17 a left-wing president. Fifty-seven percent wanted a "centrist" candidate (Ljungvall, *Kontroll*, 33, 81).

34. Feduta, *Lukashenko*, 160.

35. Sahm, "Belarus," 132.

36. Vaitovich et al., eds., *Belarus*, 266.

37. Human Rights Watch, *Republic of Belarus: Violations of Academic Freedom* 11, no. 7 (July) (Washington, DC: Human Rights Watch, 1999), 5

38. Andrej Kotljarchuk, "The Tradition of Belarusian Statehood: Conflicts about the Past of Belarus," in *Contemporary Change in Belarus, Baltic and East European Studies*, vol. 2, ed. Egle Rindzeviciute (Huddinge, Sweden: Baltic and East European Graduate School, 2004), 62.

39. Shushkevich, *Neokommunizm v Belarusi*, 37.

40. Human Rights Watch, *Republic of Belarus: Turning Back the Clock* 10, no. 7 (July) (Washington, DC: Human Rights Watch, 1998), 7.

41. Ljungvall, *Kontroll*, 48.

42. "President Lukashenko: in quotes," *BBC News Online*, July 10, 2004, http://news.bbc.co.uk/2/hi/europe/3881341.stm.

43. Jan Maksymiuk, "Analysis: Lukashenka Prepares Ground for Life Presidency," *Radio Free Europe/Radio Liberty*, October 19, 2004.

44. "Lukashenka Tells Voters You Will Elect Me," *Radio Free Europe/Radio Liberty*, November 4, 2005; "Belarus Takes Legal Steps against 'Colored Revolutions,'" *Radio Free Europe/Radio Liberty*, November 25, 2005.

45. Anna Brzozovska, "Discourses of Empowerment: Understanding Belarus' International Orientation," in *Contemporary Change in Belarus, Baltic and East European Studies*, vol. 2, ed. Egle Rindzeviciute (Huddinge, Sweden: Baltic and East European Graduate School, 2004), 103; Pavel Sheremet and Svetlana Kalinkina, *Sluchainyi Prezident* (St. Petersburg: Limbus, 2004), 37; "Belarusian president wants nuclear weapons back," *BBC News Online*, February 26, 1999.

46. Brzozovska, "Discourses," 96–97.

47. Blacker and Rice, *Problematic Sovereignty*, 229, 249.

48. Stephen Dalziel, "EU ambassadors back to Belarus," *BBC News Online*, January 18, 1999, http://news.bbc.co.uk/2/hi/europe/257252.stm.

49. "President Lukashenko: in quotes"; "Warsaw Recalls Ambassador from Minsk," *Radio Free Europe/Radio Liberty*, August 3, 2005.

50. "Lukasjenko hotar Västeuropa med 'droger och illegala invandrare,'" *Dagens Nyheter*, November 13, 2002.

51. David R. Marples, "Europe's Last Dictatorship: The Roots and Perspectives of Authoritarianism in 'White Russia,'" *Europe-Asia Studies* 57, no. 6 (September 2005): 895. Interestingly, far worse human rights abusers, such as Turkmenistan, Uzbekistan, China, Libya, Sudan, and Saudi Arabia, did not make it to Rice's list.

52. David R. Marples, "Belarus: The Last European Dictatorship?" (p. 43); and Heinz Timmermann, "The Union of Belarus and Russia in the European Context" (pp. 283–86), *The EU and Belarus: Between Moscow and Brussels*, ed. Ann Lewis, 31–44, 277–302 (London: Federal Trust for Education and Research, 2002).

53. Heinz Timmermann, "*Koloboks* Union: Belarus und Rußland am Wendepunkt?" *Konturen und Kontraste: Belarus sucht sein Gesicht, Osteuropa* 2, no. 54 (February 2004): 221.

54. Michael Winiarski, "Putin-utspel enar vitryssar," *Dagens Nyheter*, September 18, 2002; Timmermann, "*Koloboks* Union," 221, citing BelaPan, October 31, 2003.

55. Michael Winiarski, "Putins utspel svårt bakslag för Lukasjenko," *Dagens Nyheter*, August 18, 2002.

56. "Belarus president waves iron fist," *BBC News Online*, January 8, 2005, http://news.bbc.co.uk/2/hi/europe/4157611.stm.

57. "Belarus President Lukashenko Orders Foreign Music Off Radio," *Moscow News*, October 1, 2005; "Lukashenka Issues Call for More Belarusian Babies," *Radio Free Europe/Radio Liberty*, February 8, 2006.

58. Jan Maksymiuk, "Analysis: Stuck in a Rut," *Radio Free Europe/Radio Liberty*, February 15, 2005; "Lukashenka Unveils Memorial To Dzerzhinskii," *Radio Free Europe/Radio Liberty*, October 8, 2004.

59. "Lukashenko v razreze: Po chastiam tela," *Moskovskii Komsomolets*, April 30, 2005.

60. Human Rights Watch, *Violations of Academic Freedom*, 12.

61. Iury Drakakhrust, "Chamu liudzi halasuiuts' za Lukashenku?" *Radio Free Europe/Radio Liberty Belarus, Ukraine, and Moldova Report,* February 14, 2006.

62. Shushkevich, *Neokommunizm v Belarusi,* 50.

63. Michael Winiarski, "Putin-utspel enar vitryssar," *Dagens Nyheter,* September 18, 2002.

64. Shushkevich, *Neokommunizm v Belarusi,* 27–28.

65. Marples, "Kuropaty," 29.

66. Jan Maksymiuk, "When bread is sweeter than freedom," *Radio Free Europe/Radio Liberty Belarus, Ukraine, and Moldova Report,* February 28, 2006.

67. Steven Lee Myers, "Bringing down Europe's Last Ex-Soviet Dictator," *New York Times,* February 26, 2006.

68. David Marples, "Independence Day March Turns Violent in Minsk," *Eurasia Daily Monitor,* March 27, 2006.

69. Erik Ohlsson, "Kritiken växer mot Lukasjenko," *Dagens Nyheter,* March 23, 2006; Ohlsson, "Vitryssland gotar införa restriktioner mot EU," *Dagens Nyheter,* March 25, 2006.

4

Post-Soviet Moldova's National Identity and Foreign Policy

Steven D. Roper

Over the past half-decade, there has been a realignment in Moldovan foreign policy. As European Union (EU) and North Atlantic Treaty Organization (NATO) borders have changed, Moldovan foreign policy orientation has moved farther westward. The irony is that after the 2001 parliamentary elections, in which the Moldovan Community Party (PCM) received more than 50 percent of the vote and approximately 70 percent of the seats (and elected Vladimir Voronin president), many analysts believed that the country would further integrate into the Commonwealth of Independent States (CIS) and a Russian zone of influence. The 2001 PCM electoral platform outlined several policy changes that would have further solidified Russian influence in the country (e.g., the elevation of the Russian language as an official state language and Moldovan membership in the Russian-Belarusian union).

Instead, under the leadership of President Voronin, the country increased diplomatic and economic links with the EU and EU member states, which ultimately resulted in the signing of the EU-Moldova Action Plan in February 2005. This policy reorientation from Russia toward the EU and Europe has been accompanied by a steady increase in public support for EU membership. While Moldovan foreign policy has become more aligned with Europe, economic considerations, especially concerning gas imports from Russia, have forced the country to balance competing needs and foreign policies. President Voronin has often spoken of the special relationship between Moldova and Russia and has avoided making foreign relations among Russia, Europe, and Moldova a zero-sum game; however, the status of the breakaway region of Transnistria is one of the focal points of Moldovan domestic and foreign policy and an issue that demonstrates for many the conflicting foreign policy agendas of Europe and Russia, as well as institutions such as the Organization for Security and Co-operation in Europe (OSCE).

While short-term factors such as the 2004 presidential elections in Ukraine and Romania can partially explain the change in Moldovan foreign policy, there are more fundamental economic, demographic, and sociological changes that account for the changing perspectives on domestic and foreign policy. As Moldovan identity has evolved over the past decade, there has been a noticeable shift in the cultural and social affiliation of Moldovans. This chapter explores these changes and the relationship between foreign policy and Moldovan identity. To understand the reorientation of attitudes and policies, this chapter traces the evolution of Moldovan identity during the end of the Soviet Union and throughout the 1990s and the 2000s and focuses on the interaction between identity and foreign policy formation and ultimately Moldovan relations with Russia and Europe.

Moldovan Identity: Caught between Romanianization and Russification

To understand the development of twentieth- and twenty-first-century Moldovan identity, it is vital to examine Moldova's contemporary history. Moldova's geography and history have shaped the current debate over identity as well as the status of the breakaway region of Transnistria. Following the Russo-Turkish war of 1806–12 and the conclusion of the Treaty of Bucharest, the Moldovan area between the Prut and the Dniester Rivers (known as Bessarabia) was annexed by Russia in 1812. At this time, Moldovans made up 86 percent of the population, and by the mid-nineteenth century, Russia began to actively assimilate the local population. The Russian language supplanted the Romanian language in all legal proceedings, and an influx of Russians and other ethnic groups significantly reduced the percentage of the ethnic Moldovan population. While still the largest language group, by the beginning of the twentieth century, the Moldovan population had been reduced by almost 40 percent and only made up 14 percent of the urban population. At this time, Wim van Meurs argues that "the Bessarabian population had no mature identity, and they identified themselves . . . only in a territorial, non-ethnic sense."[1]

World War I and the Russian Revolution provided Bessarabia's pan-Romanian nationalists with an opportunity to press their claims for self-determination and ultimately integration with Romania. Unlike the rural Bessarabian population that van Meurs describes, the urban Bessarabian elites demanded greater administrative, cultural, and economic autonomy. By spring 1917, in public meetings held throughout Bessarabia, individuals called for the replacement of the Cyrillic alphabet with the Latin alphabet and for the freedom to use Romanian. The cultural demands soon gave way to political aspirations, and in December, the national assembly voted to form the independent Moldovan Democratic Republic of Bessarabia.[2] The Republic's borders extended from the Prut to the Dniester River. Significantly, the area of modern-day Transnistria was not included in this new formation. Two months later, in March 1918, the assembly voted to unite with Romania, and by the end of 1918, the areas of Bukovyna and Transylvania had joined Bessarabia to form so-called "Greater Romania."

To integrate the newly acquired population into Romania, the state promoted Romanian language acquisition in primary and secondary schools; however, Russian linguistic and cultural influences were still dominant during this period. The Romanian government was not very successful in its efforts at Romanianization, partly due to the influence of Soviet propaganda. In 1924, Soviet authorities created the Moldovan Autonomous Soviet Socialist Republic (MASSR) within the Ukrainian Soviet Socialist Republic by combining Transnistria with territory in present-day Ukraine. The MASSR served as a propaganda vehicle and base for Soviet activities in Romanian-controlled Bessarabia.[3]

In August 1939, Germany and the Soviet Union signed the Molotov-Ribbentrop Pact, which included secret protocols that conceded the Soviet Union's special interest in Bessarabia. By July, all of Bessarabia and Northern Bukovyna were under Soviet control. The Soviet Socialist Republic of Moldova was formed by joining Bessarabia with six counties that had constituted the MASSR. Thus, Moldova inherited a large Russian-speaking community from the MASSR, and immigration particularly of industrial workers furthered the Russification of Moldova's urban areas. Due to the Soviet immigration policy, the percentage of ethnic Russians in Moldova almost doubled from 6.7 percent in 1941 to 13 percent by 1989.[4] As elsewhere in the Soviet Union, ethnic Russians enjoyed disproportionate representation in important political and economic institutions. Ethnic Moldovans perceived themselves to be underrepresented in the more desirable professions and in the Communist Party structure.

Throughout this period, the Soviet leadership encouraged the creation of a distinct Moldovan nation in order to emphasize close cultural ties to Russia. As part of the Russification policy, the alphabet for the Romanian language in Moldova was changed back to Cyrillic in 1939, and Russian once again became the language of interethnic communication, higher education, and public life. Soviet linguists were instructed to find fundamental differences between the Romanian and Moldovan languages. A new mythology was created: Soviet scholars spoke of a distinctive Moldovan language that was the foundation of a distinctive non-Romanian Moldovan nation, which reinforced the idea of two separate nations.[5]

Moldovan Identity during the Late 1980s

As elsewhere in the Soviet Union, reforms introduced by Mikhail Gorbachev in the mid-1980s provided an opportunity for the Moldovan titular majority to express its desire for greater cultural freedoms and its resentment over Russification policies. In 1987, Moldovan intellectuals organized informal discussion groups that focused on greater cultural and linguistic freedom. The initial movement included broad cultural, educational, and linguistic issues that encouraged the participation of nonethnic Moldovans, such as ethnic Ukrainians and ethnic Gagauzi. By mid-1988, these informal pro-reform groups had organized the Democratic Movement in Support of Restructuring to press for democratization and redress for discriminatory practices imposed upon the ethnic majority and certain ethnic minority populations.[6]

While the Democratic Movement pressed for the recognition of Moldovan as the official state language (using the Latin alphabet), it also articulated a linguistic agenda that focused on cultural and linguistic freedom for ethnic Gagauzi, Ukrainians, and Bulgarians. At the beginning, the reform movement was not organized primarily around the issue of identity or ethnicity (e.g., Russian- and Romanian-speakers). Several disadvantaged ethnic groups had joined with ethnic Moldovans to press their claims. Instead, the division in the society was between entrenched political elites and those who aspired to power in order to pursue a pro-reform agenda. As Pål Kolstø, Andrei Edemsky, and Natalya Kalashnikova argue, "it is a gross simplification to present the conflict as a showdown between ethnic Moldovans and the 'Russian-speaking' part of the Moldovan population . . . [the conflict] is essentially political in character."[7]

In May 1989, individuals from the Democratic Movement, the Democratic League of Moldovan Students, the Ecological Movement, and other associations organized the Popular Front, which quickly became the leading Moldovan opposition force promoting linguistic and cultural freedom. While the Popular Front opposed Soviet policies of Russification, several leading Front members were actually ranking Communist Party functionaries. These party leaders recognized that to maintain power they would have to shift their policies.

In August 1989, the Moldovan Supreme Soviet proclaimed Moldovan (using the Latin alphabet) as the state language. Afterward, the Front adopted a more radical platform than the earlier Democratic Movement. The reform agenda of the Democratic Movement was rejected in favor of a pro-Romanian agenda. This shift in focus and the exclusive elevation of the Moldovan language touched off an immediate response by the Russian-speaking community. The promotion of the Moldovan language, particularly in Transnistria, threatened elites. By September 1989, Gagauzian leaders proclaimed the creation of an independent republic in the southern part of the country, and ethnic Ukrainians and ethnic Bulgarians left the Front and united with ethnic Russians to form the Internationalist Movement for Unity, or *Edinstvo* (a pro-Russian organization). Edinstvo joined with associations in Tiraspol to organize factory strikes and demonstrations against the language law. As King argues, Transnistrians were the group most opposed to the language law because it was the clearest sign of the shifting balance of political power away from Russian-speakers to Romanian-speakers.[8]

This shift in power was also evident during the 1990 election for Moldova's last Soviet-era parliament. Following the election, the Popular Front formed a parliamentary coalition with other parties, which held approximately 66 percent of the seats. The parliament confirmed a government composed almost entirely of ethnic Moldovans. Mircea Snegur, a leading Front supporter, was elected president by the parliament, and Prime Minister Mircea Druc was a strong advocate of union with Romania. During this period, Front MPs and the Druc government pursued a pro-Romanian and pro-unionist agenda that alienated the Russian minority within Moldova as well as Transnistria.[9]

In May 1990, the elites who controlled the city governments of Tiraspol, Bender, and Răbniţa refused to accept the legitimacy of the new parliament and asserted sovereignty over all local institutions. During the next two years, the status of Transnistria was the single most important domestic issue facing the Moldovan government. After the formation of the Transnistrian Moldovan Soviet Socialist Republic in September 1990, the conflict between Chişinău and Tiraspol quickly accelerated, particularly after Moldova declared independence in August 1991. In September, Transnistria declared its independence from Moldova, and during 1991 and 1992, there was a transfer of personnel and weapons from the Russian 14th Army to the Transnistrian paramilitary force. During 1992, several clashes between the Moldovan and the Transnistrian paramilitary took place along the Dniester River with more than a hundred people killed. As the Transnistrian separatists consolidated their position, nationalist elites inside the Moldovan parliament became increasingly militant. This brought intense pressure on President Snegur to undertake decisive action to resolve the conflict. In late March 1992, a state of emergency was declared and an effort was made to disarm the separatist units. This attempt met with armed resistance and intensified the conflict.

By this time, Russian nationalists viewed Transnistria as a test case for Russians in the near abroad.[10] By May 1992, the level of violence had greatly increased. The heaviest fighting occurred close to the border between Moldova and Transnistria. There are various estimates of the number of casualties but perhaps as many as one thousand died during this period. The civil war, and particularly the violence in Bender, had an immediate impact on Moldovan domestic politics. In July, almost all the members of the government resigned. The irony is that while the civil war forced a fundamental change in the Moldovan government, the conflict entrenched the Transnistrian leadership. As King notes, the conflict in Bender became part of the mythology of Transnistria.[11] Those who were associated with the conduct of the war in Transnistria were able to solidify their positions and maintain power throughout the 1990s and into the next decade.

Moldovan Foreign Relations with Russia

The political fallout from the civil war continued throughout the 1990s and forced a reorientation in Moldovan domestic and foreign policies away from Romania toward Russia. In the 1994 parliamentary elections, the Democratic Agrarian Party (a party of former *nomenklatura*) captured an absolute majority of seats. This party and President Snegur promoted a foreign-policy realignment with Russia while relations with Romania and much of Europe languished. In April 1994, Moldova joined the CIS (although the country refused to join the military component of the organization). The foreign policy orientation toward Russia during the 1990s was not surprising given Moldovan economic trade links with CIS countries. As shown in Table 4.1, Russia was Moldova's largest export market by a significant margin. Especially after the 1996 election of pro-Russian President Petru Lucinschi, Moldovan exports to Russia continued to grow until the Russian economic collapse of 1998. Table 4.2 indicates the percentage of Moldovan imports by country and shows that Moldovan imports from Russia were significant until 2000. These data do not break down the specific categories of imports, but most Moldovan imports from Russia were in the energy sector. During the twenty-first century, however, Moldovan economic relations with Russia have gradually deteriorated. Not only has Russia significantly increased the price of gas exports to Moldova, but in April 2006, the country banned Moldovan wine imports, for supposed health reasons. After the import ban, President Voronin announced that Moldova would reorient its wine exports to markets in the EU as well as China. Aside from bilateral economic relations, Moldova has also increasingly turned away from Russian-dominated multilateral organizations. For example, in 2003, President Voronin announced that Moldova would not join the Common Economic Space (a trade organization established among Russia, Kazakhstan, Ukraine, and Belarus), and that this organization demonstrated the failure of the CIS to coordinate and to stimulate economic activity.

In addition to the economic links between Russia and Moldova throughout the 1990s, the continuing presence of Russian troops on Moldovan soil provided another important source of Russian leverage over Moldovan domestic and foreign policies. Moldova has had considerable difficulty with Russia in resolving the status of the remaining Russian forces in Transnistria. The agreement to withdraw all Russian forces was initially signed in 1994, and while there are fewer than 2,500 troops remaining by 2007, there is still a massive amount of ammunition and equipment in Transnistria. While Russia has destroyed several tons of ammunition and has transported equipment from Transnistria via a program sponsored by the OSCE,

Table 4.1 Moldovan Exports, 1994–2004

	1994	1995	1996	1997	1998	1999	2000	2001	2002	2003	2004
Russia	51*	48	54	62	53	41	45	44	37	39	35
Ukraine	12	8	6	5	8	7	8	10	10	7	7
Romania	15	14	9	7	10	9	8	7	9	11	10
EU	—	12	10	10	13	21	26	25	27	27	39

Source: Compiled by the author from International Monetary Fund reports as well as reports from the EU. In order to be consistent, the data were rounded to whole numbers.
*Data are percentage of total.

Table 4.2 Moldovan Imports, 1994–2004

	1994	1995	1996	1997	1998	1999	2000	2001	2002	2003	2004
Russia	47*	33	27	29	23	24	15	16	15	13	13
Ukraine	19	27	27	18	15	14	14	17	20	22	24
Romania	6	7	7	9	11	14	15	11	9	7	8
EU	—	14	17	20	28	27	36	36	35	36	46

Source: Compiled by the author from International Monetary Fund reports as well as reports from the EU. In order to be consistent, the data were rounded to whole numbers.
*Data are percentage of total.

the status of these forces has not changed fundamentally since 1995. Moldova's dependency on Russian energy and the Russian market limited the country's ability to resolve the status of these forces or press for a conclusion to a basic treaty. Thus, the Russian commitment in the OSCE Istanbul Declaration to remove all forces from Moldova by the end of 2002 was viewed as a significant development. In the Istanbul Declaration, Moscow committed to remove its forces without any conditions and without any connection to resolving Transnistria's status. The Russian Foreign Ministry has since consistently argued, however, that a military withdrawal must coincide with a political agreement on Transnistria. The status of Transnistria has become a focal point of the EU's efforts to promote economic development and stable borders in the region. Since the late 1990s, the EU has become increasingly involved in settling the conflict, but the EU's relationship with Moldova involves broader issues concerning the European definition of security, as well as foreign relations with Russia and Ukraine.

Moldovan Foreign Relations with the EU

While Moldovan foreign policy during the mid- and late 1990s was oriented toward Russia, Moldovan elites attempted to place the country within a European geography in the hopes of stimulating economic links. In 1993 and 1994, President Snegur sent letters to the EU Commission, urging the EU to develop a framework for relations with Moldova. With the war raging in the former Yugoslavia, EU foreign policy was less than receptive to formalizing relations with a country that had just experienced a civil war; however, Moldovan leaders continued to press for more formal relations with the EU. In 1996 and 1997, President Lucinschi also addressed the EU Commission and expressed Moldova's desire to become an associate member of the Union by 2000. The EU and EU member states refused to respond to this request, and instead in 1998, the EU implemented a Partnership and Cooperation Agreement (PCA) with Moldova, which established a legal framework for closer collaboration between the EU and Moldova, as well as the implementation of the Technical Aid to the Commonwealth of Independent States assistance program.

During the 1990s, neither the EU nor the Moldovan leadership was willing to commit to specific actions. The Moldovan leadership's desire to fully integrate within Europe and the EU was limited due to the nature of the domestic political environment. For example, the government of Ion Sturza declared European integration as its foreign policy priority; however, by late 1999, the PCM parliamentary group (joined with another parliamentary group) brought down the Sturza government, and Moldova never achieved any significant steps toward European integration. The division within Moldovan domestic politics reflected a deeper division within the society over the orientation of the country. Just as the EU was divided in how to deal with southeastern Europe, Moldovan elites were equally divided over whether to pursue a pro-European foreign policy or a pro-Russian one. Ultimately, the results of the parliamentary election in 2001 indicated a triumph for those who wanted closer cooperation with Russia.

Moldova after the Election of the Communists in 2001

In the 2001 parliamentary election, the PCM received 50 percent of the vote, which translated into 71 seats (of a total of 101). Only two other parties/coalitions were able to pass the 6 percent threshold. After a change to the constitution (which restructured the political system from a semipresidential to a parliamentary regime), Voronin was elected president by the parliament; in April 2001, he nominated Vasile Tarlev as prime minister. The PCM-dominated government, and particularly the Ministry of Education, attempted to enact several of the electoral pledges made by President Voronin and the PCM. At the end of 2001, the government proposed replacing the study of the history of Romania with that of the history of Moldova and making the teaching of the Russian language compulsory.[12] The education reform plans were criticized by several noted scientists and educators, and starting in January 2002, the opposition organized a series of protests in Chişinău in an attempt to block the proposed changes and to demand the resignations of both the government and the parliament. Protests were held almost daily on the main street of the capital with attendance ranging from several hundred to several thousand. A demonstration held at the end of March was attended by more than fifty thousand people. The protests compelled the government to cancel the proposed amendments to the education system. Since 2001, however, education and language instruction have emerged as central political issues and have been used by various groups to define Moldovan identity in terms of Moldova's geopolitical orientation. While earlier the ruling PCM had promoted the use of the Russian language and Moldovan integration within the CIS, opposition parties had promoted the use of the Moldovan language and Moldovan integration within European structures. Thus early in the twenty-first century, there were competing political notions of Moldovan identity expressed within the education system and through language instruction.

In late July 2001, the PCM-dominated parliament adopted a law on the legal status of national minority organizations, stipulating that the state guaranteed members of national minorities the right to education at all levels in Moldovan, Russian, and their mother tongue. President Voronin asked the state-run radio and television stations to refer to the country's official language as Moldovan, not Romanian. In December 2001, Moldovan education officials adopted a decision requiring compulsory Russian language instruction in all schools (beginning in the second grade) to be implemented in January 2002. The Russian language had been taught as an optional foreign language since Moldova gained independence from the Soviet Union in 1991. These domestic policies had implications for Moldovan foreign policy, particularly relations with Russia and Romania.

The Romanian government was, predictably, critical of the initial PCM decision to make Russian language instruction compulsory. The Romanian Foreign Ministry called the decision "political interference in education and culture meant to give the Russian language a privileged status."[13] The Romanian government's criticism of Moldovan education policy reflected the tense relations between the two countries since the PCM had come into power. The poor historical relationship between the two countries contributed to a concern among Moldovan-speakers that, eventually, the country would revert to a pre-1989 status quo in which Russian was the dominant and preferred language of communication. This fear, combined with impending EU restrictions on Moldovan travel, created a huge demand for Romanian passports.

In 2001, the EU pressured the Romanian government to require an international passport for all Moldovan travelers. Moldovans began to worry that the Romanian border would once again be closed to them (as it was during the Soviet period) and began to apply for Romanian citizenship. It was a not-so-well-kept secret that many Moldovans held dual citizenship in countries such as Romania, Ukraine, and Russia. Indeed, unofficial data in 2001 indicate that as many as two hundred thousand Moldovans held Romanian citizenship.[14] Although dual citizenship was illegal, the number of Moldovans applying for Romanian citizenship in 2001 and 2002 increased dramatically, and eventually the Romanian Embassy in Chișinău enacted a passport moratorium. For many Moldovans, the passport moratorium and dictate from Brussels effectively isolated them from Europe and contributed to the concern among many Moldovans that, with Europe closed, Russia's already considerable influence would grow. The issue of dual citizenship became an increasingly important one following the 2003 local elections, and in November 2003, the Moldovan parliament passed a law that allowed Moldovans to hold dual citizenship. While Romania had been pressing for this reform for some time, Moldovans who held Ukrainian and Russian passports also benefited from this change. The amendment eliminated the previous prohibition on holding dual citizenship and demonstrated that an individual could be both Romanian and Moldovan simultaneously, which further oriented Moldova toward the West.

The struggle over Moldovan identity involves more than just education policy and language; the issue of identity concerns the orientation of the country. For some, Moldova is a European country that should embrace its Romanian heritage and integrate into Western institutions. For others, Moldova is a country in which the best markets and relationships remain with Russia and the CIS, and therefore the Russian language and Russian-dominated institutions remain the best options for the country. Most of the opposition parties accept the former description, while the members of the PCM have traditionally tended to embrace the latter. However, events concerning Transnistria caused a fundamental shift within the PCM leadership toward Europe, the EU, and EU-based institutions.

The Fallout from the Kozak Memorandum: Reorientation toward Europe

Following the election of President Voronin in early 2001, there was a great deal of optimism that a conclusive status could be negotiated for Transnistria. The negotiations between Voronin and Transnistrian leader Igor Smirnov were initially successful. In May 2001, Transnistria released Romanian-Moldovan nationalist Ilie Ilaşcu from a Transnistrian jail, following his imprisonment on charges of terrorism in 1992. The release of Ilaşcu had been a long-standing demand of the Moldovan government, and Voronin and Smirnov met on subsequent occasions to negotiate on a range of issues. By late 2001, however, Voronin had concluded that Smirnov had no real interest in changing the status quo, and the negotiations produced no lasting agreement to resolve the conflict.

In July 2002, the first signs of possible progress in the negotiating process were finally discernible. Mediators from Russia, Ukraine, and the OSCE submitted a new draft agreement to the Moldovan and the Transnistrian sides that constituted the most detailed and far-reaching proposals thus far. Fundamentally, the so-called "Kiev agreement" envisioned the federalization of Moldova with state-territorial formations (specifically Transnistria) to exercise local power over a range of issues, subordinate to the Moldovan central administration.[15] The proposals included plans for the creation of a bicameral parliament with an upper house that would represent the territorial formations.[16] Although the proposal was well received by President Voronin and leading members of the PCM, opposition parties were very critical of federalization. There were concerns that the proposal did not specify the number of territorial formations to be created and that it failed to provide a mechanism for constitutional revision.

The Kiev agreement continued to serve as a basis for discussion between Moldovan and Transnistrian officials throughout 2003. In February of that year, Voronin proposed the adoption of a new constitution based on the federal principles of the Kiev agreement. Voronin established a Joint Constitutional Commission charged with drafting a new constitution (in collaboration with Transnistrian representatives) that was to be submitted to a national referendum and that, if passed, would result in new elections to all nationwide offices. Although the OSCE, the EU, and Western states such as the United States were in favor of the federalization of Moldova, most opposition parties remained firmly opposed to both the principle of federalization and the Kiev agreement. From the opposition's perspective, the proposed federalization of the country represented a status quo that would legally enshrine Transnistria's status. However, international organizations such as the OSCE argued that federalization was the only basis for ending the long-standing conflict, but the negotiations made only limited progress. While Voronin was publicly committed to the principles laid out in the 2002 Kiev agreement, he secretly entered into negotiations with Russia. The First Deputy Chairman of the Russian presidential administration, Dmitri Kozak, was appointed by President Vladimir Putin to mediate between Moldova and Transnistria and produce a memorandum that would serve as the basis for a new constitution.

For several months in mid-2003, Kozak was engaged in shuttle diplomacy between the authorities in Moscow, Chișinău, and Tiraspol. In November 2003, Russia presented the OSCE and Ukraine with a final draft of what became known as the "Kozak Memorandum." The document provided for the establishment of an upper house in which thirteen of the twenty-six members of the chamber were to be elected within Transnistria and Gagauzia. In effect, this chamber provided these regions, particularly Transnistria, with the ability to veto national legislation. Moldovan civil society and opposition groups were vocal in their criticism. They regarded proposals for federalization as detrimental to their national interests and expressed concerns that the Kozak Memorandum undermined the Moldovan state. The international community was equally concerned about the document and the method by which it was negotiated.

Soon after the Kozak Memorandum was formally announced, a flurry of diplomatic effort was centered on Chişinău. Voronin realized that the memorandum had only limited domestic and international support and declined to approve the document. From 2003 to 2005, the failure to approve the Kozak Memorandum, as well as Romanian language school closings in Transnistria in 2004, increased tensions and led to a sharp war of words between the Transnistrian and the Moldovan leadership. More fundamentally, the failure of the Kozak Memorandum led President Voronin and the government to view the West as a much more reliable partner than Russia. Increasingly, Voronin's relationship with President Putin became strained, and Voronin repositioned himself, the PCM, and Moldova toward the West.

Moldovan Integration into Europe

Moldova has instituted a number of reforms and policies designed to facilitate European integration. In November 2000, Moldova established a National Commission for European Integration that developed the "Concept of Integration of Moldova into the EU." This document would later form the basis of discussion concerning the EU-Moldova Action Plan. In addition, the Moldovan parliament created a Committee for European Integration while the Ministry of Foreign Affairs created a Department for European Integration, as well as ministerial and departmental subdivisions in charge of European integration.[17]

Leading up to the 2005 parliamentary elections, the Moldovan leadership intensified discussions with the EU concerning economic and political coordination. Before the elections, the EU and the

Moldovan government announced the agreement of an EU-Moldova Action Plan, designed to facilitate the coordination of Moldovan legislation with EU norms. The Action Plan was signed in February 2005 and covers a timeframe of three years. Its implementation is designed to fulfill the provisions in the PCA (implemented in 1998 but never having a significant influence on Moldovan-EU relations) and encourage Moldova's further integration into a European economic space. As shown in Tables 4.1 and 4.2, the amount of trade between Moldova and the EU increased steadily after 2000. The Action Plan contributed to expanding economic ties with the EU and with Romania (as it is now a member state of the EU).

Since the 2005 parliamentary election, in which a PCM majority was returned to parliament, EU relations with Moldova have intensified. In March 2005, the EU Council appointed Jacobovits de Szeged as EU special representative to deal with the Transnistrian issue. Later in that year, the EU proposed a Border Assistance Mission to Moldova and Ukraine that has since monitored the border between the two states. During the meeting of the "five-sided mediation process" in Odesa in September 2005, the EU and the United States were invited to join as observers. A first meeting of the so-called "5+2" format occurred in October 2005 and coincided with the opening of a new Delegation of the European Commission to Moldova.

Conclusion

The reorientation of Moldova toward the EU has generally broad support among all political forces in the country. While the Moldovan opposition has articulated a pro-European view for quite some time, the change in the attitudes of the PCM and President Voronin in favor of stronger ties with the EU and Europe since the Kozak debacle has resulted in a consensus that improved relations with Europe are fundamental for economic and national security reasons. Because of energy needs, the government must balance relations between Europe and Russia; however, increasingly, the dialogue in Moldova has become more pro-European. As shown in Table 4.3, the change in political elite attitudes toward the EU and Europe has occurred as civil society has re-evaluated attitudes toward Europe and EU membership.

Undoubtedly, this change in social attitudes has occurred as contacts between Moldovans and Europe have increased (not the least

Table 4.3 Moldovan Public Opinion Concerning
European Union Membership

Year	In favor	Don't know/No alliance
2001	47%	18%
2002	38%	24%
2003	68%	22%
2004	66%	20%
2005	64%	13%

Source: Compiled from various public-opinion polls
commissioned by Soros Foundation Moldova between
2001 and 2005. Certain response categories have been
omitted while others have been combined.

because of the large number of legal and illegal Moldovan workers in
Europe). Given the nature of Moldovan politics and society, however,
it seems that civil-society attitudes toward Europe have become
much more receptive as political elites (especially those in the PCM)
increasingly embrace European institutions. Not surprisingly, civil-
society research by White and McAllister shows that in comparison to
other CIS countries (including Russia and Belarus) Moldovan society
is much more supportive of EU and NATO membership.[18] The question for Moldova is whether the enthusiasm for Europe and the EU
will continue without tangible signs of economic and social improvement. The EU is unlikely to accept Moldova as an accession candidate
in the foreseeable future, and, as the earlier citizenship issue with
Romania demonstrated, the EU must ensure that its new borders do
not close doors to Moldova as the country continues to move
toward European integration.[19] However, negotiating the status of
Transnistria forces the Moldovan government to re-examine its relationship with the EU and Russia. By 2007, indications are that
President Voronin has become impatient with the 5+2 format and
instead relied once again on secret one-on-one negotiations with
Russia. Unless the EU and the West are able to provide more significant economic and political benefits to the Moldovan leadership,
there will always be the possibility that Moldova might return to a
more pro-Russian foreign policy. While opposition politicians and
much of the population are decidedly pro-West, many within the
PCM may still view Russia as a more reliable partner. In the end,
Moldova today is still caught between East and West and the foreign
policy priorities of the EU, the United States, and Russia.

Notes

1. Wim van Meurs, "Carving a Moldavian Identity out of History," *Nationalities Papers* 26 (1998): 39–56, 41.

2. Irina Livezeanu, *Cultural Politics in Greater Romania: Regionalism, Nation Building, and Ethnic Struggle, 1918–1930* (Ithaca, NY: Cornell University Press, 1995), 4.

3. See Charles King, "Ethnicity and Institutional Reform: The Dynamics of 'Indigenization' in the Moldovan ASSR," *Nationalities Papers* 26 (1998): 57–72, 62.

4. V. Trebici, "Basarabia și Bucovina: Aspecte demografice," in *Sub povara graniței imperiale*, ed. A. Pop (Bucharest: Recif, 1993), 6.

5. Alla Skvortsova, "The Cultural and Social Makeup of Moldova: A Bipolar or Dispersed Society?" in *National Integration and Violent Conflict in Post-Soviet Societies: The Cases of Estonia and Moldova*, ed. Pål Kolstø (Lanham, MD: Rowman and Littlefield, 2002), 173.

6. See William Crowther, "The Politics of Ethnic-National Mobilization: Nationalism and Reform in Soviet Moldavia," *The Russian Review* 50 (1991): 183–203, 185–90.

7. See Pål Kolstø, Andrei Edemsky, and Natalya Kalashnikova, "The Dniester Conflict: Between Irredentism and Separatism," *Europe-Asia Studies* 45 (1993): 973–1000, 975.

8. Charles King, *The Moldovans: Romania, Russia, and the Politics of Culture* (Stanford, CA: Hoover Institution Press, 2000), 178–208.

9. Nicolae Enciu and Ion Pavelescu, "Un miracol istoric: Renașterea romanismului in Basarabia," in *Istoria Basarabiei: De la inceputuri pînă in 1998*, ed. Ioan Scurtu (Bucharest: Semne, 1998), 45.

10. See Stuart Kaufman, "Spiraling to Ethnic War: Elites, Masses, and Moscow in Moldova's Civil War," *International Security* 21 (1996): 108–38, 115.

11. King, *The Moldovans*, 194–98.

12. See Lucan A. Way, "Pluralism by Default in Moldova," *Journal of Democracy* 13 (2002): 127–41, 133.

13. *RFE/RL Newsline*, January 18, 2002.

14. *Basapress*, April 13, 2001.

15. See Oleh Protsyk, "Federalism and Democracy in Moldova," *Post-Soviet Affairs* 21 (2005): 72–90, 80.

16. Steven D. Roper, "From Frozen Conflict to Frozen Agreement: The Unrecognized State of Transnistria," in *De Facto States: The Quest for Sovereignty*, ed. Tozun Bahcheli, Barry Bartmann, and Henry Srebrnik (New York: Routledge, 2004), 115.

17. Nicu Popescu, "The EU in Moldova—Settling Conflicts in the Neighborhood," Occasional Paper No. 60 (European Union Institute for Security Studies, 2005), 10.

18. Stephen White and Ian McAllister, "Moldova and the Politics of Meso-Areas," in *Emerging Meso-Areas in the Former Socialist Countries: Histories Revived or Improvised?* ed. Kimitaka Matsuzato (Sapporo, Japan: Slavic Research Center, Hokkaido University, 2005).

19. See Alina Mungiu-Pippidi, "Beyond the New Borders," *Journal of Democracy* 15 (2004): 48–62, 51.

5

The Donbas—The Last Frontier of Europe?

Hiroaki Kuromiya

The Donbas, situated in the far east of Ukraine, is often portrayed as the last frontier of Europe in both a literal and symbolic sense. Far from the heart of Europe, bordering on Russia and heavily Russophone, the Donbas appears, to many observers, to represent the least European area—the area least amenable to European civilization and democracy (whatever "European" may mean). Few people in Ukraine or elsewhere associate the Donbas with "respectable" culture: the Donbas is a coal-and-steel industrial center, the hallmarks of which are not airy theaters or philharmonics, but dark and dangerous coal waste dumps. The Donbas' notoriety was clinched in 2004 by Ukrainian presidential election fraud, perpetrated by and for Viktor Yanukovych, a politician from the Donbas region who had previously served two jail terms for violent crimes. Moreover, the apparent regionalist tendencies in Donbas politics, which challenge the power of Kyiv, are interpreted by many observers as anti-Ukrainian and pro-Russian separatism. Nevertheless, few people, even ardent Ukrainian patriots, would write off the Donbas. It is possible that the Donbas is too valuable an economic asset to dismiss easily. According to 2002 data, the Donetsk province accounts for only 9.9 percent of the population of Ukraine, but 12.4 percent of the Ukrainian GDP, 22 percent of Ukrainian industrial production, and 22.5 percent of total Ukrainian exports. Another Donbas province, the Luhansk province, accounts for 5.2 percent of the population, 4.2 percent of the GDP, and 5.1 percent of total exports. Together, the two regions account for almost 30 percent of total exports.[1]

Although it may be that the split of Ukraine into a pro-Russian east and a patriotic west has become more pronounced as a result of the Orange Revolution than it was, say, in 1999 at the time of the previous presidential election,[2] there are also signs that, for the first time in recent history, Ukrainians—particularly Ukrainian intellectuals—have begun to want to understand the Donbas and its significance. In other words, even though the Donbas had long been the problem child of Ukraine, as long as it remained merely a child, it could be dismissed. Now it appears that the child has grown up and must be taken seriously. How this troublemaker will fit into a still young Ukrainian state remains to be seen, but the wide recognition of its significance would seem to bode well for the political future of Ukraine. Paradoxically, the Donbas with its weak Ukrainian identity may have the potential to break through narrowly nationalist, regionalist, or pro-Russia politics to push Ukraine decisively toward Europe.

Historical Background

The Donbas has always enjoyed the reputation of being free but unmanageable. Its freedom stems in large part from its frontier character. The region is situated in the area of the "wild field" (*dyke pole*), where the lands of the Zaporozhian Cossacks and the Don Cossacks intersected. Far from the metropolises of Muscovy (Russia), the Polish-Lithuanian Commonwealth, and even Kyiv, the wild field has always attracted criminals, fugitives, freedom seekers (from political, economic, religious, and other persecution), fortune-hunters, and the like.

When the Russian empire extended its control over the Black Sea and then over the Caucasus in the late eighteenth and early nineteenth centuries, the Donbas ceased to be a frontier area. Nevertheless, when it developed into a major industrial center, a magnet for people fleeing to a new life, the Donbas once again became known as a frontier, at least symbolically. Even at the height of Stalinism, the attraction of the Donbas was evident. In nearly every tale one reads of collectivization and de-kulakization in Ukraine, one encounters peasants fleeing the countryside for the Donbas, seeking a livelihood and freedom from persecution. The Donbas was hard hit by Stalin's terror for the very fact that it harbored numerous suspected "enemies of the people." But the extent of the terror was likely mitigated by the importance of the Donbas as the "All-Union coalfield." Post–World War II reconstruction again drew freedom seekers to the Donbas. In 1947, the father of Anatoly Shcharansky, unable to find work in Odesa because of an imposed quota on Jews, was told to go to the Donbas: "Try your luck in Stalino [later Donetsk, the capital of the Donetsk province]." He and his family moved to Stalino in 1947.[3] In late 1947, when the Ukrainian Insurgent Army (UPA) faced defeat in its fight against the Soviet government in western Ukraine, "the UPA command ordered [its members] to escape, either by posing as workers being resettled in the Donbas or by fighting their way to the American occupation zones in Germany and Austria."[4]

Whatever freedom the Donbas may have offered, by the 1950s and 1960s, it had ceased to be as attractive a haven for freedom seekers as it had been before, because the Donbas coal industry no longer provided the opportunity that it once had. If the Donbas had previously functioned as an "exit" (as opposed to the "voice" and "loyalty" in Albert Hirschman's apt phrase[5]), by the 1970s, it no longer symbolized such an exit. Regardless, Donbas industry continued to expand in other areas, with the result that today the Donbas is one of the most urbanized regions in Ukraine. (The urban population of the Donetsk province accounts for more than 90 percent of the province's total.)

The Donbas has also been known as an unmanageable place, alien to culture and civility. Exploitation, poverty, and violence may not have been unique to the Donbas, but the region's political life baffled outsiders and many insiders as well. While Baku, an oil-drilling center in present-day Azerbaijan (where economic conditions—ethnic diversity and the dominance of foreign capital—were similar to those of the Donbas), developed in tsarist times a semblance of "normal" labor-management relations in the form of collective bargaining and collective agreements, the Donbas saw no such developments before the Bolshevik Revolution. At the time of the Revolution and the Civil War, the Donbas miners, like the peasants, often rejected Bolshevik visions or accepted them selectively, in spite of the relative popularity of the Bolsheviks. While people nearly everywhere else on the periphery of the former Russian Empire were preoccupied by national issues, the Donbas remained indifferent.

The Donbas was also known for political violence. On the one hand, workers frequently physically attacked the formerly privileged, and the phenomenon of "specialist-baiting" in the Donbas was a constant threat to Soviet industrial authority in the 1920s. On the other hand, few organized political groups were able to capture the hearts and minds of the Donbas workers. Ivan Maistrenko, who was sent to the Donbas in the early 1920s by the Ukapisty (the Communist left wing of the Ukrainian Social Democrats, which was absorbed by the Bolsheviks in 1925), later recalled: "the Ukapisty appeared to have more support among the Donbas workers than did the Bolsheviks. Yet those workers who supported the Ukrainian Communists had no sense of nationality issues. They just wanted to see how the Ukrainian Communists would improve their lives, their thought being 'Well, if nothing comes of the All Russian party (Bolsheviks), let's try the Ukrainian one.'"[6] Ten years later, Maistrenko categorically refused to go back to the Donbas ("this culturally joyless province") to work.

This is not to say that the idea of democracy was alien to the Donbas. In fact, the Donbas had its own sense of democracy, an inclusive democracy as opposed to an exclusive nationalism. During World War II, Yevhen Stakhiv, who worked in the Donbas as a secret organizer of the Organization of Ukrainian Nationalists, noted that Dmytro Dontsov, a Ukrainian nationalist ideologue, was seen as a fascist in the Donbas. In response to the political climate in the Donbas, Stakhiv, who had once idealized Spain's Franco regime, "abandoned a narrowly defined Ukrainian nationalism and embraced the ideal of a democratic Ukraine without discrimination against its national minorities." Stakhiv later claimed that he was grateful to the Donbas people for his conversion.[7] Toward the end of the Soviet regime, when the Donbas miners went on strike en masse, all sorts of political groups sought to extend their influence over the militant workers. The Communists had been discredited, but Rukh, or the Ukrainian Popular Movement for Perestroika, also found itself largely rejected by the Donbas miners, who showed no inclination to organize an alternative political group or trade union similar to the Polish Solidarity. Rukh activists sent to the Donbas "found the Donbas miners very indifferent to its [Rukh's] cause and referred to them as 'sausage people': one miner said to a Rukh activist, 'It's all the same to us what language we speak, as long as there is sausage.'"[8] After the 1991 independence of Ukraine, the people of the Donbas, like the old Cossacks, appeared utterly unprincipled, often allying themselves with the Communists whom they had earlier rejected. During the strikes of the early 1990s, they even allied themselves with regional authorities against the national government in Kyiv.[9]

It has always been difficult for outside observers to comprehend Donbas politics. The Donbas appears to be the province least European in its outlook and policy—neither liberal democrat nor nationalist. Its politics, like its geographic position, help to define it as the last frontier of Europe.

Contemporary Images of the Donbas

Given the province's historical background, it is no surprise that images of the Donbas are less than positive. Some depictions by outsiders are particularly striking. On the political scene in Donetsk in 2002, one Ukrainian publicist observed rather prophetically:

> A region with an important concentration of capital but totally devoid of any democratic parameters is a dangerous problem for a state which has learned to at least imitate civilized behavior and pretend that it formally recognizes the need for certain democratic values. But in Donetsk the authorities do not even appear to bother with appearances. These are the people who are the main bulwark of the declining president [Kuchma], his most reliable long-term partners. The party list (proportional) [sic] electoral results show the authorities' real strengths, while their manner of implementing the elections in the individual (majority) districts show to what lengths they were willing to go in the agonizing struggle for their own political survival. They used violence, bribery, intimidation, and electoral fraud: the whole gamut. But even in this respect, Donetsk is an exceptional case in point. The totalitarian "values" which are so carefully preserved in this region in their practical, and not only historical, applications as the foundation of its way of life may very well become determinant for all of us. If all the other political forces, clans, and individuals do not fully apprehend this danger, it might turn into reality.[10]

The Donbas would seem to represent tyranny and totalitarianism to some outside observers. This is a far cry from its historical reputation as a haven for freedom seekers.

This perspective is a far from isolated one. For example, the noted Ukrainian poet Yurii Andrukhovych, who is of western Ukrainian origin, wrote of the "Ukrainian East" (a euphemism for the Donbas):

> Sarmatia is to the east and the south of the Dnieper river, in the South and the East of Ukraine. It is an outcry,
> For all Ukraine Sarmatia is an outcry, because
> it is plain and dry
> speaks mainly Russian

is dense, anachronistic, depressively industrialized
proletarianised and traditionally criminalised.
Always was and will be the territory of fugitives—for example from
Turkish slavery, and after that of homeless recidivists, unemployed
gatherers of hemp and poppy and such godless anarcho-Orthodox
types (who are mostly loyal to the authorities as a whole unless they
touch their proletarian monuments).
Easily succumbs to political manipulation in connection with a black-
and-white view of the world
Drinks vodka 'Colliers' with beer 'Sarmat.'
Doesn't like or at least doesn't like enough everything western, for
Europe is too far, too satiated, comfortable and too contrived. Europe
was contrived in Kyiv in order to annoy the brain. Europe for it doesn't
exist, for Europe could only betray
scoop unlawful coal from unlawful mines with the hands and spines of
old women and underage kids.
Is an indivisible totality of zones—of industry and prison, closed, pro-
hibited, *free economic* zones.
Alludes to a Dreamland—a big proto-cultural wasteland which it very
much wants to fill with something.
But with what can it be filled?[11]

Elsewhere Andrukhovych has noted the "colossal social-civil lag of
the Donbas behind the rest of Ukraine," the contrast between the
Donbas' "medieval-feudal" or "Cro-Magnon–Neanderthal" people and
the "modern-bourgeois" people of the rest of Ukraine. Dialogues with
the Donbas species, if possible at all, have been "always extremely complicated," and most often people of the Donbas abandon "the possibility of a dialogue and cover their ears": "With all the doggedness and all
the spiritual ardor of medieval man, 'they' simply don't want the 'aliens'
in their 'final territory.'" The "ballast of the Donbas" could become an
impediment to Ukraine's integration into Europe.[12] To be fair to
Andrukhovych, as will be discussed later, he conjures up these images
only to reach a conclusion very different from what they imply—that
the Donbas may well become very "European."
    Similar images are legion in the Ukrainian press. During the
Orange Revolution, the Internet was full of "blogs" describing the
Donbas (Donetsk in particular) as a "fascist city" or a "bandit city"
and denouncing its "thug culture." Viktor Tkachenko, writing in
March 2005 for *Narodne slovo*, a newspaper of the Ukrainian Popular
Party (an offshoot of the Rukh), represented the Donbas as a "Soviet
cesspool." He first recounts his own experience of post–World War II
orphans being taken to the Donbas against their will and being left to

the mercy of criminals who, he maintained, had also been dumped there by the Soviet authorities. Those orphans who fled the Donbas were caught and punished. He contended that Russified Ukrainians in the Donbas filled the "fifth columns" in Russian-occupied Ukraine. Even today, "speaking Ukrainian in the Donbas is not safe for one's health and life." There is "Russian Nazism" in the Donbas, which is "one of the most backward areas in a technological sense" in Ukraine. Therefore, it is imperative to "raise the cultural and living standards of its residents."[13] Tkachenko seems not to know that the industrial technology of the Donbas is not so backward, that in general one can safely speak Ukrainian in the Donbas, and that now the per-capita GDP in the Donetsk province is higher than the national average.

In a sense, these images of the Donbas are a reflection of the equally negative images the Donbas has of western Ukrainians as Nazi collaborators.[14] In any case, Tkachenko's lament is yet another testimony to the widespread perception of the Donbas as a sinister and corrupting force undermining everything Ukraine wants to achieve.

The Donbas in Post-Independence Ukrainian Politics

Such was not the image of the Donbas in 1991. The Donbas, like the rest of the country, overwhelmingly supported the independence of Ukraine in the 1991 referendum, a sharp swing from the mood of 1989. A sense of profound alienation from Moscow inclined the Donbas toward the belief that it would be better off in an independent Ukraine. In the December 1991 referendum, 83.9 percent of the voters of the Donetsk province voted for independence (the turnout rate was 76.7 percent), and the corresponding figures for the Luhansk province were equally high: 83.86 percent and 80.7 percent, respectively. Even the Crimea, where ethnic Russians accounted for as much as 67 percent of the population, voted for independence: 54.19 percent with a turnout of 67.5 percent.[15]

Yet the post-independence economic woes, aggravated by Kyiv's reluctance and inability to reform the economy, sharply changed the mood in the Donbas and images of the Donbas. The post-independence economic decline was "one of the deepest post-Soviet recessions experienced by any of the transition economies not affected by war"; in 1993, "the retail price inflation in the country reached its record level of 10,156% a year, the Donbas' industrial output collapsed by

25% and the average real wages decreased by about 80% from the 1990 level."[16] The Donbas exploded once again. This time, the Donbas attacked Kyiv, accusing it of favoring western Ukraine at the cost of the Donbas. The 1993 Donbas colliers' strike assumed anti-Kyiv, regionalist characteristics, supported by most major regional actors (including political elites and mining and industrial managers). One strike committee leader noted in 1992, "Our view of independence was always the destruction of the centre, the Kremlin, and getting the party out of economic life." Yet it so happens that "we have changed from one political machine to another, with practically the same people. This was not our view of Independence." [17] (Ukrainian President Leonid Kravchuk was indeed the former chief of ideology of the Central Committee of the Communist Party of Ukraine. Many other dignitaries of the young Ukrainian state formerly belonged to the Soviet bureaucracy.) Another strike leader noted in a similar vein:

> The Center had just moved from Moscow to Kiev. We didn't want that. . . . We wanted power to be given to the localities, enterprises, cities. We wanted the living standard of the population to improve rather than Kiev concentrating the reins of government in its fist.[18]

Thus the 1993 Donbas strike, which appeared to some observers to threaten the survival of Ukraine as a united, independent state, became "a struggle between the Donbas region and the rest of the country."[19] It is noteworthy that the Donbas, contrary to widespread assertions, did not advocate a return to old-style Communist management, even though it voted in the Communists whom it had earlier chucked out of government office. On the contrary, it wanted free economic zones. Although the Donbas' demand for regional independence was not immediately satisfied, it extracted significant economic and political concessions from Kyiv, capturing state power through its representatives. (For example, Yukhim Zviahilskyi, until then the Donetsk mayor, served as acting prime minister from September 1993 to June 1994).

Leonid Kuchma was elected in 1994 as the new president of Ukraine, in large part due to the support of the Donbas and other eastern regions. In so doing he defeated the first president of independent Ukraine, Kravchuk, who was supported by the more nationalistically minded regions in the west. Kuchma's economic reform was devoid of vision, inconsistent, constantly reconfigured to count conflicting interests, and satisfactory to none but "bandits" who made fantastic fortunes from privatization and property redistribution. Perhaps the greatest achievement of his economic reform was the successful launch in 1996 of the new Ukrainian currency, *hryvnia*, and the largely successful maintenance of its stability, under the supervision of the Ukrainian central bank, headed by Viktor Yushchenko. Yet this meant that vast state subsidies to the Donbas' coal mines and other industries were curtailed, and wage arrears reached astronomical levels. So the Donbas miners' strikes continued throughout the 1990s. Under pressure from western democracies (the World Bank), unprofitable mines were closed. Mine closures threatened to destroy many communities in the Donbas "company towns," in which nearly every resident's life was closely connected to the main enterprise of the town. The 1999 presidential elections brought some relief to the Donbas, as Kuchma used economic concessions to the Donbas (including the authorization of free economic zones and "priority development territories") to secure political loyalty. It is not known whether election fraud was committed, but Kuchma was elected owing in part to the Donbas' support. After the election, however, Kuchma appointed Yushchenko, no friend of the Donbas, as prime minister.

By Kuchma's second term, the unity of the Donbas economic interests had disintegrated. Kyiv's strategy of "divide and conquer" had split the Donbas trade unions (using political repression when necessary, as it did in 1996).[20] More importantly, the economic reforms and restructuring in the mid- to late 1990s, along with privatization and property redistribution, had created large industrial holding companies (conglomerates), such as the Industrial Union of the Donbas (founded in 1995 and now headed by Vitalii Haiduk, an energy tycoon) and System Capital Management (founded in 2000 and headed by Rinat Akhmetov, regarded as the richest man in Ukraine), which encompassed energy, coal, and metallurgy industries as well as R&D and banks in the regions. The conglomerates accumulated enormous and poorly regulated wealth and power, which led to corruption. Moreover, the consolidation of regional interests led to conflict with other regions such as Dnipropetrovsk, a major industrial center just west of the Donbas. One of the most dramatic results was the murder of some of the powerful politicians and industrialists involved. In any case, the interests of the Donbas "clan," composed of these holding companies, regional politicians (Yanukovych served as the governor of the Donetsk province from 1997 to 2002), and other regional bigwigs, did not coincide with the particular interests of the striking Donbas miners. Kyiv's government, now headed by Yushchenko, found no reason to give in to Donbas miners not supported by the Donbas clan. In fact, Kyiv had every economic reason to promote the restructuring of the Donbas coal mines. It probably hoped that the restructuring would weaken the power of the Donbas clan. But Yushchenko was dismissed in 2001, owing in part to the influence of the clan. In 2002, Yanukovych was appointed by Kuchma to the position of prime minister, signaling the dramatic rise of the Donbas clan.

The formation of the Donbas clan (and other regional clans) in Ukraine in the 1990s is often described as a "takeover" (very different from "exit," "voice," and "loyalty").[21] Some Western observers go much further and describe today's Ukraine as a "captured state" (or a "captured region") and a "neo-patrimonial polity."[22] According to these views, the regional economy of Donetsk was monopolized by the clan that also controlled regional and local politics ("privatization of politics") as well as whatever still remained of state-owned industry. The nature of the clan is "pre-modern," situated above the rule of law and hindering the formation of modern social and economic organizational capital. Transparency, accountability, and dissent are alien to this "neo-patrimonial" polity, the aim of which is to safeguard and promote the particularistic interests of its own region. The region thus has become an electoral patrimony of the elite clan. The population has been manipulated into believing that it is the victim not of its own power elite but of global forces. There are no "autonomous societal actors" who can act as a counterweight to the clan, and there are no civic movements to speak of: "Trade unions either have similar ideas about maintaining the economic structure, are co-opted (or manipulated and their leaders bribed), or are marginalised." The clan's view of the region generally matches the population's self-understanding (identity).[23]

These kinds of analyses fit well with the image of the Donbas as the least democratic and the most sinister region in Ukraine.

Visions of the Future

The political scientist Vlad Mykhnenko, himself from the Donbas, takes issue with the neo-patrimonial interpretation. The Donbas did extract economic favors from Kyiv. Yet, according to Mykhnenko, far from living on the vast subsidies extracted from Kyiv under the threat of strike and living at the cost of others, the energy-intensive Donbas economy has begun to achieve a significant degree of efficiency: from 1997/98 onward, two years before Ukraine's industry began its recovery, the Donbas economy had returned to growth while reducing its electricity consumption. From "rent-seeking" and "rent-taking," the Donbas industrialists had turned decisively capitalist, toward profit-making and capital accumulation through investment. This resulted in a "steady increase in gross fixed capital investments, growing in total during the last 6 years by 60%." If "in 1988, at the end of state socialism, the provincial GDP per capita [was] 32.5% lower than the Ukrainian average," then by 2002, "the GDP per capita in the Donbas was 26.7% higher than the national average." This growth caused real wages in the Donetsk province to grow steadily.[24]

The economic growth in the Donbas was accompanied by economic growth in Ukraine. The growth has led to an impressive growth in exports as well. In both respects, Yanukovych's administration was particularly successful. The GDP grew by 9.6 percent in 2003 and 12.1 percent in 2004, while exports grew by 28.5 percent and 41.6 percent in 2003 and 2004, respectively.[25] Obviously the Donbas clan played a major role in this growth.[26] Its capitalist spirit is apparent. For example, Vitalii Haiduk, the head of the Industrial Union of the Donbas, a former deputy minister of fuel and energy (January 2000–April 2001) and now the president of the Industrial Group consortium in Kyiv (founded in 2004), rejected Yushchenko's 2006 gas deal with Russia on the grounds that the negotiated gas price did not reflect the actual costs: that is, the price is a "political price." Haiduk stated that Yushchenko asked him to take the post of vice minister again, but that he did not accept.[27] Is this the Donbas clan's notorious pro-Russian and anti-Ukrainian conspiracy? Unlikely. It is almost capitalist logic (if it can be said that Enron and the alleged Houston clan operated according to capitalist logic). From the interview Haiduk gave to the BBC in January 2006, it is evident that he is serious about economic efficiency, cost reduction, and energy independence. The Industrial Union of the Donbas is not confined to the Donbas. In 2005, the Union beat the British-Indian Mittal Steel Company and bought the privatized Polish Huta Czstochowa Steelworks. (Mittal, however, acquired the Kryvyi Rih Steel Mills in eastern Ukraine shortly thereafter.)

It is understandable that, given economic progress, Yanukovych was popular in the Donbas (and in other regions in eastern Ukraine). One Donbas mine supervisor told a reporter for the *Los Angeles Times*, "When Yushchenko was prime minister, he basically told us, 'I don't need your people. It's easier to shut down your mines and buy coal from abroad.'" Another Donbas mine foreman said, "When Yushchenko was prime minister, I hadn't been paid my salary for a year. There were interruptions in the electricity supply; we would sit for days without power here. And when Yanukovich became prime minister in this country, it became much easier to live."[28]

What we do not know clearly is how the economic gains are being distributed in the country and in the Donbas. Has inequality increased in recent years? Or is the region heading in the direction of slow yet steady prosperity? In any case, many observers contend that the Donbas people are being manipulated and deceived by the clan that monopolizes economic gains. The 2004 election frauds are a prime example of the clan's deception. Perhaps surprisingly to outsiders, some 44 percent of the Ukrainian population (and 93.54 percent of the Donetsk population and 91.24 percent of the Luhansk population) still supported Yanukovych (who was said to be the figurehead of the clan).

If and when the clan becomes useless to the Donbas people, however, it is likely that they will turn against it. Mykhnenko is absolutely right that "it *is* still clear who is the boss in post-Communist countries. And it is the behaviour of the boss that matters."[29] Such has been the pattern of the "deceived and manipulated" Donbas people. It is somewhat puzzling that the Polish Solidarity movement and the Orange Revolution attracted so much Western sympathy and support while the Donbas miners' movements did not in the 1980s and 1990s. The miners were not hailed with fanfare as signs of an emerging civil society in independent Ukraine. Instead, nearly every Western commentator deplored the lack of civil society (and civility) in the Donbas. According to commentators, in the Donbas, manipulation and deception obtained.[30] Instead of a modern rule of law, market relations, and social associations, informal clientele networks and personal rewards are said to dominate the region.

Yet in one critical respect, the Donbas may well have much more of a future than the rest of Ukraine, particularly the western regions of Ukraine. The Donbas is often portrayed as the bastion of pro-Russian separatism. Yet nearly every poll ever taken in independent Ukraine seems to speak otherwise. Despite a host of scholarly works emphasizing regional (two-way, three-way, eight-way, and other) splits, the polls suggest that even the citizens of the most disaffected Donetsk think of their future in terms of an independent Ukraine. Even in 1994, the year of post-independence hardship, as many as

70.9 percent of those interviewed agreed with the statement "My region has a common destiny with the rest of Ukraine."[31] This position had not changed five years later.[32] Equally important is the issue of identities: the polls clearly demonstrate that "social identity in the [western] Lviv region tends to be ethnically based, while in the Donetsk region it is mainly civic."[33] One wonders if civic identity should not be preferable in an independent Ukraine that was explicitly established not in ethnic but in civil-juridical terms. The Donbas' desire for closer ties to Russia is perfectly rational economically and socially. To speak otherwise would be the equivalent of telling Canada to distance itself as much as possible from its southern neighbor because of its allegedly deep cultural, social, and political differences and the bullying nature of the latter's government. According to Yevhen Holovakha, a Ukrainian sociologist, two graduate students from Kyiv who studied under him reached an interesting conclusion after studying the dynamics of values in Lviv and Donetsk for ten years: the Donbas is evolving toward democracy faster than Lviv.[34] I suspect that Lviv's historical consciousness, with its deeply nationalistic tone, may be less flexible than the Donbas' civic, non-nationalistic, and non-ethnic collective identity, particularly at a time when globalization is leading inevitably to a greater integration—rather than division—of nations.[35] This is particularly the case with the European Union that Ukraine now strives to join.

Conclusion

Andrukhovych now admits that ten or even five years ago he would have said that the Donbas should be left to join Russia (although it is not known whether Russia would have wanted that). Yet since the Orange Revolution, Ukrainians have become more optimistic and wish to preserve the country's territorial integrity. So the Donbas cannot possibly be let go.[36] Asked about his passage on Sarmatia quoted earlier, Andrukhovych responded that it was not so much political as aesthetic: it was not propaganda against the Donbas but an "artistic condensation of ideas and images tied to this region," a condensation that is "ambivalent and contradictory."[37] Andrukhovych says that he has a proposition for a new Donbas, a "different East," which he still cannot formulate in words. Yet he adds that the "vogue of the Donbas" is inevitable—the unmistakable attraction of a post-Soviet, post-industrial space that is in essence not yet filled with anything. He hopes it is there that the "Centre of Europe" will be located.

He wants a new "Europe from Lisbon to Luhansk."[38] Andrukhovych is mistaken in thinking Donbas is an empty land. That it has "no history," unlike, say, Lviv, is a prevalent myth.[39] In fact, Andrukhovych himself has written of its rich history, as quoted earlier. Yet he may well be right that the Donbas is flexible, that is, that its political mood can change rapidly. In exploring the future of the Donbas, Andrukhovych was struck by the photo exhibition of Viktor Marushchenko, "Dreamland-Donbas,"[40] in particular by one photograph of three colliers, full of humanity and "artistism." Yet soon he noticed that it was in fact a photograph of "horror": these were not men but female miners who illegally descend deep into closed mine shafts (more than a thousand feet) to make a dangerous but meager living by selling the extracted coal on the black market. They (and their children) risk their lives to earn $60 per month at most.[41] After seeing this horror, Andrukhovych says in retrospect that nothing else has any meaning.[42]

Dire poverty is no monopoly of the Donbas. Yet the region's horrific poverty exists not in a traditional landscape but against the backdrop of modern industry.[43] People in the Donbas, like people elsewhere, struggle for daily existence while holding onto dreams. The 2004 presidential elections may have highlighted the sinister aspects of life in the Donbas, but the Marushchenko exhibition humanized it. Indeed, the apparent anger in the pro-Yushchenko regions against the Donbas in the wake of the election fraud was accompanied by a rise of interest in the Donbas.[44] Even the fiercely nationalistic émigré press began to publish sympathetic articles on the Donbas as a "Ukrainian" land.[45] Now it has dawned on people outside the Donbas that inhabitants there have the same aspirations that they do: for a better life and a better, stable, and peaceful future.

It is only recently that Western observers such as Samuel Huntington and Padraic Kenney have unequivocally stated that western Ukraine, with its history of "western" civilization, is inherently different from eastern Ukraine with its history of "Orthodox" civilization. Ukraine, according to these observers, is a "cleft country": western Ukraine is rich with potential for democracy, and eastern Ukraine is not.[46] Yet the Orange Revolution has demonstrated that central Ukraine, with Kyiv as its center (an area belonging to eastern Ukraine according to Huntington and Kenney), is capable of staging something extraordinarily democratic. If the center is capable, why not the east as well? In fact, it has done so repeatedly. Needless to say, few observers in the West have even noticed the significance of the challenge to the state by earlier mass, direct actions by the Donbas miners.

The political situation in Ukraine is fluid, and there is no way of knowing if the young, independent state will develop into a stable democracy. Will the Donbas remain politically relevant? Given the Donbas' past, people were—and still are—apprehensive of the Donbas. In the March 2006 parliamentary elections, Yanukovych's "Party of Regions" turned out to be the most popular, winning more than 32 percent of the vote, supported mainly by the Donbas and other Russified eastern regions, and beating Yushchenko's "Our Ukraine" (which won approximately 14 percent of the votes) by a wide margin. The Party of Regions achieved this result in part by replacing its former Russian advisers with "a team assembled by US Republican party campaign virtuoso Paul Manafort."[47]

Leon Trotsky, himself from the Russified Kherson province of Ukraine, once noted the difficulty of managing the Donbas: "One cannot go to the Donbas without a [political] gas mask."[48] The poet Nikolai Domovitov wrote some time ago:

Neither Ukraine nor Rus
I fear, the Donbas, I fear you.[49]

Now there is a broad consensus in Ukraine that the Donbas will remain an integral part of Ukraine. Fear remains, however. Some of this fear is due to the Donbas' legendary potential for mass actions. It also has to do with the fact that the Donbas industrialists, following the logic of capitalism, are rapidly transcending national borders, to say nothing of regional boundaries within Ukraine. This means that even though the Donbas may be the last of Europe's frontiers, it may well jump ahead of western Ukraine to embrace a capitalist and democratic Europe.

Notes

1. Here I rely on the data on the Donetsk province on http://ipa.net.us.
2. For this view, see Dominique Arel, "Paradoksy Pomaranchevoi revoliutsii," *Krytyka*, no. 4 (2005): 2–4.
3. Hiroaki Kuromiya, *Freedom and Terror in the Donbas: A Ukrainian-Russian Borderland, 1870s–1990s* (Cambridge: Cambridge University Press, 1998), 325.

4. John A. Armstrong, *Ukrainian Nationalism*, 3rd ed. (Englewood, CO: Ukrainian Academic Press, 1990), 221.
5. Albert O. Hirschman, *Exit, Voice, and Loyalty: Responses to Decline in Firms, Organizations, and States* (Cambridge, MA: Harvard University Press, 1970), 107.
6. Kuromiya, *Freedom and Terror*, 124, quoting Ivan Maistrenko, *Istoriia moho pokolinnia. Spohady uchasnyka revoliutsiinykh podii v Ukraini* (Edmonton: CIUS, 1985), 171.
7. Kuromiya, *Freedom and Terror*, 282, quoting Ievhen Stakhiv, *Kriz tiurmy, pidpillia i kordony. Povist moho zhyttia* (Kyiv: Rada, 1995), 133–34, 308.
8. Kuromiya, *Freedom and Terror*, 332–33.
9. See Vlad Mykhnenko, "State, Society and Protest under Post-Communism: Ukrainian Miners and Their Defeat," in *Uncivil Society? Contentious Politics in Post-Communist Europe*, ed. Peter Kopecký and Cas Mudde (London: Routledge, 2003), 93–114.
10. From Mykola Riabchuk, "Ukraine: One State, Two Countries?" *Transit*, no. 23 (2002), quoting Tatiana Korobova, "Strana voskhodiashchego zastoya?" *Grani*, no. 13 (2002).
11. Yurii Andrukhovych, "Atlas. Medytatsii," *Krytyka*, nos. 1–2 (2006): 10–11 (emphasis original). The English translation is my own. "Free economic zones" refers to the fact that, in 1999, then president Kuchma allowed the Donetsk province to create free economic/trade zones in exchange for the Donbas' support for his election bid. Kuchma was elected with the strong support of the Donbas, which in turn benefited from the tax breaks provided by the zone.
12. Yurii Andrukhovych, "Shukaiuchy Dreamland," *Krytyka*, nos. 1–2 (2005): 2.
13. Viktor Tkachenko, "Shcho robyty z Donbasom?" *Narodne slovo*, March 5, 2005, http://www.slovo-unp.com.
14. Note some interesting episodes in Ivan Dziuba, "Spohady i rozdumy na finishnii priamii," in *Rukopys*, vol. 1 (Kyiv: Vyd-vo Krynytsia, 2004), 35; and Vasil Stus, *Lysty do syna* (Ivano-Frankivsk, Ukraine: Lileia-NV, 2001), 10.
15. Taras Kuzio and Andrew Wilson, *Ukraine: Perestroika to Independence* (Edmonton, AB: CIUS Press, 1994), 189, 194, 198.
16. Mykhnenko, "State, Society and Protest," 101; and Vlad Mykhnenko, "From Exit to Take-over: The Evolution of the Donbas as an Intentional Community," paper presented at Workshop No. 20, "The Politics of Utopia: Intentional Communities as Social Science Microcosms," April 13–18, 2004, Uppsala, Sweden, 26.
17. Lewis H. Siegelbaum, "Freedom of Prices and the Price of Freedom: The Miners' Dilemma in the Soviet Union and Its Successor States," *Journal of Communist Studies and Transition Politics* 13, no. 4 (1997): 17–18.
18. Ibid.

19. Ibid.
20. Mykhnenko, "State, Society and Protest," 105.
21. See Mykhnenko, "From Exit to Take-over."
22. See Claudia Šabić and Kerstin Zimmer, "Ukraine: The Genesis of a Captured State," and Kerstin Zimmer, "The Captured Region: Actors and Institutions in the Ukrainian Donbas," in *The Making of Regions in Post-Socialist Europe—The Impact of Culture, Economic Structure and Institutions. Case Studies from Poland, Hungary, Romania and Ukraine*, vol. 2, ed. Melanie Tatur (Wiesbaden, Germany: VS Verlag, 2004); and Hans van Zon, "Neo-Patrimonialism as an Impediment to Economic Development: The Case of Ukraine," *Journal of Communist Studies and Transition Politics* 17, no. 3 (2001): 71–95.
23. See van Zon, "Neo-Patrimonialism," 72–74; quotation from Zimmer, "The Captured Region," 346–47.
24. Mykhnenko, "From Exit to Take-over," 35–39.
25. The World Bank Group Project Information Document, Report No. AB1755, http://www-wds.worldbank.org.
26. Mykola Azarov, then the head of Ukraine's tax administration, noted in 2001 that "It is from the Donbas that the rebirth of Ukraine began" ("'Donteskii klan' uverenno vkhodit vo vlast," *Nezavisimaia gazeta*, August 15, 2001).
27. Note his interview by the BBC, January 17, 2006, http://www.bbc.co.uk/ukrainian.
28. Kim Murphy, "Ukraine's East and West Are Miles Apart on Issues," *Los Angeles Times*, December 3, 2004.
29. Mykhnenko, "State, Society and Protest," 169.
30. Back in the 1970s, even Andrei Sakharov, the champion of human rights movements in the Soviet Union, dismissed the Donbas independent union movement, treating its leader as mentally unhealthy (Kuromiya, 331).
31. George O. Liber, "Imagining Ukraine: Regional Differences and the Emergence of an Integrated State Identity, 1926–1994," *Nations and Nationalism* 4, no. 2 (1998): 204.
32. Nataliya Chernysh, "Cities of Donetsk and L'viv: Convergence or Divergence?" *The Ukrainian Weekly*, January 21, 2001.
33. Ibid.
34. "Pora ukrainskoho vyboru: mizh revolintsiieiu ta reformoiu," *Krytyka*, no. 12 (2004): 7.
35. For Lviv's inflexible "nationalism connected with religion and the peasantry" and its "weakness of civic tradition," see Claudia Šabić, "The Ukrainian Piedmont: Institutionalisation at the Borders of East Central Europe," in *The Making of Regions*, esp. 146–57.
36. Andrukhovych, "Shukaiuchy Dreamland."
37. From his interview in *L'vivska hazeta*, January 5, 2006, http://www.gazeta.lviv.ua.
38. Andrukhovych, "Shukaiuchy Dreamland," and "Atlas. Medytatsii," 11.

39. See Zimmer, "The Captured Region"; and Melanie Tatur, "Comparative Conclusion," in *The Making of Regions in Post-Socialist Europe—The Impact of Culture, Economic Structure and Institutions. Case Studies from Poland, Hungary, Romania and Ukraine*, vol. 2, ed. Melanie Tatur (Wiesbaden, Germany: VS Verlag, 2004), 356–95.

40. The best online report on this seems to be the Polish site http://www .sekcja.org/miesiecznik.php?id_artykulu=84.

41. There is a very fine report on this in *The Christian Science Monitor*, May 15, 2002 ("Ukraine: Digging for black gold").

42. Andrukhovych, "Shukaiuchy Dreamland."

43. Note the collection of stunning photographs capturing poverty in Donetsk in Boris Mikhailov, *Case History* (Zurich and New York: Scalo Publishers, 1999).

44. See, for example, Andrii Portnov, "Svoboda ta vybir na Donbasi," *Krytyka*, no. 3 (2005): 5–6.

45. See Yurii Kurylko, "Donbas moiei iunosty," *Svoboda*, January 13, 2006; and Kurylko, "Iaku Ukrainu my liubymo? Dumky donetskykh ditei," *Svoboda*, March 24, 2006.

46. Samuel P. Huntington, *The Clash of Civilizations and the Remaking of World Order* (New York: Simon and Schuster, 1996); Padraic Kenney, *A Carnival of Revolution: Central Europe 1989* (Princeton, NJ: Princeton University Press, 2002).

47. Frederick Kempe, "Democracy Takes Root in Ukraine," *The Wall Street Journal*, March 21, 2006, p. A6.

48. Kuromiya, *Freedom and Terror*, 3, 334.

49. Quoted in *Donbass*, no. 8 (1993): 235.

6

In the Minority in Moldova: (Dis)Empowerment through Territorial Conflict

Hülya Demirdirek

The Question of National Minority

Despite the commonalities between various forms of majority and minority nationalisms, the social and political contexts in which a national entity and its relationship to significant others are envisioned may differ from case to case. Furthermore, these social and political relations can themselves play a decisive role in shaping nationalist ideologies. Some nationalist movements arise in response to the imperatives of capitalist industrialization and represent the commonalities of a majority community; others arise in response to the demands of minority communities incorporated within a wider nation-state. The character of a specific nationalist ideology (for example, its stress on equality within the national community or the forms of exclusion outside of it), can be shaped by whether the nationalist identity represents relations between a majority community and the state or minority aspirations within it. In their extreme form, majority nationalisms may, for instance, incorporate ideologies and practices of violence against minorities. In any case, notions of majority and minority are situational, relational, and change through time—a minority community in one context may be a majority in another context.

The autonomous territory of Gagauzia and the quasi or de facto state of the Transnistrian Moldovan Republic (TMR) within the territory of the Republic of Moldova[1] are illustrative of the situationality and relational character of the minority construction and the associated territorial conflicts that may ensue. In this article, I argue that both of these minority entities display a clear legacy of the Soviet Union. In each case, the Soviet experience is drawn upon to create new minority and smaller, nation-like units, yet this continuity manifests itself in two very different ways in Gagauzia and the TMR. Furthermore, the leadership of both entities, though claimed by different types of groups, also carries the legacy of Soviet rule. The way power is allocated and the access of particular groups to certain kinds of resources have had enormous impact on the fate of both entities. In formal politics and larger political constellations, the TMR (firstly) and Gagauzia (secondly) have greater prominence than other minorities in the Republic of Moldova. In this chapter, I provide only a brief overview of the other minorities, offer a background for the events in the early 1990s in Moldova, and focus principally on the Gagauz case.

From the Moldavian SSR to the Republic of Moldova

In the early 1990s under the political heat of reaction against the Soviet Union, Moldovans were strongly reunified with Romania. Historically, it is understandable that Moldova's ethnic Moldovans might classify themselves as Romanians. Formal state borders do not always correspond to the population they encircle; this was the case in the historic territory of Bessarabia. If it had not been annexed by Soviet power in 1940 and again in 1944, much of the Bessarabian population would today readily identify itself as Romanian, as it would be living within Romania's national borders. Allowing for short periods of changes of rule, however, the population of the current Republic of Moldova has not been part of Romania for close on two hundred years. Since the early nineteenth century, Bessarabia had been a meeting place for various peoples and ideas, not least a place for a high number of inter-ethnic marriages. These numbers were significant enough to give rise to a distinctive Moldovan identity. Consequently, it is not surprising that after the initial wave of excitement had subsided, 95 percent of voters in a 1994 referendum rejected reunification with Romania and chose to stay independent as the Republic of Moldova.

Bessarabia has a long history as a multiethnic region. The earliest ethnic violence against Jews in the twentieth century goes back to

April 1903, when 49 Jews were killed and several hundred injured (mainly by Russians rather than Moldovans) during the Chişinău pogrom. In the north, Moldovans and Ukrainians have lived together peacefully for centuries and share common cultural traits. In its recent history, Moldova rarely experienced ethnic violence until the early 1990s.

Present-day Moldova has approximately 4.2 million inhabitants.[2] In the 2004 census,[3] 78.2 percent of the population was Moldovan, 8.4 percent Ukrainian, 5.8 percent Russian, 4.4 percent Gagauz (a Christian Orthodox Turkic people), 1.9 percent Bulgarian, and 1.3 percent other nationalities, mainly Jews, Belarussians, Poles, Greeks, Germans, and Roma (gypsies). Historically, the Ukrainian population has lived mainly in the north and east of the country, while Gagauz and Bulgarian settlements are concentrated in the southern Budjak region.[4] The Russian population (predominantly workers and professionals who came to Moldova after World War II) is concentrated in Chişinău, Bălţi, and the industrial zones of Transnistria. The total migration loss in Moldova between 1990 and 1996 was some 105,000 persons, with Jews, Ukrainians, and Russians the most likely to leave.[5] Comparison of the 1989 and 2004 census figures reveals an increase of 13.7 percentage points in the Moldovan portion of the population.

Minority Ethnic Movements in Moldova

Of the ethnic minorities in Moldova, only the Gagauz (and, to a limited extent, the Bulgarians) had organized ethno-nationalist movements during the collapse of the Soviet Union. It is more difficult to label the grouping and actions of the people who went on to form and subsequently rule the TMR. Those who came into conflict with the Moldovan army in 1992 were Russians, Moldovans, and Ukrainians. They were not members of a particular political movement organized along ethnic lines.

The territory of the former Moldovan Soviet Socialist Republic has witnessed two territorial conflicts following the collapse of the Soviet Union: the Gagauz and the Transnistrian. The Gagauz conflict ended peacefully and was one of the least bloody territorial conflicts in the entire former Soviet Union. The Transnistrian conflict, however, resulted in a great deal of bloodshed within a short time period. In legal terms, this conflict has yet to be settled. I shall first outline the events that led up to the establishment of the TMR and Gagauzia, and then undertake an in-depth analysis in which I shall refer back to these events.

The formation of Gagauzia and Transnistria took place against the backdrop of the ethnic tensions and nationalist movements of the late 1980s, factors that were commonplace throughout the former Soviet Union. Clashes between central leaderships and local administrators crossed ethnic lines. Local governments made up of Russian-speaking officials were unwilling to accept decisions coming from central government; this was especially true of the Russian-speaking cities on the other side of the Dniester River, such as Bender and Tiraspol. First the Gagauz and then later the Transnistrian leaders formed their own unrecognized republics in 1990. Central power fell into the hands of pan-Romanian factions, and reunification with Romania became a highly charged issue over the next five years. Pan-Romanian sentiment was symbolic of the resentment against Russian domination. Strong support was forthcoming from Romania and the political discourse evolved along ethnic lines of division, while there was also a marked urban/rural distinction that corresponded to language ability and preference: Russian speakers predominated in the cities, whereas in the countryside (except for Transnistria and Gagauzia), Moldovan was widely spoken. The Popular Front leaders, who had enjoyed privileges in the Soviet era as prominent intellectuals, successfully mobilized anti-Russian sentiment. The tension between those who considered themselves Moldovans and those who saw themselves as non-Moldovans increased in various parts of the republic. Although bus loads of Moldovan volunteers traveled to the Budjak area in response to the Gagauz claim for independence, this event did not escalate into conflict or bloodshed. The cultural and political rivalries moved in another direction in Transnistria, where the combined majority population is not ethnic Moldovan but rather Russian/Ukrainian. This region of Moldova was part of Ukraine prior to 1940, when it was amalgamated with Bessarabia under Stalin's policy. Armed clashes in the spring of 1992 resulted in numerous casualties, with the Russian 14th Army still present in the background. Not all parts of Transnistria were rocked by violence. The eastern bank of the Dniester, where the majority of the Russian-speaking community lives, was not exposed to these armed clashes.[6]

In the Transnistrian conflict, unlike the Gagauz conflice, Moldovans and non-Moldovans fought on both sides, against each other: one side was supported by Chişinău forces; the other was backed by the pro-Soviet forces in Tiraspol (including the Russian 14th Army stationed there). More than a thousand people were allegedly killed, and approximately one hundred thousand people fled their homes in an atmosphere akin to civil war. All these events served to reinforce pan-Romanian sentiment among Moldovans. But although the first post-independence government of Moldova was in the hands of the pan-Romanians, the political constellation changed rather quickly. The Popular Front lost power, and the problems in both Transnistria and Gagauzia attracted international attention and involvement. The economic benefits of controlling Transnistria were (and still are) significant, and Russia supported the breakaway republic in various ways. The new Moldovan constitution of 1994 safeguarded the rights of minorities. The same year also saw the granting of autonomy to the Gagauz. The status of Transnistria remains an unresolved issue, although there has been a prolonged absence of explicit conflict.

Nationalisms and Minority Nationalisms

Many nationalist movements stress the creation of a common past and a shared culture in the construction of "imagined communities" of nationhood.[7] To this end, a variety of symbols (language, shared kinship, blood, soil, the nation imagined as a family, etc.) may be used to create a sense of community and cohesion of the internal collectivity. These symbols operate in relation to those in response to which one's identity has been formed. This means that expression of identity is context-specific, according to the constructed other. For example, in one instance a Turkic language alongside Christianity can mark Turkicness (as with the Gagauz in Moldova), while in another case Islam alongside the Bulgarian language may imply a Turkic identity (as with the Pomaks in Bulgaria). In another scenario, a shared recent experience of struggle to attain independent status, as in Transnistria, may be invoked in order to establish a "quasi state," a nation-like unit, among the Transnistrian people.

Nationalist movements often arise in the context of the break-up of empires, as occurred with the former Soviet Union and with the British and French Empires after the Second World War. The character of the resulting nationalist movement can vary according to how the "ethnic" community was envisaged prior to the break-up of the larger imperial unit. Indeed, one could argue that the way in which national entities are constituted after the break-up of empires partially reflects earlier categories. Nationalist movements emerging after the disintegration of empires, like many counter-ideologies, are derivative of the political imaginings of those empires.[8]

In the case of formerly colonized countries, colonization has been accompanied not only by the denial of statehood, but also by the denial to its citizens of the full rights of citizenship. Colonized individuals were objects of the state, not full legal subjects with the rights of enfranchisement. Indigenous languages and cultures were typically devalued, while attempts were made to spread the culture of the colonizers (typically understood as a modernization project) to at least an influential minority of the population (through education and other means). The culture of modernization assumed the status of universality and homogeneity; cultures of the colonized were constituted mainly in terms of their lack (for example, their lack of modernity). Consequently, the process of forging a national identity assumed a dual role: on the one hand, that of criticizing the culture of modernity and showing it to be partial rather than universal and, on the other hand, that of creating a sense of a shared "culture" among the colonized peoples, where previously little shared culture had been assumed to exist. This process of creating "something" out of a previous "nothing" is perhaps most marked in anti-colonial revitalization movements.

There are, however, differences between postcolonial movements that emerged as a reaction to the colonial regimes and those movements that have emerged following the break-up of the Soviet Union. In the latter case, for example, minorities were allowed to express identity prior to the dissolution of the Soviet Union through the notion of ethnos, an identity manifest in the teaching of local languages and history.

I have argued elsewhere[9] that the Soviet Union was less repressive than Western European nation-states and other colonizers in terms of the way it used modernization and civilization projects to create a literate public that could embody simultaneously a national identity and a socialist identity. Yet, in going through the processes of adapting to and withdrawing from Russian dominance, ethnic categorization and stratification experienced radical transformations.

Bearing this in mind, I consider the historical construction of the formative elements in ethnic and national identity politics, and examine how certain notions are cultivated in order to generate ethnic consciousness. The force of this consciousness depends on the strength of the connection between people's experiences and the language that shapes the ideologies of belonging. These ideologies are employed by agents (here the nation-builders) seeking to generate the emotions necessary to create national subjects.

Ethnic Units and Minority Policies of the Soviet Union

As indicated above, the Soviet Union was in many ways less repressive and less homogenizing than the nation-states of Western Europe. Leninist and Stalinist ideas of nations and their interpretations, in which ethnic and national characteristics were regarded as innate, created room for "national forms," which had to be filled with "socialist content." Soviet policies on nationalities and minorities fluctuated over time and varied across different groups. Thanks to their use of the census (like other colonial states[10]), first the Russian empire and later the former Soviet Union created a certain legitimacy for ethnic groups of different sizes—despite suppressing them in other regards.[11] Bruce Grant sees this as a sign of both diversification and unification, trends that he attributes exclusively to earlier periods of Soviet nationality policy.[12] Despite fluctuations in these trends, I would argue that they continued later, too. It must be noted, however, that there was always a system of ethno-national units in the Soviet Union. This concept can be seen as analogous to the Russian nesting doll or *matryoshka*, a doll that contains a series of smaller dolls, each smaller doll inside a larger one. While population size was an important element in achieving recognition as a nation (that is, a "nation" was more than one hundred thousand people), such recognition was also dependent on historical and territorial circumstances. Nations were entitled to statehood in the form of union republics with greater autonomy, while smaller units had a lower administrative status.[13] The situation was not straightforward, however, and the administrative status of smaller units changed over time. The formula introduced by Krushchev in 1961 contained the elements of "flowering," *rapprochement*, and "merger" (in Russian, *rastvet, sblizhenie, sliianie*), but the relative importance of each element varied in particular circumstances. Even the number of ethnic groups in the former Soviet Union changed from time to time (194 in 1929, 109 in 1939, 196 in 1970, 101 in 1979 and—as listed by the Academy of Sciences—128 in 1989[14]), with some periods witnessing heavy repression (for example, scholars could be labeled nationalist merely because they were studying a local language, especially during the Stalin period). In periods when it was possible to promote education in the student's native language (for example, in the 1960s), patriotism for one's native region was compatible with patriotism for the Soviet Union.[15]

The practice of the socialist project and the practice of nationalist projects thus have many features in common. Just as national days are celebrated within the dynamic of the local community in Norway, for instance, local achievements were used to praise the glory of the Soviet Union. Involvement in activities supporting the prosperity of one's region and one's people, when undertaken within the discourse of Soviet patriotism, was one way of showing love for the Soviet Union. Such a context provided scope to foster and idealize patriotic work aimed at enhancing the prosperity of a particular culture (with a capital and a lower-case "c"). This ensured continuity between the people and activities relating to issues of identity politics.

During the Soviet period, it was the intelligentsia who cultivated this sense of patriotism. In the post-Soviet context (as in colonial territories, in which large merchants and industrial entrepreneurs were rare or rarely acknowledged, at least initially),[16] the intelligentsia took the vanguard role in nation-building or -restoring processes. Those involved in the cultural politics of the Gagauz and the Bulgarians in the 1960s would become the political activists of the Gagauz and Bulgarian struggle in the 1980s. They were representative of their respective cultures in each period. In studies of nationalism, these intellectuals are usually referred to as national elites. These elites established a system of justification that held that if a population were a "nation," then it was entitled to certain rights, if not full statehood. In the struggle to assert Gagauz nationhood or a Transnistrian supra-national collectivity, the nation-builders created an ideological space within which they built the framework for justifying the nationalization of the entity they were trying to establish.

While the ethno-national unit system classified groups on the basis of ethnic origin, scholars acknowledged the importance of socio-economic and politico-historical processes in the formation of units. But this understanding was accompanied by a belief in the manipulation of social processes of the past, the present, and the future. On one hand, traditions and religions, ethnic compositions, and collective memory were all regarded as highly open to manipulation through central planning. On the other hand, ethnic and national characteristics were also regarded as innate. These commonly held views went hand in hand, and both constituted some of the fundamental ingredients of ethnic and national revival.

This ideological climate gave rise to a belief in the possibility of manipulating further developments in a desired direction. The break-up of the Soviet Union allowed for the emergence of social actors and the creation of entities that could be recognized as legitimate possessors of rights, land, and other national "belongings."

The Making of a Nation and a Place

I refer to the Gagauz as a "nation-in-the-making" since Gagauz activists were seeking recognition as a nation despite being within the territory of another nation-state. It is difficult to call this process national reconstruction since the region's previous history of national construction is rather ambiguous and hidden from the Gagauz public. To this extent, the making of Gagauzia is about emergent ethnic/national mobilization and construction within the framework of the legacy of the former Soviet Union.

Numerous territorial conflicts in the former Soviet Union, in Europe, and elsewhere in the world are addressed as problems of minority rights, nationalism, and ethnicity. In many instances, cultural idioms, genealogy, religion, language, territory, and history are used to differentiate particular groups from each other. The Gagauz example is similar in many ways to other cases in the manner in which difference is defined and boundaries established. After all, many anthropologists have acknowledged that nationalisms are externally alike.[17] But the Gagauz nation-building process also exhibits certain less usual features.

Firstly, Gagauzia is not a contiguous territory: only those villages and towns that voted to be included in Gagauzia make up the autonomous territory. Some villages (for example, some of those in which the Gagauz population makes up only a minority) did not vote to be included in the new territory. Thus, there are gaps in the map of Gagauzia. Today, Gagauzia is marked on maps as an international legal entity, but it has no formal border-crossing points. In contrast, the TMR—which is not an internationally recognized entity—is not included on formal maps yet has strict border-crossing points.

Secondly, the Gagauz share their religion with the other ethnic groups that live in the same region or together with the Gagauz in the same villages and towns. Budjak is inhabited not only by the Gagauz but also by Bulgarians, Moldovans, Roma (gypsies), Ukrainians, and Russians. Budjak contains ethnically mixed villages as well as villages that are relatively homogeneous. The most obvious difference that many Gagauz perceive between themselves and other groups is their language.

Thirdly, the Gagauz population as a whole did not go through the kind of systematic nation building that took place in many parts of Eastern Europe prior to the socialist regime[18] and the Soviet Union.[19]

Finally, the most significant difference between the Gagauz struggle and many other territorial conflicts in Eurasia in the past
decade—first within Gagauz's unrecognized self-proclamation as a
republic and subsequently during its attempts to secure an
autonomous territory—is that the latter Gagauz struggle did not
result in bloodshed. Unlike the Transnistria conflict within the territory of the Moldovan SSR, which erupted in violence in 1992, the
Gagauz conflict was resolved at the negotiating table. As elaborated
elsewhere,[20] this outcome is related to macro-political processes and,
perhaps, contingencies. The shared historical and cultural experience
of the people who live in Moldova can also be seen as a "peace-keeping factor," although this term could be applied equally to the population living on the other side of the Dniester. Yet during the 1992
conflict, this shared experience did not prevent violence from flaring
up. Such violent conflict makes it all the more necessary to consider
the unique socio-political constellation in each case.

From Budjak to Gagauzia

I now turn briefly to the development of Gagauz identity politics. The
cultural activists of the Gagauz in the late 1960s—who worked with
and for the language—became politically active in the 1980s and
formed different groups, which competed with each other over technical linguistic and historical issues, as well as personal and political
matters. These activists were ethnographers, painters, poets, teachers,
and various other academics. Among other projects, they compiled
an anthology of Gagauz folklore and published volumes of Gagauz
short stories, poems, and other literature. Those who worked with
Gagauz cultural issues or wrote in the Gagauz language were colleagues and knew each other personally. Their activity must be seen
in light of the status of knowledge and intellectual activity in the
1960s and 1970s in the Soviet Union. This era saw the flourishing of
Soviet culture, with political and economic stability, and a generally
thriving intellectual community. One important mission for intellectuals was to contribute to the cultural prosperity of their people. In
those days, one could combine one's patriotism for one's native city
and one's patriotism for the Soviet Union.

Gagauz cultural activists operated as if "Gagauz culture" were a
generally accepted and understood concept, without ever generating
discussion as to what Gagauz culture comprised. Activists sought to
shape the development of the Gagauz language and history and, at

the same time, tried to define the scope of the self-proclaimed republic and its subsequent autonomous status. In the early 1980s, the activists had no economic clout, but their struggle was less motivated by economic interests than it was by the desire to attain formal political power.

Gagauz cultural workers and activists in the areas of language and education would maintain their commitment to social reform, but the meaning of their activities changed as political circumstances changed. In the late 1980s, together with other non-Moldovans, the Gagauz were in the position of defending themselves against the Moldovan nationalist movement as symbolized by the Moldovan language law. The Moldovan language law was a reaction to repressive Soviet Russian policies and an assertion by Moldovans of Romanian identity. The law initially hinted that it might penalize those who did not speak the official state language (in many official contexts, the Moldovan or Romanian language is referred to as the "state language," without actually being named. The number of Gagauz who are fluent in Romanian is very limited (4 percent). Under the threat of mandatory "state language" use, some activists took a more aggressive stance. But despite the Moldovan government's move to increase the population's proficiency in the Romanian language following independence, Russian remained the primary language of administration, commerce, and instruction in Gagauz areas. But even with increasing empowerment of Romanian language practice, the Moldovan state did not pursue exclusionary activities such as proficiency tests and other markers of language use.

A parliamentary report produced by the Moldovan government in 1990 briefly summarizes the context of the struggle over the understanding of ethnic categories. The report claimed that the Gagauz and other non-Moldovans were not indigenous to Moldova, adding that the Gagauz homeland was Bulgaria and that the Gagauz thus had no national territory of their own.[21] This report provoked an angry reaction from the Gagauz: the Gagauz were not an ethnic minority (*etnicheskoe men'shinstvo*), they argued, but a people (*narod*). Ever since the late 1980s, the Gagauz leaders argued with the Moldovan government about the wording of the draft laws, insisting on being recognized by the government as a nation and appealing to international organizations as such. Still, debates over ethnic categorizations and entitlements were a hallmark of the transitional period. As indicated above, in the late 1980s and early 1990s, reunification with Romania was a hotly debated topic. Though support for this idea has gradually waned, it has had a great influence on the political attitudes of the minorities in the country.

The Gagauz struggle for autonomy took place in a rich landscape of political change, leading to a few armed clashes and international involvement. After five years of active political struggle, the Moldovan parliament passed a law on the special legal status of Gagauzia, thus recognizing Gagauz autonomy, on December 23, 1994. This can be seen as one of the most peacefully solved territorial conflicts in the former Soviet Union. With the law on autonomy, a new officially recognized territory emerged: Gagauz Yeri ("the place where the Gagauz live"), otherwise known as Gagauzia.

For the purposes of this discussion, there are two significant factors in the Gagauz efforts to achieve autonomy. Firstly, the entire cultural and political struggle to achieve autonomy took place against the backdrop of the Transnistrian conflict. Secondly, the territory of Gagauzia did not have the industry or the financial potential of Transnistria. This meant that, although not easily achieved and heavily dependent on Gagauz political mobilization, Gagauz autonomy has always been more about the control of a rural territory than about industry or economic interests.

New Unit, New Friends, and Old Habits

Gagauz nation-builders insisted on the recognition of the Gagauz as a nation rather than as a national minority. They pursued the logic of Soviet taxonomy to redefine and generate a national unit, with all the unit's respective rights. Before the break-up of the Soviet Union, the Gagauz were citizens of the Moldovan SSR. In many cases, the new concern at the end of Soviet rule was to categorize people in terms of common ethnic origin and to communicate these categories to the public. This was part of the process of downsizing the Soviet imagination to a national level. But Gagauz leaders for the most part did not feel the need to pass on this message, nor did the general population's immediate interests leave much room for such a concern. Thus, achieving greater recognition in terms of personal and national identity has been no easy task for Gagauzia.

I turn now to the situation in Gagauzia following the granting of autonomy, with special reference to language practice. The official languages in Gagauz Yeri are Moldovan, Gagauz, and Russian. Russian is used actively in the handling of bureaucratic tasks, while Gagauz serves as the symbolic language in the naming of administrative bodies. The Gagauz terms for "governor," "popular assembly," and "executive committee" are used irrespective of the language being spoken. There is, however, no such consistent use of Gagauz terms for other official bodies.

According to the law of Gagauzia, which was adopted in 1995, the Gagauz governor (who is elected locally) must be at least thirty-five years years old and must speak Gagauz. A 1998 amendment to this law stipulates that the governor must live or have lived in Gagauzia. These relatively liberal conditions show the theoretically inclusive attitudes taken by the Gagauz Popular Assembly. Although it is not, in reality, very likely, a non-Gagauz—by virtue of language knowledge and regional belonging—may be entitled to become governor. On this basis, it can be seen that the key idioms in the Gagauz assertion of nationhood are territory and language.

Language stands at the heart of the Gagauz educational sphere, both as an ideological and a practical concern. I should point out that there are several problems affecting lower and higher education: pedagogical programs in Gagauz are lacking for all subjects, textbooks are in short supply, and academic terminology is only just beginning to become established. Programs currently available were designed in Russian. Some subjects in further education can be studied only in Romanian, while many fields can still be studied in Russian. Thus, the prospects for Gagauz students seeking to enroll in university depend heavily on their language abilities. Yet for all the difficulties they may face in Moldova, their Gagauz language competence opens up alternative prospects for study in Turkey. Gagauz and Turkish are mutually understandable (with some perseverance and effort), and the Gagauz have been more exposed to Turkish in the past few years, due to personal contacts, as well as the availability in Moldova of Turkish television channels. Turkey is a source of both political and financial support for the Gagauz language revival.

Due to their insufficient experience with Gagauz scientific and political rhetoric (and a paucity of Gagauz terminology), many politically active people in Gagauzia are more fluent in Russian than in Gagauz. Gagauz political meetings are frequently conducted in Russian, both because many participants are more at ease in Russian and because some non-Gagauz speakers are usually present (this fact is often used to justify the use of Russian after the initial formal introduction has been made in Gagauz). This tendency to use Russian, prevalent in many parts of the former Soviet Union, has created tension among the politically active people who came together to "save their language and culture from fading away." Those who passionately support literacy in the Gagauz language are not always those who have the best grasp of Gagauz. Likewise, some recent converts to Moldovan nationalism, who had been Russian speakers themselves, were very aggressive in their suppression of Russian after Moldovan became the state language.

Conclusion

The type of analysis I have offered in relation to the Gagauz case has implications for the historical and political understanding of the region as a whole, not only of post-socialist Moldova. There is, for example, a close connection between the points made here and an understanding of identity politics and ethnic conflict in the TMR.[22] The major issues in common are the strong historical continuities and legacies of the past (however transformed they may be and however divergent the directions they take), the importance of the location of political power, and the status of ethnic consciousness.

In the Gagauz case, through its Soviet-educated leadership, an already existing minority makes use of a new situation (namely, the break-up of the Soviet Union) by drawing on the Soviet classification system to create a new national unit. In the case of the TMR, local elites (the products of Soviet power structures, who hold political power and therefore have access to economic power) mobilize an ethnically mixed population by embracing Soviet internationalism in order to create a regional identity not based on ethnicity (and which later becomes a quasi-state). The Soviet legacy is plainly visible in both cases, albeit manifesting itself quite differently in the creation of the national unit. The leaders are products of the Soviet system: In the Gagauz case, they use existing ethnic minority sentiments to further raise consciousness against the backdrop of Moldovan nationalism; in Transnistria, they create a non-ethnically based unit against the backdrop of Moldovan nationalism.

Despite having the ethnic composition necessary to encourage ethnic consciousness and political mobilization, the Gagauz leaders had to work hard to mobilize the Gagauz population for the establishment of Gagauzia, and this development was not accompanied by widespread violence. The TMR, however, had no ethnically based political mobilization force, yet the struggle for the control of resources was so fierce that ethnically mixed Transnistria was mobilized to take up arms alongside the Russian 14th Army. The Transnistrian case serves to check those assessments that take for granted ethnic con-sciousness as a political mobilization tool. If one considers more recent developments in the TMR, and the partial success of efforts to create a "Transnistrian people," Hroch's scheme (as discussed by Yekelchyk in this volume) may be more persuasive. One of the biggest differences between Gagauzia and the TMR is their differing financial potential. While there was little to be lost by letting the Gagauz lead-ership take control of the rural non-industrial Budjak, the heavy industry on the other side of the Dniester was too important to be relinquished by the Moldovan state. In both cases, though, one could argue that, for the most part, the struggle was a struggle to national-ize a *territory*, whether that territory was a rather dry region of vine-yards or a region of industrial complexes.

These two conflicts surely influenced each other. The struggles between the central government and the Gagauz leadership and between the Moldovan state and TMR leadership for control of terri-tory illustrate well the political complexity of the region. Neither eth-nic consciousness nor a quarrel over rich resources can serve as the sole explanation for either conflict; instead, both derive from partic-ular social, political, and historical circumstances. Soviet Moldova was transformed into a post-Soviet ethno-territorial federation through the actions of minority elites. Yet the strategies used to appropriate or re-appropriate the territory in Gagauzia differed from those used in Transnistria. Territorial conflicts within Moldova empowered these minority entities, which also contained minorities. Although some would argue that the collective consciousness created in both Transnistria and Gagauzia has reached a "point of no return," politico-economic conditions can still influence the future direction of these entities. As both cases demonstrate, collective consciousness must be built on a history, yet it is also open to manipulation.

Notes

1. The TMR is located along the eastern banks of the Dniester and has a population of 660,000 people (or 15 percent of the Moldovan total). Gagauzia is not a contiguous territory. It covers large patches of terri-tory in the area in southern Moldova, traditionally known as Budjak. Gagauzia has approximately 150,000 inhabitants.
2. United Nations Fund for Population Activities, *2006 State of World Population: A Passage to Hope*, http://www.unfpa.org/swp/swpmain .htm (accessed April 28, 2007).

3. Central Intelligence Agency, *The World Fact Book 2007*, https://www .cia.gov/cia/publications/factbook/geos/md.html (accessed April 28, 2007).

4. H. Demirdirek and Claus Neukirch, "Moldova," in *Countries and Their Cultures*, ed. M. Ember and C. R. Ember (New York: Macmillan Reference, 2001), 1477–88.

5. Ibid.

6. Ibid.

7. Benedict Anderson, *Imagined Communities* (London: Verso, 1983); Richard Handler, *Nationalism and the Politics of Culture in Quebec* (Madison: University of Wisconsin Press, 1988).

8. The way in which we approach postsocialist phenomena is also a reflection of our own perception of this part of the world as seen from the capitalist West. Because of the different political regimes that divided the West from the East, the countries behind the Iron Curtain represented a collective other to us in the West. Despite this fairly recent conceptual and historical divide, it is hardly possible to ignore Soviet socialism as the formative context of particular nationalisms in the East, just as we can scarcely disregard the historical development of nationalisms (including such events as the dissolution of the Ottoman Empire, the Habsburg Empire, and the Romanov Empire). The legacy of these empires in the form of a combination of cultural and territorial autonomy is not, of course, specific only to former socialist countries. It has been argued, for example, that the Catalan and Basque movements of the political left in Spain—which were reinvigorated by the Spanish Civil War and subsequent persecution under the Franco regime—can also be seen as the indirect legacies of Habsburg socialism.

9. Hülya Demirdirek, *(Re)making of a Place and Nation: Gagauzia in Moldova*, unpublished doctoral thesis (Department of Social Anthropology, University of Oslo, 2001).

10. Anderson, *Imagined Communities*.

11. There was surely a hierarchy among the ethnic groups during the era of the Soviet Union, and the Gagauz were among those who felt a sense of stigmatization. But this sense is also related to the rural background of the population. Some people who lived in the cities or in other parts of the Soviet Union hid their Gagauz background, and the fact that some people claimed that others hid their Gagauz background was certainly a topic of conversation.

12. Bruce Grant, *In the Soviet House of Culture: A Century of Perestroikas* (Princeton, NJ: Princeton University Press, 1995), 5.

13. Valery Tishkov, *Ethnicity, Nationalism and Conflict in and after the Soviet Union: The Mind Aflame* (London: Sage, 1997), 33.

14. Anatoly M. Khazanov, *After the USSR. Ethnicity, Nationalism, and Politics in the Commonwealth of Independent States* (Madison: University of Wisconsin Press, 1995), 98; Tishkov, *Ethnicity*, 15–21.

15. The children who went to school learned there that their country was the Soviet Union and their republic was the Moldovan SSR. This is how the subject of Geography was taught. In one part of the curriculum, focusing on what was then called "native region" (in Russian, *rodnoi krai*), students studied the history of their region. In this curriculum, their region did not have clear-cut borders. Students learned the ethnic diversity of their own region as well as that of the Soviet Union. The population of their own region was one among many other populations referred to as "ethnoses." In this approach, territory, language, and mentality were inherent features of ethnic groups. In the school books, individual groups were usually illustrated wearing "folkloric" clothes, alongside the agricultural and other products associated with their republics. The people depicted in the texts included not only members of titular nations of republics but also those of less populous ethnic groups, of a size similar to the Gagauz or Avars.

16. Anderson, *Imagined Communities*, 106.

17. Michael Herzfeld, *Cultural Intimacy: Social Poetics in the Nation-State* (London: Routledge, 1997), 11; Bruce Kapferer, *Legends of People, Myths of State: Violence, Intolerance, and Political Culture in Sri Lanka and Australia* (Washington, DC: Smithsonian Institution Press, 1988), 3.

18. Holy Ladislav, *The Little Czech and the Great Czech Nation: National Identity and the Post-Communist Social Transformation* (Cambridge: Cambridge University Press, 1996); Katherine Verdery, *National Ideology under Socialism, Identity and Cultural Politics in Ceausescu's Romania* (Berkeley: University of California Press, 1991).

19. Hülya Demirdirek, *Dimensions of Identification: Intellectuals in Baku, 1990–1992*, unpublished dissertation, University of Oslo, 1993.

20. Demirdirek, *(Re)making.*

21. Daria Fane, "Moldova: Breaking Loose from Moscow," in *Nations & Politics in the Soviet Successor States*, ed. Ian Bremmer and Ray Taras., 121–53 (Cambridge: Cambridge University Press, 1993), 144.

22. Because my own field work is primarily in Gaugazia, for analysis of ethnographic work on the TMR, I have relied on the conclusions drawn by others.

7

The Promise of Europe: Moldova and the Process of Europeanization

Oliver Schmidtke and
Constantin Chira-Pascanut

Introduction

At first glance, the European Union (EU) seems to have established a rigorous system of inclusion and exclusion defined by full membership status and fortified external borders (captured by the image of a *Fortress Europe*). Yet considering its strategic interests with respect to the new neighbors to its east and south, the EU has recently developed a more differentiated set of policies designed to build partnerships and associational agreements. After the collapse of Communism, the EU's pledge of membership for the states in Central and Eastern European (CEE) has motivated them to embark on the road of political and democratic reforms in order to meet the restrictive Copenhagen criteria.[1] The close association with and potential membership in the EU represented the most stimulating incentive to this group of states putting in place painful economic and political reforms. The process of "Eastern enlargement" is on its way to completion now that Bulgaria and Romania have joined the EU.[2] Yet as the Treaty of the European Union provides,[3] every country that is part of the European continent can apply for membership. This entitles other states to envision their participation in the EU.

Such is the case for the former Soviet republic Moldova, whose leaders recently decided to follow the European pathway. The "promise of Europe"—the attractiveness of its values and standard of living—has become once again the spur for democratic reforms. Moldova will soon find itself not just at the eastern edge of the EU but also at the crossroads between the EU and Russia, two competing political and economic models. In fact, Moldova is an exemplary case of loyalty split between East and West. Its history entitles it to claim a place in Europe, together with Romania, while the first years of independence demonstrated Moldova's attachment to a Russian blueprint. Moldova recently began to proclaim its European aspirations, however, assiduously implementing democratic and economic reforms to meet the European criteria.

To consider the influence of Europe and the EU throughout CEE by focusing on Moldova is promising for two reasons. First, historically Moldova has been a country with strong ties to both Eastern and Western Europe. It exemplifies the—politically often contested—strategic choice that countries in this part of Europe face in terms of their external relations and the model of governance and reform they intend to follow. Second, as a country governed by a Communist party, Moldova has recently made a remarkable shift in its foreign policy by endorsing partnership with the EU. This chapter will address this surprising development in the context of the growing influence of the EU in the region. First, it will introduce the EU's approach to CEE and its key policy, the European Neighbourhood Policy (ENP). Second, it will analyze the case of Moldova with respect to the country's competing loyalties to the East and the West. This analysis will provide a more differentiated insight into the role the EU plays in the region. Against this background the chapter considers the following questions: Beyond full membership, how influential has the EU become in CEE? Can the "promise of Europe" as redefined by the ENP produce outcomes similar to the conditionality criteria put in place by the Copenhagen European Council if its incentives—a privileged relationship—are less attractive?

European Enlargement and the Expansion of the European Union in Central and Eastern Europe

With the transformation of geopolitical realities in the post–Cold War world, the EU has had to dramatically redefine its political identity. After 1945, the division of the European continent provided the

Western European community with a clear sense of its borders and sphere of influence with respect to its external relations. Yet with the disappearance of the Iron Curtain, new criteria and procedures had to be developed in terms of who could legitimately claim membership in the exclusive club that was the EU. From being a group of Western European states with a common interest and identity, essentially defined by the external geopolitical realities and the ideological divide of the Cold War, the EU had to reinvent itself primarily as a community bound together by a set of norms and forms of governance.

On this basis, it was clear that the recent enlargement of the EU eastward was the only feasible response to the claims of the aspiring new member states. Before 1989, the rhetoric of the European Community was that the continent suffered from an artificial and politically tragic division. The countries behind the Iron Curtain were said to belong to the rest of Europe and not to the sphere of influence of the Soviet Union. This support for the inclusion of countries in CEE in the EU was and is politically framed in terms of overcoming "obsolete boundaries" and welcoming the former Communist countries into the "European family." The move to extend the EU eastward is seen as an important and integral part of a broader political structure for peace in Europe. The dominant framing in public discourse follows this line of thought: the fundamental transformation of the political landscape in CEE and the enlargement of the EU are unique opportunities to overcome the division formerly marked by the Iron Curtain. In light of recent historical events, former Communist countries are now being included as potential members of the EU, which is depicted as a community sharing a basis of values and interests. Europe is portrayed as the political and cultural umbrella under which countries from both sides of the former Iron Curtain are to find an entirely new path of cooperation and exchange.

Against this backdrop it is not surprising that in the early 1990s the political elites in EU member states invited formerly Communist countries in CEE to join the community of European nations and adopt their principles of liberal democracy and market economies. Largely innocent about the practical implications of this open invitation, issued in the atmosphere of enthusiasm after the collapse of Communism, the EU was "rhetorically trapped"[4] into following up on its promise and, once basic conditions were met, accepting new member states. From the perspective of the EU and its member states, the collapse of Communism meant unexpected opportunities and challenges. On one hand, the EU seized the opportunity to be a major player in redesigning the geopolitical realities of the continent. With the expansion of NATO and then the acceptance of many countries in CEE as new members in 2004 and 2007, the EU has extended its sphere of influence and has become a decisive force promoting political change in the former Communist Bloc. After 1989, by insisting on universal criteria for domestic and international conduct as a precondition for any membership negotiations (as well as a decisive goal for the process leading up to full membership), the EU actively engaged in a process of exporting political norms, practices, and institutions.

On the other hand, the EU has come to realize the challenges of accepting countries with differing political legacies and economic fundamentals. In this respect the latest round of enlargement has proven to be more difficult than expected, both in terms of its implications for key (distributive) policies and governance issues, and in terms of popular support for accepting new member states. The recent, failed referenda in the Netherlands and France can be interpreted in large part as an indication of how skeptical, if not outright hostile, the population in the old member states is with respect to the process of enlargement. As a result, the EU has embarked on a strategy to develop forms of partnership with neighboring countries, promising select privileges and benefits from the EU in return for cooperation, while not promising a path to full membership. In short, the EU perceives expansion of its influence in CEE to be a priority in terms of interest and policy. At the same time, it is highly reluctant—given the current overall political climate—to invite more countries to initiate accession negotiations. Bulgaria and Romania may be the last countries to join the EU for a long time.

European Neighborhood Policy—The "Carrot" of European Union Membership

Reluctance to invite additional countries to embark on accession negotiations sparked an initiative on the part of the EU to consider a more cautious strategy with respect to those countries in CEE that have not (yet) gained membership status but with whom the EU still intends to have very close relations. Furthermore, with the latest round of enlargement the EU has had to develop policies that respond to the fact that Ukraine, Belarus, and Moldova share a border with the EU. The response to these challenges was the ENP, introduced at the beginning of 2004. Based on a 2003 strategic paper[5] by the European Commission on how the EU should relate to its non-member state neighbors, this policy has two central goals. First, beyond establishing good relations with those countries, the main concern driving the development of the policy was to create an area of security and stability in CEE and other countries on the Mediterranean Sea. In particular, the risks related to unstable or failed states and government structures, terrorism, organized crime, and regional conflicts have—with heightened attention after September 11, 2001—driven the agenda of the EU in this respect. This also accounts in part for the commission's strategic statement that the privileged partnership established under the ENP is meant to "build on mutual commitment to common values principally within the fields of the rule of law, good governance, the respect for human rights, including minority rights, the promotion of good neighbourly relations, and the principles of market economy and sustainable development."[6] Based on these "common values," the ENP seeks to establish cooperation and exchange, particularly in those areas seen to be critical in terms of the security concerns of the EU. With the ENP, the EU claims explicitly to go beyond simple cooperation with the participating countries and to promote a "considerable degree of economic and political integration."[7]

The second, related goal is to promote socio-political change in those countries that are part of the ENP. The promise to cooperate with such countries in the context of the ENP, to make financial aid available to them, and to give them access to the European market is tied to their complying with the standards that the EU has set for democratic governance and the rule of law. The emphasis on market reform and democratic and human rights was an integral part of EU external relations through much of the 1990s and shaped the earlier Partnership and Cooperation Agreements (PCAs) with countries in CEE. Yet under the ENP, this "conditionality" is enforced more rigorously, making the participating countries subject to a monitoring process; further cooperation with the EU depends on countries in CEE producing annual reports, similar to the "progress reports" for accession countries.[8] Over and over again, the European Commission has underlined that the benefits associated with the ENP and the country-specific Action Plans are conditional on compliance with democratic and legal reforms. This conditionality is employed in a much stricter sense than in the partnership agreements preceding the

ENP; until 1995, the bilateral agreements with noncandidate countries in CEE (i.e., Trade and Cooperation Agreements) were almost exclusively economic in nature and lacked a political component.[9]

There seems to be a certain ambiguity, however, in how the EU seeks to enforce compliance with basic democratic values and practices while at the same time avoiding inviting more countries to embark on the process toward full membership. For many countries that are part of the ENP, there are considerable costs involved in complying with the principles of democratic governance and the rule of law.[10] Various countries are governed by parties and leaders whose power is rooted in practices and institutional arrangements in open opposition to EU principles. In these countries, complying with EU norms might mean putting their own systems of political power at risk. Against this background, it cannot come as a major surprise that the incentive to comply with the conditions laid out by the EU depends to a large degree on a credible membership perspective, as recent scholarship in this area has shown[11] (though for a more skeptical view on the effectiveness of these incentives, see Lavenex 2004). Belarus provides a striking illustration of this fact: the country's motivation to comply with EU norms and practices is relatively low because President Lukashenka has much to lose, while the benefits promised by the EU are somewhat uncertain and the prospect of Belarus' membership in the EU highly unlikely.[12] Still, in many countries, the ENP is often perceived as a first step toward full membership in the EU. The EU, however, sees this policy as a surrogate for this status.[13]

In spite of the limited reach and attractiveness of the ENP as a key instrument of how the EU designs its external relations in this part of Europe, it would be misleading to assume that the EU's exclusive influence is restricted to enforcing compliance with the principles laid out in this policy. This chapter provides an illustrative case study focusing on Moldova's somewhat surprising recent endorsement of the EU as its main external partner for crafting the country's future. This case study will enable us to conceptualize more appropriately how, beyond membership negotiations or direct political pressure, the EU exerts authority in CEE, and how it has become a vehicle for political change—at times against the ruling elite in those countries. Moldova's response to proposed partnership with the EU provides us with a more differentiated and generalizable insight into the role that the EU and the "promise of Europe" has played in the transformation of post-Soviet countries in CEE.

Post-Soviet Moldova: The U-turn in Moldova's Foreign Policy and the Surprising Devotion of a Communist Country to the European Union

Moldova, a disputed territorial space between Romania and Russia, still struggles after more than a decade of independence to define its identity and to identify its place between East and West. Moldovan history, language, and culture tie it to the so-called western Moldova, a territory that is at present part of Romania. Yet in the past two hundred years, this region was (for more than a century and a half) part of tsarist Russia or Soviet Russia. This gave birth to Moldova's mixed feelings with regard to Romania and Russia and, ultimately, to an ambiguous Moldovan identity. In 1991, Moldova entered a stage never before experienced in its history—the territory that had historically moved back and forth between Romania and Russia faced the challenges of independence. In this context, the process of defining the Moldovan identity became of critical importance. During the state's first years of independence, Moldovan foreign policy oscillated between Moscow and Bucharest. Indeed, this new phase demonstrated and even accentuated Moldovan political and cultural ambivalence.

A contested Moldovan identity is a relatively new phenomenon, for until the early nineteenth century, Moldova, or Bessarabia (the territory between the Prut and Dniester Rivers—the present-day independent Republic of Moldova), had a historical record similar to that of the area situated on the western bank of the Prut River, which is today part of Romania and also called Moldova. In fact, prior to 1812, these two regions together formed the Principality of Moldavia. For most of its existence the Principality of Moldavia was a vassal state of the Ottoman Empire. It maintained its autonomous status by paying tribute regularly. The late eighteenth century witnessed Russia's westward expansion under Catherine the Great and Tsar Alexander I. It was in this context that the eastern half of the Principality of Moldavia was incorporated into the tsarist Empire.[14] During negotiations after the Russo-Ottoman War (1806–12), which led to the signing of the Treaty of Bucharest (1812), the Sublime Porte agreed to cede the so-called "Bessarabia,"[15] without clarifying the meaning of this term, which was used historically[16] to describe the southeast area of the Principality of Moldavia. Since tsarist Russia had already occupied the space between the Prut River and the Dniester River, and the term was not clearly defined, Russia granted this term a new meaning, maintaining its territorial occupation of the whole eastern Moldova, roughly the territory of the current Republic of Moldova. This period witnessed an intensive process of Russification of the Moldovan population. While the native population was moved to other parts of the Empire, other ethnic groups were encouraged to move or moved by force into Moldova. In fact, "14 percent of the population . . . is a new population brought by the Russian Empire."[17] The outcome of this process was that the number of Moldovans decreased substantially, as the figures of the censuses show.

The confusion created by the Russian Revolution and the stampede of Russian soldiers left Moldova in an unexpected situation. After a brief period of independence, the representative body of Moldova, the *Sfatul Țării*, voted for union with Romania, a move seen by many as a natural process of unification. In 1859, western Moldova and Walachia merged and created the United Principalities, which later became the Kingdom of Romania (1881). As a result, western Moldovans officially became Romanians. The Soviet Union never recognized post-Versailles Romanian borders, considering Bessarabia an occupied territory. In response, Moscow created in 1924 the Moldovan Autonomous Soviet Socialist Republic (MASSR) on the territory of the Trans-Dniester (Transnistria) Republic. The Soviet aim was to prevent Romanian expansion and to preserve Moldovan identity. Moscow sought to use this space to spread its new "Moldovan language theory" and to create a unique Moldovan identity. Moldovan grammars and dictionaries were published in Transnistria as part of an attempt to demonstrate the individuality of "proletarian Moldovan language," "based on peasant speech patterns,"[18] in contrast with the "bourgeois Gallicized Romanian," "not quite Romanian, not quite French."[19] These projects were abandoned in the late 1920s, as it was futile to try to demonstrate differences between the Moldovan and Romanian languages, other than the script used to write them. In this context it became increasingly hard to define Moldovan identity. On one hand, the Principality of Moldavia no longer existed, and its inhabitants were officially Romanians. On the other hand, after more than a century of Russian rule, the inhabitants of Bessarabia felt increasingly closer ties to Russia than to Romania. During interwar Romanian rule, the majority of Bessarabian students preferred to study in Russian rather than in Romanian.[20]

Moldova changed hands again in 1940 when, by implementing the Ribbentrop-Molotov Pact, the Soviet Union incorporated Bessarabia.

The Soviet administrative reorganization of Moldova aimed to fully integrate Moldova into the Soviet system and, above all, to reduce the possibility of its subsisting independently if its inhabitants sought independence or unity with Romania. Under its new appellation, the MASSR had its boundaries redrawn. It came to include Transnistria, a territory that was never before part of Moldova but was considered by Moscow to be vital to its exercising influence in the area. As a further safety measure, Bessarabia was landlocked: the southern territory that had given it access to the Black Sea was incorporated into Soviet Ukraine. Also, Moscow continued its policy of identity building in this region, seen as the first step toward the establishment of "a 'society without nations' that [would be] linguistically and culturally a Russianized one."[21]

After the collapse of the Soviet Union, Moldova faced two options: unity with Romania, or independence while cultivating strong ties with Russia under the umbrella of a new organization, the Commonwealth of Independent States (CIS). A third alternative, European integration—fully embraced by the Baltic States—did not seem to attract the attention of the Chişinău leaders in the aftermath of Moldovan independence.[22] These mixed feelings were partly due to the fact that newly independent Moldova could not count on a national identity that would entitle it to adopt one of the other options.

During this period, the undefined Moldovan identity was used to achieve Chişinău's diplomatic objectives. In the period immediately after its independence, when Moldova looked toward Bucharest, the country's linguistic law recognized "Moldo[van]-Romanian linguistic identity."[23] Other acts were envisaged to emphasize Moldovan-Romanian common identity and to secure close relations with Romania. Moldova adopted the Romanian "tricolor," anthem, and currency name. But when Moldova openly made its strategic move toward Moscow, relations with Bucharest worsened, and the "concept of 'two Romanian states' (accepted in 1991) was abandoned."[24] In this new context, it became important once more to reaffirm Moldovan separateness. The Moldovan Constitution (adopted in 1994) declared that "the national language of the Republic of Moldova is Moldovan,"[25] the history of Romanians would become the "history of Moldova," and the interwar Transnistrian projects to publish a Moldovan-Romanian dictionary were revived.

Fully integrated into the CIS economic system, Moldova did not consider other alternatives in foreign affairs for more than a decade.

By signing the CIS treaty,[26] Moldova made public its strategy in foreign policy. This granted it economic privileges—special trade arrangements with Russia and other member states. But in the early 2000s, Moldova was gradually excluded economically from the CIS, and the country saw its initial economic privileges effaced. In 2001, Russia "went so far as to exclude 14 categories of goods accounting for 47 percent of Moldova's exports."[27] In this tense context, the Yalta CIS summit (September 2003) was seen by Chişinău as crucial: "Moldova hoped to get a better deal . . . but no such agreement was signed in Yalta and, even worse for Moldova, Kazakhstan, Russia, Belarus and Ukraine created a 'Common Economic Area' without Moldova."[28] Moscow's decision to increase the gas prices for Moldova at the end of 2005 continues the same political line. No doubt Moldova had ceased to be a strategic partner for Russia.

Isolated Moldova began to consider other options without delay. Indeed, 2003 can be considered the turning point of Moldovan foreign policy, as President Vladimir Voronin proclaimed:

> Until last year we did not openly declare our priorities in foreign affairs. But the examination of the events from the beginning of 2003 has determined our strategic option—*Moldova's European integration* [s.n]. This option was chosen because four of the most powerful states of CIS—Ukraine, Belarus, Russia and Kazakhstan—have opted for an alternative model of integration, as members of the CEA [Common Economic Area], and Moldova cannot find its place in this organization.[29]

In its isolation, Moldova saw European integration as the most appropriate and immediate alternative. This line of foreign policy was reiterated by the Moldovan president, in the context of an extremely tense relationship with Moscow,[30] when he underlined that European integration was an "irreversible"[31] objective for Chişinău.

Moldova turned toward Europe, although this option forced Chişinău both to rebuild its relationship with Romania as a new EU member state, seriously damaged in the early years of Voronin's rule, and to engage in a long process with uncertain results—that is, European integration. Moldova now wants to make the most of its "special relationship" with Romania, which is to become its interior voice and supporter in Brussels. Likewise, its citizens want to use their right to acquire Romanian citizenship as a means to access the EU labor market. And although Romania has implemented strict measures for Moldovans, such as the introduction of visas from January

2007, this does not mean that Romania will not remain a staunch supporter of Moldovan European aspirations, as more and more voices in Bucharest speak about offering "unconditional"[32] support for Moldova. Moldova's recent choice is fully supported by all parliamentary political parties and the large majority of its citizens.[33] During the last parliamentary elections (March 6, 2005), all major Moldovan political parties acknowledged European integration as a key strategic objective for Moldova. While the Communist Party of the Republic of Moldova underlined the necessity of "Moldova's transformation into a state of European standards,"[34] the Moldovan Democratic Bloc[35] and the Christian Democratic Peoples Party,[36] the other two parties represented in the Moldovan unicameral parliament, pledged their European aspirations as well.

Moldova's relations with the EU are based on the PCA signed on November 28, 1994, which entered into force on July 1, 1998. This agreement was dormant for the most part of its validity until Moldova decided on its European path. One of the first states to sign an agreement with the EU under the ENP,[37] Moldova now looks toward Brussels as the ultimate solution for its diplomatic crisis. On March 16, 2005, following the invitation of Moldovan foreign minister Andrei Stratan, the EU sent a special representative, Adriaan Jacobovitz de Szeged, to participate in the negotiations of the settlement of the Transnistrian conflict. By signing the Memorandum of Understanding for the EU's Border Assistance Mission on October 7, 2005, Moldova and Ukraine agreed that "a mission of 60 customs and border guards officials from the EU member states will monitor the whole Moldovan-Ukrainian border, inclusively its Transnistrian segment, starting from December 1st [2005]."[38] These actions, together with the opening of the Delegation of the European Commission in Chişinău on October 6, 2005, are signs that the EU is fully committed to protecting its new eastern border after the adhesion of Romania, by stabilizing the situation in Moldova and by securing its borders. Conversely, Moldova began recently a process of intensive adoption of European standards in order to demonstrate its belonging to Europe and its European values. As the following declaration of Moldova's Ministry of Foreign Affairs underlines, this strategic reorientation of the country's external relations is perceived as a choice between allegiance to one or the other of the two "great poles of power"—politically between Russia and the EU, and culturally between the East and the West:

Under the conditions of the new world system's configuration around the great poles of power it is obvious that the Republic of Moldova cannot remain aside, becoming vital [to orient its foreign policy towards] one of these poles . . . in order to guarantee its development perspectives and national security. In this context the advisable pole for the Republic of Moldova is the European Union, whose political and economical weight is undoubted in comparison with other regional organizations. Thus, the Republic of Moldova promotes the idea of a United Europe, a Europe without division lines.[39]

Similar to other post-Soviet republics, Moldova had thus hoped to alleviate its transition by cultivating strong ties with Moscow, vigorously encouraged by the last Communist government. But Moldova's historical record, similar to that of western Moldova, entitled it in the early 1990s to examine a potential union with Romania. An ill-defined Moldovan identity, the subject of various experiments, played an important role in this uncertainty and did not allow the newly independent state at first to follow a straightforward option in foreign affairs. After more than a decade of uncertainty, however, Moldovan leaders and citizens agree that Moldova has finally found its place. It belongs to Europe geographically, politically, and culturally, and it is now—at least rhetorically—committed to doing whatever is necessary to demonstrate this.

Conceptualizing Europeanization and the Transformative Role of the European Union in Central and Eastern Europe

The scholarly discussion on the link between the transnational political sphere of the EU and domestic, national areas has focused mainly on EU member states.[40] Even with respect to processes within the EU, some observers have pleaded for caution when it comes to assuming that there is a compelling drive toward convergence with a European approach to key policies and forms of governance.

Political Inclusion—Transfer of Legislation
and Forms of Governance

The reform of the political system and structures of governance in accordance with EU standards is at the heart of the objectives of the ENP and earlier partnership agreements. The EU aspires to gain a direct impact on institution building and institutional adjustments, including constitutional and administrative legislative provisions. The transformation of formerly Communist countries into liberal democracies is widely perceived as the most successful strategy to achieve the EU's external relations objectives in the region, namely stability and mutually beneficial cooperation.

To achieve the desired reforms, the EU has various policy instruments at its disposal, ranging from normative pressure and assistance to conditionality and coercion (sanctions). The latter two options attach punishments and incentives to demands for democratic reforms. Comparable to the negotiation process with accession countries, the ENP allows conditional incentives to be gradually upgraded in terms of a country's association status and further integration into the *acquis communautaire*, the body of legislative provisions governing the EU. Integration progress is then rewarded with various forms of financial and technical assistance, as well as market incentives (see next point).[41] In a way, these mechanisms are closely patterned on the basis of the accession process, whereby applicant countries are subject to rigorous monitoring and conditionality. Yet democratic and administrative reform under the ENP is not rewarded by the promise of eventual membership, but only by a "privileged partnership."

The first results of the Action Plans implemented in the current seven partner countries seem to indicate that the principle of conditionality works. Although these three- to five-year plans do not focus primarily on political reforms, the first priorities are clearly targeted at strengthening democratic institutions, the rule of law, and electoral reforms (including human rights issues, the freedom of media and expression, and so on).[42] Some of the demands on the participating countries relate to the implementation of broad democratic rules; however, the plans also foresee quite concrete and measurable priorities in political reforms.[43] Moldova is an example of how these demands for actions are endorsed and have become a driving force in domestic institutional and political reforms (see the following section). One additional component in terms of the EU's involvement in domestic politics is peculiar to Moldova: the European Commission has committed to the settlement of the Transnistrian conflict.[44]

Beyond the transfer of institutional and legal provisions to the countries in CEE, there is also the more benevolent option to encourage political change and reform through persuasion and assistance to civil-society actors. These options are more in line with the self-perception of the EU as a "soft" power in international relations,[45] one that exercises its influence through diplomacy and a strong commitment to democratic values. Over the course of the past fifteen years, the EU has spent considerable resources on providing technical and financial support to democratic political institutions or civil-society actors. For instance, in the past year, financial assistance for Belarus went exclusively to activities designed to democratize the country and provide reform-minded forces with opportunities in their political struggle.

In Moldova, the stick-and-carrot policy of the EU seems to work, instigating far-reaching legislative and political change in the country. It is still early to determine if the 2005 EU-Moldova Action Plan will bring Moldova quickly closer to West European standards. Yet, in terms of both official declaration and initial legal results, Moldova seems to have embarked on a far-reaching and multidimensional reform process, as listed in the government's internal report on the plan:

> legislative reforms in the field of justice, public administration, educational system; measures taken in order to prevent money laundering, illegal migration; regulatory reform regarding the activity of entrepreneurs, the consolidation of financial, banking and fiscal systems; the adjustment of regulations in the field of inland water transport to international standards.[46]

As this citation indicates, the reform process reflects the priorities of the EU; it ranges from restructuring the legal system (the adjustment of national legislation to European standards) and amendments to the constitution (implementation of fundamental rights, electoral reforms, etc.) to promoting democratic reforms (independence for mass media, dialogue with civil society, gender equality, etc.) and addressing security concerns (organized crime, corruption, migration, etc.). Regardless of how thorough these reforms will be in the long run, the EU has been successful in defining the reform agenda and setting benchmarks for success.

Market Inclusion—Expansion of the Common Market and Financial Assistance

Economic incentives are a critical—and, as some would argue on the basis of a realist perspective, the most successful—component of the EU's strategy to gain influence in nonaccession countries in CEE. With the difficult transition process toward a capitalist economy, and with crisis-ridden economic relations with Russia, the EU promise to provide these post-Communist countries access to the lucrative West European market might seem almost as enticing as full EU membership. Acknowledging the attractiveness of this incentive, the European Commission stated in its document on a "wider Europe,"

> In return for concrete progress demonstrating shared values and effective implementation of political, economic and institutional reforms . . . the countries . . . should be offered the prospect of a stake in the EU's Internal Market and further integration and liberalization to promote the free movement of persons, goods, services and capital.[47]

The ENP's Action Plans offer a series of incentives in this respect, the most important of which are a substantial degree of integration in the EU's internal market, the reduction of tariffs on trade and, as a result, strengthened trade and economic relations with EU member states. What appears on the horizon as the economic "carrot" is a free-trade zone, perhaps similar to EFTA, which would allow participating countries in CEE to seize enormous economic opportunities and redefine their priorities in terms of export markets. And there are clear economic incentives laid out by the EU: beginning in early 2006, the list of Moldovan goods that benefit from tax-free access to the EU market has been extended.[48]

In public discourse this prospect of closer economic ties to the EU resonates with hopes of prosperity associated with images of Western lifestyles and consumption patterns. Regardless of how beneficial such an inclusion in the European market would actually be, the promise of access and participation in the prosperity of Western Europe carries considerable political weight in domestic politics. Popularly, the "promise of Europe" is shaped largely by images of a better life in material terms.

Normative Inclusion—Norm Setting and Socializing Effects

Beyond the direct political pressure or change imposed from outside, there is a more subtle and often more successful way in which the EU has become a source of promoting change. In this respect, one needs to conceptualize the relationship between institutions and political behaviors in terms of socializing and cultural effects. This approach encourages us to see the "constitutive, identity-forming role"[49] of institutions, a perspective prominently developed in neo-institutionalist approaches. These perspectives go beyond the focus on strategic interests and instrumental schemes of preference formation (the bargaining game played by political elites in countries in CEE). Rather, they shed light on the critical role that institutions play in defining issues, molding patterns of political legitimacy, and thus shaping interests.

In broader cultural terms, a subtle, albeit powerful, process of Europeanization works through permanent communicative interaction (personal as well as media-based) and a related diffusion of knowledge, ideas, and norms in public discourse. Checkel[50] conceptualizes this as a "diffusion of norms," a gradual dissemination of ideas and preferences whose rationale has exceeded the framework defined by purely "national interests." European institutions establish a normative script with a distinct set of expectations in which national actors form their preferences. In this respect one can think of the European polity also in terms of an "epistemic community"[51] distinguished by a distinct set of shared perceptions of reality and norms. In line with Easton (1953), it seems legitimate to describe the EU as the source of an "authoritative allocation of values" that form a normative script providing considerable authority for national initiatives.[52]

One simple yet often overlooked aspect of this transfer of norms and institutional practices is the socialization and learning process for which institutions provide a constitutive framework as far as regulating political behavior is concerned. This becomes manifest in the formation of a transnational community of experts, administrative elites, and policy-makers beyond the classical national-international divide. In some of the countries participating in the ENP, administrative elites come into regular contact with the EU bureaucracy, and the resulting knowledge about European practices and norms informs and potentially changes their routines and expectations.

In broader political terms, Vachudova (2001) has pointed to the fact that the track record of the EU's impact on authoritarian governments is not very impressive. Yet, at the same time, noncompliance with the EU plays out forcefully in domestic politics. A conflict with the EU over issues related to democratic, human, or minority rights, for instance, can be a notable tool for instigating the protest of the opposition. European norms establish a widely shared reference point, which can be neglected or violated, and which can be portrayed as a legitimate cause for dissatisfaction with the government. Vachudova points to the fact that the widespread sympathies for the EU within the population should be considered an important factor in shaping domestic political conflicts, in particular if the incumbent government is seen to prevent a *rapprochement* to, if not outright membership in, the EU. Here again images of accordance with European norms or standards become an important tool in domestic politics in terms of legitimizing or discrediting political actors. At least in certain segments of the populations in the countries under investigation, Europe and the EU have become identified as representing standards of democratic life and governance against which domestic practices can be measured and opposed. Representing an influential socio-economic model, the EU becomes a vehicle for political modernization beyond direct intervention in domestic affairs.

Identitarian Inclusion—Patterns of Belonging and Identity

Less tangible in terms of its measurable effects on domestic politics and governance of countries in CEE, yet of critical importance to what shapes their relationship with the EU, is the last aspect of Europeanization—namely, the symbolic power of a European identity. After the collapse of Communism, these countries had to rethink how to define their national communities culturally, politically, and socially. The developments leading to the collapse of the Communist regimes in CEE, as well as the enlargement of the EU, can be seen as powerful factors in this need to renegotiate the collective memories and identities that have structured Europe's postwar reality. The public debate on whether a country "belongs to Europe" and whether it should be part of an emerging European identity has become a focal point in the discussion of the country's long-term normative ideas about its political community, its concept of justice, the common good, and democratic life. In this respect, EU enlargement is far more than the simple inclusion of sovereign countries into an international organization. Beyond mere strategic national interests, the request for EU membership or partnership is often driven by images of the country's long-term future as a political community.

Again, the general, seemingly abstract images of collective identity and belonging easily become a polarizing and mobilizing force in politics. In public discourse, as well as in the strategies of political elites, the matter of where the nation belongs and how it defines its collective identity with reference to the international community is critical. The decision about whether a country's appropriate place is closer to Moscow-led Eastern Europe or to EU-represented Western Europe has repeatedly developed into a political controversy over competing political institutions, cultural norms, and economic interests.

The public debate over forms of belonging and loyalty to these competing models is often framed as rooted in historical experience and (revived) collective memory. Populations in the former Soviet Bloc have different ties and historical experiences in terms of their position within the traditional divisions of the European continent. The case of Moldova is pertinent in this respect as the country has such strong historical ties to Western Europe that it was easily politicized at the end of the twentieth century.

The Moldovan political elite seems to have recognized the popular attraction of European identity as a reference in defining the country's political future. Still, their political rhetoric is often shaped by the deep ambivalence that Moldovans feel, as they are torn between two worlds. One way of reconciling competing loyalties to the West and the East is to depict Moldova as a country in the center of Europe, as a kind of bridge between the two worlds. Moldova's former Deputy Minister for Foreign Affairs Ion Stăvilă stated: "Moldova may have been geographically placed in the centre of Europe, but this has not stopped people traditionally including it in their minds in the East European area, along with Ukraine, Belarus and Russia."[53] Similarly, President Vladimir Voronin announced: "Geographically we are in the centre of Europe."[54]

Conclusion

The process of Europeanization fueled political and economic reforms in states in CEE in the late twentieth century with an accelerating speed since 1989, becoming a vehicle for democratic change in this region. The trade-off between adopting EU standards and becoming a member of the EU was fully embraced by the states involved in the most recent wave of enlargement and by the ones that have joined in 2007. Yet the process of exporting EU standards did not stop here. The ENP is based on the unequivocal understanding that this policy foresees a privileged partnership without the perspective of joining the EU in the near future. Nonetheless, this inducement is less appealing than the one offered to the more fortunate states in CEE, namely that of admittance into the EU. But the "promise of Europe" is still producing the desired results. Despite the vagueness of some of the ENP's policies and incentives, Moldova has embarked on the road to implement intensive democratic reforms in order to meet the EU requirements. The principle of conditionality highlighted at the Copenhagen European Council was applied to the candidate states and now applies to a certain extent to the participating states in the ENP. Yet it is not entirely clear what Moldova will gain in exchange. Financial and diplomatic support from Brussels on its own is less appealing than the promise of becoming a member of the European club. Even though the leaders from Chişinău hope that Moldova will soon be recognized as a candidate state, the diplomatic signals from Brussels are rather discouraging, as more representatives recommend putting the process of enlargement on hold. Despite these signals, Voronin sees the current situation as the last opportunity for Moldova: "now we have the chance, metaphorically speaking, to get aboard a railway wagon of European standards. They have even stopped the European train for us, for Moldovans. Now everything depends on us. If this train leaves, it will depart forever."[55] The EU has become once again the vehicle for change, for democratic transformations. Nonetheless, Moldova's situation remains unpredictable as it continues to rely economically on Russia, and there is ambiguity about whether this is a point of no return for Moldova or whether the country's status is still ambiguous despite the political discourse and the population's will.

Notes

1. At the Copenhagen Summit (1993), the EU leaders highlighted the conditions that need to be fulfilled by a state before it becomes a member of the European Union, the so-called "Copenhagen Criteria." The accession criteria include three aspects: political (a democratic political system, the respect of rule of law, and human rights); economic (a functioning market economy); and the full adoption of the *acquis communautaire*.
2. See article 45 of the Treaty of the European Union.
3. "The accession of Bulgaria and Romania will mark an historic achievement: The completion of the fifth enlargement of the European Union." José Manuel Borroso, President of the European Commission, Presentation of Bulgaria and Romania accession report, European Parliament, Strasbourg, September 26, 2006, Reference: SPEECH/06/535.
4. Frank Schimmelfennig, "The Community Trap: Liberal Norms, Rhetorical Action, and the Eastern Enlargement of the European Union," *International Organization* 55, no. 1 (2001): 47–80.
5. See http://europa.eu.int/comm/world/enp/pdf/strategy/strategy_paper _en.pdf (accessed February 14, 2006).

6. For the security concerns of the EU, see the paper "European Security Strategy" (March 23, 2003), http://ue.eu.int/uedocs/cmsUpload/78 367.pdf (accessed February 14, 2006).

7. Idem.

8. Communication from the Commission of the European Communities, European Neighbourhood Policy Strategy Paper, COM (2004) 373 final (Brussels, May 12, 2004).

9. The Partnership and Cooperation Agreements—which entered into force in 1998 for Moldova and Ukraine—gradually introduced the principle of political conditionality. Yet in hindsight these agreements turned out to be rather ineffective in promoting democratic reform. See Andrei Zagorski, "Policies towards Russia, Ukraine, Moldova and Belarus," in *European Union Foreign and Security Policy: Towards a Neighborhood Strategy*, ed. Roland Dannreuther (London: Routledge, 2004).

10. Frank Schimmelfennig, Stefan Engert, and Heiko Knobel, "Cost, Commitment and Compliance: The Impact of EU Democratic Conditionality on Latvia, Slovakia and Turkey," *Journal of Common Market Studies* 41, no. 3 (2003): 495–518.

11. Schimmelfennig and Sedelmeier (2005) have developed a "bargaining model" based on such a cost-benefit analysis. In their interpretation, the degree of compliance with EU demands depends essentially on the credibility of the threats and promises that the EU is able to make.

12. Hans-Georg Wieck, "The OSCE and the Council of Europe in Conflict with the Lukashenko Regime," in *The EU and Belarus: Between Moscow and Brussels*, ed. Ann Lewis, 261–75 (London: Federal Trust for Education and Research, 2002).

13. In February 2005, the EU's External Relations Commissioner, Benita Ferrero-Waldner, was clear that there was no point in Ukraine and Moldova seeking to start the process of joining the European Union: see http://europa.eu.int/comm/external_relations/ukraine/intro/bfw_210205.htm and http://europa.eu.int/comm/external_relations/moldova/intro/bfw_220205.htm (accessed February 20, 2006).

14. For a detailed account of Russian rule in Bessarabia, see George F. Jewsbury, *The Russian Annexation of Bessarabia, 1774–1828: A Study of Imperial Expansion* (New York: East European Quarterly, 1976).

15. For a detailed account of this term, see Ion Nistor, "Localizarea numelui Basarabiei în Moldova transpruteană," *Analele Academiei Române Memoriile Secțiunii Istrice* (Bucharest: Academia Română, București) 3/24, no. 1 (1943–44): 1–27.

16. Named after the Walachian/Romanian king (*domn*) Basarab I (1310?–52).

17. Ștefan Ciobanu, *Basarabia. Populatia, istoria, cultura* (Chișinău: Editura Știința; București: Editura Clio, 1992), 25.

18. See p. 119 of Charles King, "The Ambivalence of Authenticity, or How the Moldovan Language Was Made," *Slavic Review* 58, no. 1 (1999): 117–42.

19. King, "Ambivalence," 124.
20. "Russian sections filled up, while the Romanian ones remained empty" (Irina Livezeanu, "Urbanization in a Low Key and Linguistic Change in Soviet Moldavia," *Soviet Studies* 32, no. 3 (1981): 332.
21. Livezeanu, "Urbanization," 327.
22. For a comparison of post-1991 Moldova with the Baltic States, see Liliana Viţu, "Moldova and the Baltic States: Lessons of Success and Failure," in *The EU and Moldova: On a Fault Line of Europe*, ed. Ann Lewis, 155–59 (London: Federal Trust for Education and Research, 2004).
23. "Identitatea lingvistică moldo-română realmente existentă," Legea Parlamentului Republicii Moldova cu privire la funcţionarea limbilor vorbite pe teritoriul RSS Moldoveneşti, Nr.3465-XI din 01.09.89, Veştile nr.9/217, 1989.
24. Oleg Serebian, "'Good Brothers,' Bad Neighbours: Romanian/Moldovan Relations," in *The EU and Moldova: On a Fault Line of Europe*, ed. Ann Lewis, 149–53 (London: Federal Trust for Education and Research, 2004).
25. Constitutia Republicii Moldova, adoptata la 29 iulie 1994 Monitorul Oficial al R.Moldova nr.1 din 12.08.1994.
26. In December 1991, Russia, Belarus, and Ukraine established the Commonwealth of Independent States. Other former Soviet republics signed the agreement, including Moldova in 1991. Only the Baltic States refused to adhere to the agreement.
27. Claus Neukirch, "Moldova's Eastern Dimension," in *The EU and Moldova: On a Fault Line of Europe*, ed. Ann Lewis, 133–43 (London: Federal Trust for Education and Research, 2004), 136.
28. Idem.
29. The President of the Republic of Moldova Vladimir Voronin, interview for *Trud-Moldova*, January 30, 2004 (translation from Romanian), http://www.prm.md/press.php?p=1&s=1584&lang=rom (accessed February 14, 2006).
30. "The president Voronin recognized that the relations between the Republic of Moldova and Russia continue to be extremely tense stressing that Moscow is fully responsible for this situation." Translation from Romanian, *Preşdintele Voronin îl laudă pe Traian Băsescu*, BBCRomanian, December 21, 2005, http://www.bbc.co.uk/romanian/news/story/2005/12/051221_voronin_basescu.shtml (accessed February 14, 2006).
31. Vladimir Voronin's speech, The Parliament of the Republic of Moldova, Chişinău, July 29, 2005. Translation from Romanian, http://president.md/press.php?p=1&s=3166&lang=rom (accessed February 14, 2006).
32. Interview with the Romanian president, Traian Băsescu, BBCRomanian, December 28, 2005, http://www.bbc.co.uk/romanian/news/story/2005/12/051228_interviu_basescu.shtml (accessed February 14, 2006).

33. Seventy-seven percent of Moldovans think that Moldova should join the EU. *National Voters Studies, International Republican Institute and Baltic Surveys Ltd./The Gallup Organization,* http://www.gallup europe.be/events/l_at_l.htm (accessed February 14, 2006).

34. *Platform of the Party of Communists for the 2005 Parliamentary Elections,* http://www.pcrm.md/index_en.html (accessed February 14, 2006).

35. "European integration is possible only with a new government." *Platforma electorală a blocului "Moldova Democrată,"* http://www.alegeri 2005.md/opponents/bemd/program (accessed February 14, 2006).

36. "Moldova's European integration . . . represents a major strategic objective. . . . " *Party's Statute Objectives,* http://www.ppcd.md/ro/docs .php (accessed February 14, 2006).

37. EU-Moldova Action Plan, February 22, 2005.

38. Report of the Government of the Republic of Moldova on the Implementation of the EU-Moldova Action Plan (August–October 2005), Chişinău, http://www.mfa.md/En/EurInteg/Documents/RAP ORT%20aug-octob2005.pdf (accessed February 14, 2006).

39. Ministry of Foreign Affairs, The Foreign Policy of the Republic of Moldova, http://www.mfa.md/En/PolicyKeyElements/PolicyMainText .html (accessed February 14, 2006).

40. K. Featherstone and C. Radaelli, eds., *The Politics of Europeanization* (Oxford: Oxford University Press, 2003); Maria Cowles, James Caporaso, and Thomas Risse, *Transforming Europe: Europeanization and Domestic Change* (Ithaca, NY: Cornell University Press, 2001).

41. Funding opportunities for countries included in the ENP will be incorporated into a new Neighbourhood instrument in 2007, with the aim to manage the various forms of financial aid more effectively and to provide a more robust material incentive.

42. The strict adoption of the conditionality principle is part of the Action Plans: "The pace of progress of the relationship will acknowledge fully Moldova's efforts and concrete achievements in meeting commitments to common values." Proposed EU-Moldova Action Plan, http://europa.eu.int/comm/world/enp/pdf/action_plans/Proposed_ Action_Plan_EU-Moldova.pdf (accessed February 22, 2006). In spite of this rhetorical precision, however, there are serious doubts about how effective conditionality actually is. One key problem in this respect is that this principle is implemented according to differing criteria in various countries. Acknowledging that this practice makes it difficult to condone failure in one area by rewarding a country for success in other areas, the European Commission has gradually retreated from formulating measurable benchmarks of success. See Judith Kelley, *Ethnic Politics in Europe: The Power of Norms and Incentives* (Princeton, NJ: Princeton University Press, 2004).

43. In the case of Moldova, these immediate priorities concern the "draft legislation for Parliamentary reform in line with Council of Europe, to

approve the draft legislation for Parliamentary reform incorporating fully any comment, suggestion by Council of Europe, PACE, Venice Commission (March 2006), to draft legislation to reform electoral code incorporating fully the joint OSCE-ODIHR, Council of Europe recommendations on elections, to take decisive steps in court reform and in ensuring independence of the judiciary (March 2006), and to ratify the Rome Charter of the International Criminal Court and prepare approval of constitutional and legislative amendments foreseen thereto." Short-term priorities for the EU-Moldova Action Plan implementation (February 2005–March 2006), http://www.mfa.md/En/EurInteg/Documents/prioritati%202005-martie%202006%20eng.pdf (accessed February 19, 2006).

44. For the list of issues that the EU asks Moldova to address, see the Commission's Country Report from May 2005, http://europa.eu.int/comm/world/enp/pdf/country/Moldova_11_May_EN.pdf (accessed February 19, 2006).

45. Ian Manners, "Normative Power Europe: A Contradiction in Terms?" *Journal of Common Market Studies* 40, no. 2 (2002): 235–58.

46. Internal Report on Semestrial Evaluation of the EU-Moldova Action Plan Implementation, September 2005, The Government of the Republic of Moldova, http://www.mfa.md/En/EurInteg/Documents/Raport%2012.09.2005%20eng%20rev%20integral.pdf (accessed February 19, 2006).

47. Commission of the European Communities, "Wider Europe Neighbourhood: New Framework for Relations with our Eastern and Southern Neighbours," Strategy Paper by the European Commission, March 2003.

48. See *European Newsletter*, Ministry of Foreign Affairs and European Integration, no. 10, November 2005, http://www.mfa.md/Buletin%20European%20nr10.pdf (accessed February 19, 2006).

49. See p. 345 of Jeffrey Checkel, "The Constructivist Turn in International Relations Theory" [review article], *World Politics* 50 (1998): 324–48.

50. Jeffrey Checkel, "Why Comply? Social Learning and European Identity Change," *International Organization* 55, no. 3 (2001): 553–88.

51. Hugh Miller and Charles Fox, "The Epistemic Community," *Administration & Society* 32, no. 6 (2001): 668–85.

52. Oliver Schmidtke, "Immigration Policy in Europe: A Challenge to Established Forms of Multi-Level Governance," in *European Governance: Policy Making between Politicization and Control*, ed. G. Walzenbach, 127–46 (Aldershot, UK: Ashgate, 2006).

53. Ion Stăvilă, "Moldova between East and West: A Paradigm of Foreign Affairs," in *The EU and Moldova: On a Fault Line of Europe*, ed. Ann Lewis (London: Federal Trust for Education and Research, 2004), 127.

54. The President of the Republic of Moldova Vladimir Voronin, interview for *Trud-Moldova*, January 30, 2004, http://www.prm.md/press .php?p=1&s=1584&lang=rom (accessed February 19, 2006).

55. The President of the Republic of Moldova Vladimir Voronin, interview for "Pervyi kanal v Moldove" for the „Tochka zrenia" talk show, December 24, 2004 (translation from Romanian), http://preseinte .md/press.php?p=1&s=2520&lang=rom (accessed February 19, 2006).

8

Taking Ukraine Seriously: Western and Russian Responses to the Orange Revolution

Derek Fraser

The Orange Revolution—A Staging Post on a Long Journey

The Orange Revolution—that mass popular protest at the end of 2004 against vote rigging in the first two rounds of the Ukrainian presidential election—resulted in a largely fair third round of voting that brought to power the reformist coalition under President Yushchenko. The reformers made Ukraine a more democratic and, possibly, a more independent country. Much still has to be done, however, to realize fully the reformers' goals of assuring Ukraine's independence, achieving European standards of governance and economic freedom, and anchoring the country to Western institutions such as the World Trade Organization (WTO), the European Union, and the North Atlantic Treaty Organization (NATO). This chapter will examine what the reformers achieved and what remains to be done. It will also consider Russia's efforts to regain its influence and power in Ukraine and the role that the West might play to support reform.

The Orange Revolution was significant for several reasons. It marked a coming of age of civil society in much of Ukraine. Throughout a large part of the country, Ukrainians sloughed off their passivity toward those in authority. The uprising was the largest civic action in Europe since the Velvet Revolution ended Communist rule in Czechoslovakia in 1989. One in five Ukrainians, including 48 percent of the population of Kyiv, participated in protests against the fraudulent second round of voting on November 21, 2004.[1] The third round of voting on December 26 was notable for being one of the rare times in the history of the former Soviet republics that an election has been largely democratic, and not a carefully stage-managed affair. It was the first free election in Ukraine since 1994. The Orange Revolution and the final outcome of the election went against the prevailing trend in the former Soviet Union toward increased authoritarianism. Furthermore, the victory of Viktor Yushchenko marked the first time, since Ukraine became independent in 1991, that a non-Communist president replaced a former Soviet dignitary.

Following the Orange Revolution, its architects began a process of political and economic reform. Nevertheless, the difficulties the reformers faced suggest that their victory in the election was only a staging post on the long road that Ukraine has yet to travel to achieve their goals.

Among the results of the Revolution and its aftermath—which we treat as the period lasting up to the return to power as prime minister, in August 2006, of Yushchenko's opponent in the presidential election, Viktor Yanukovych—were the following:

- *The emergence of a structural basis for democracy.* The presidential election of 2004 and the parliamentary elections of March 26, 2006, confirmed the existence in Ukraine of two broad and, admittedly, fissiparous political streams—the Orange parties in the west and center, and the Blue or conservative parties in the east and south. Provided that future elections remain democratic, the difficulty that either tendency will have in permanently dominating the political landscape should discourage absolutism and encourage pluralism and compromise.[2] Furthermore, the competition among the various political parties, and the political fluidity it implies, should, if the experience of the ex-Communist states of Central and Eastern Europe (CEE) is any guide, stimulate political and economic reform.
- *Greater political freedom.* The application of "administrative resources," that is, the illegitimate use of state funds and methods of pressure, including assassination, blackmail, judicial and administrative persecution, and vote rigging, largely disappeared at the national level as a means of influencing the political

process, although misuse of "administrative resources" remained still a factor locally.

- *Greater media freedom.* Ukrainian television was partly de-monopolized and democratized. Gone were the censorship directives that the presidential administration under Kuchma issued to the media. National journalists could work in a freer environment, no longer fearful of arrest or violent personal attack. At the same time, the parliament, the *Verhovna Rada* (Supreme Council), passed a law prohibiting the media from offering any commentaries, assessments, or analyses during an election campaign. Furthermore, local journalists still faced difficulties. According to Viktoriia Siumar, Director of the Institute of Mass Information in Ukraine, the media reported only twelve cases of economic or political pressure in 2005, compared with sixty in 2004. There were only fourteen reported cases of censorship in 2005, compared with fifty-two in 2004.[3] In its 2005 Annual Worldwide Press Freedom Index, Reporters without Borders, the international watchdog for press freedom, raised Ukraine's ranking from the 138th spot in the previous year, to the 112th place out of 167 countries. By comparison, Russia ranked 138th.[4]

- *Economic reforms.* Ukraine moved from a government in which corruption was integral to the system to one that began a modest start in the fight against bribes. Procedures for registering new companies were simplified, and 4,500 regulations governing business activity were eliminated. To reduce the temptation to take bribes, salaries for officials were increased. Corrupt practices were prosecuted. While the government lowered the income tax rate by reducing tax evasion, it managed to increase tax revenues. As a result of these and other steps, the government shrank the shadow, or illegal, economy. The Financial Action Task Force, the international body that monitors money laundering, removed Ukraine from its black list of countries that fail to deal with the problem. Both the United States and the EU granted Ukraine market economy status. In its 2005 Corruption Perceptions Index, Transparency International, the global anticorruption association, raised the ranking of Ukraine according to the degree of corruption, from the 122nd spot in 2004, to 107th place in 2005 out of 159 countries. In the same time period, Russia dropped from 90th place to 126th.[5]

As a result of these and other reforms, Freedom House, the U.S. non-governmental organization devoted to promoting human rights and democracy, in its report "Freedom in the World 2006," judged Ukraine to be "free" instead of, as it was previously, "partly free." It raised Ukraine's marks for political rights and civil liberties, on a scale from the best to the worst standards of one to seven, from four in 2004 to two in 2006. In the same time period, Russia was classified downward from being "partly free" to "not free." Its score declined from five to six for political rights, while remaining at five for civil liberties.[6]

Much still remained to be done to overcome the burdens of Ukraine's past. The culture of patronage, in a wide variety of areas ranging from the appointment and promotion of officials to the awarding of contracts, had not yet been replaced by a culture of merit. The state bureaucracy remained largely unreformed; the legal process was not yet entirely independent; regulations were neither impartial nor clear; contracts were difficult to enforce; property rights were still not well protected; and the Ukrainian economy and political process remained largely dominated by oligarchs who could still block foreign investments. It will therefore take a while to establish conditions for promoting competition and restraining unfair trade practices.[7] The slow pace of economic reform meant that Ukraine's rating in the Index of Economic Freedom 2006, published by the Heritage Foundation and the *Wall Street Journal*, had—on a five-point scale where a score of one is highest and a score of five is lowest—improved only marginally, from 3.49 in 2004 to 3.24 in 2006. In comparison, Russia scarcely budged from its 2004 score of 3.51 to 3.50 in 2006.[8]

The break-up in September 2006 of the coalition between the two principal Orange parties—President Yushchenko's Our Ukraine and Prime Minister Tymoshenko's *Batkivshchyna* (Fatherland)—owed much to a persistence of authoritarian patterns of thought and behavior, and a poor understanding, even among the reformers who had headed the Orange Revolution, of the rules of the game of a functioning democracy and a market economy. Other factors were President Yushchenko's poor management skills and political judgement, possibly worsened by the precarious state of his health following the attempt, by apparently unknown assailants, to poison him during the election campaign.

The art of compromise does not come easily to an authoritarian culture, nor does respect for the rule of law. In forming their coalition after the presidential election, the two Orange parties had not agreed on a detailed action program or worked out an adequate system of policy coordination. Instead, the president duplicated in his administration some of the functions of the cabinet, so as, in the view of several political observers, to block the government from carrying out policies he opposed. In doing so, the president sometimes ignored the law. The prime minister interfered in the economy using methods borrowed from the Communist era. Officials of the Orange Coalition repeatedly bullied the judiciary to render favorable decisions, and attempted, through dubious means, to force some of the oligarchs associated with President Kuchma to divest themselves of their media holdings.

The president's bad judgement and his difficulties in treating his allies as equals came to the fore in his actions in the dissolution of the coalition and subsequently. The alliance between Yushchenko's party and Tymoshenko's party was essential for success in the reform programs and for victory in the parliamentary elections in March 2006. In spite of the coalition's importance, in September 2005, when one of Tymoshenko's allies brought forward what seem to have been well-founded accusations of corruption against particular officials in the president's administration, Yushchenko dismissed Tymoshenko after she refused to place her party under his control.[9]

This split, coupled with Yushchenko's lack of experience in mustering support in parliament, forced him, in order to get parliamentary approval for Yurii Yekhanurov as her successor, to enter into a tactical alliance with the man who had been his opponent in the presidential election in the previous year: Viktor Yanukovych. Yanukovych had a criminal record and, as prime minister at the time, was implicated in the political oppression and monstrous electoral frauds that had led in the first place to the Orange Revolution. One of the terms of Yushchenko's agreement with Yanukovych was that members of the previous regime would not be prosecuted for their crimes. Yushchenko's break with Tymoshenko and his agreement with Yanukovych may have rescued Yanukovych from marginalization. Certainly both events contributed to a serious decrease in public support for Yushchenko in the parliamentary elections in March 2006.

Membership in the WTO is central to Yushchenko's policy of joining Western economic institutions. Although it was important that the Verhovna Rada should pass in the autumn of 2005 a series of bills that were a condition for Ukraine's admission, Yushchenko did not do the necessary lobbying. As a result, half the bills were defeated.

A similar scenario played out in January 2006. As a result of the lack of support from members of Yushchenko's own party, due in part to a lack of lobbying by the government and the presidential administration, the Verhovna Rada passed a motion of nonconfidence against the government for its handling of a gas dispute with Russia.

After the parliamentary election in March 2006, the inability of the reformist parties to agree on a program for a new government, and especially the political ineptitude of the president, eventually resulted, in August 2006, in Yushchenko offering the post of prime minister to Viktor Yanukovych, in spite of his past. The gap between the political values and goals of the two men became apparent in the fact that Yanukovych disregarded much of the political Action Plan he had negotiated with Yushchenko as a condition for his appointment and began to reverse many of the reforms of the Orange Revolution.

The slow pace of reform in Ukraine since its independence in 1991, compared with that in the ex-Communist countries in CEE, such as the Czech Republic, Hungary, and Poland, can be better understood when one takes into account the differences between Ukraine's history and that of former Communist countries in Central and Eastern Europe. Unlike the states in CEE, Ukraine was only obliquely affected by the evolution of political structures in the Western world during the past five hundred years from authoritarianism to pluralism. As a result, Ukraine has had no culture of pluralism or memory of democracy to draw on. It also has had no knowledge of a market economy. In addition, Ukraine had experienced no previous period of existence as an independent state to give it a sense of national cohesion. At the moment of its declaration of independence, it also lacked much of the apparatus of a state, since the sole function of the limited governmental structure in place at the time of the Ukrainian SSR had been to carry out the decisions of the Central Committee of the Communist Party of the Soviet Union.

If Ukraine's past and present are a prologue to its future, Ukraine's progress toward a stable democracy and a prosperous market economy may, in spite of the Orange Revolution, continue to be slow.

The Russian Big Brother

Another factor that acts as a brake on Ukraine's progress along the road of reform is Russian interference. Most Russians find it difficult to conceive of a Russia without Ukraine. For the Russians, Kyiv was the first Russian capital: the tsars buried there were Russian, St. Sophia Cathedral (in Kyiv) was the first Russian cathedral, and the Kyivan Caves Monastery was the first Russian monastery. The Treaty of Pereiaslav of 1654, which for many Ukrainians signifies the beginning of Russian domination, is regarded by Russians as the restoration of the unity of the Russian lands, destroyed by the Mongol invasion in the thirteenth century.[10] As a consequence, public opinion polls in Russia have shown that about three-quarters of the population thinks that Russia and Ukraine should form a single country. According to a September 2005 poll carried out by the Levada Center in Moscow, 71 percent of Russians favored a united state with Ukraine. Only 24 percent were opposed.[11]

The prevailing attitude of the Russian government toward Ukraine can perhaps be discerned in statements made by President Vladimir Putin and his Ambassador to Ukraine, Viktor Chernomyrdin. In the interview accorded by President Putin to the Russian newspaper *Kommersant* on April 12, 2005, while he was visiting Germany, the president spoke out against Ukraine's membership in the EU. If Ukraine entered the Schengen zone of visa-free travel, among some EU countries, he declared, "there will be a certain problem. As far as I know, at least 17 percent of the population living there are Russian. This is the division of a people. It recalls the division of Germany into East and West." Although Putin carefully limited his statement to ethnic Russians, it has been interpreted as referring to Russia and Ukraine as a whole.[12]

Somewhat later, Chernomyrdin, according to *Ukrainska pravda*,[13] remarked, "Ukraine and Russia have never lived as two sovereign states. Ukraine has never been a sovereign government. Now we have to learn how to perceive her as such." In an interview with the Russian newspaper *Izvestiia*, three weeks before the Orange Revolution, the ambassador was apparently somewhat franker: "Russia was always an independent state. Ukraine never was. There never was such a country."[14]

Beyond a disinclination, derived from history, to regard Ukraine as a separate, equal, and sovereign state, the Russians have had, especially since President Putin came to power determined to restore Russian strength, a concrete reason for seeking to dominate Ukraine—control of Ukraine would be highly advantageous to the recovery of Russia's earlier power and influence:

- Ukraine's population of 46 million is about one-third the size of Russia's population of 143 million.

- In Soviet times, Ukraine possessed about 37 percent of the Soviet Union's military and industrial complex.
- Tutelage over Ukraine would give Russia once again access to Ukraine's long border with areas of former Soviet influence—Central Europe and the Balkans—as well as to the northern littoral of the Black Sea.
- The compliance of Ukraine with Russian economic plans might determine the success of President Putin's efforts to bring key former Soviet republics together in a common market, known as the Common Economic Space (CES), in which all the central institutions are under Russian control.
- The subordination of Ukraine to Russian foreign policy would block the eastward expansion of the EU and NATO.

For several reasons, therefore, Russia has devoted considerable effort to bringing Ukraine under its tutelage. It has repeatedly interfered in Ukrainian politics so as to make the Ukrainian government compliant to its interests. The Russian government used to put pressure on Yushchenko's predecessor, Kuchma, to dismiss certain ministers regarded as unfriendly. Ukrainian candidates for high office still go to Moscow to seek the Kremlin's blessing. The Kremlin has encouraged Russian companies to buy up key Ukrainian companies, notably in the energy field. It has repeatedly pressured to have the gas pipeline transporting Russian and Central Asian gas to Western Europe put under effective Russian control. Russia successfully took advantage of Kuchma's weak position, resulting from his apparent implication in the 2000 murder of dissident journalist Heorhii Gongadze, and other crimes, to pressure Ukraine into joining the CES. Had Yushchenko not, on assuming office as president, limited the extent of any Ukrainian association with the CES to that of a free-trade zone, Ukraine would have been prevented from joining the WTO or the EU, except in tandem with Russia. Since Viktor Yanukovych became prime minister in August 2006, Russia has resumed its pressure on Ukraine to become a full member of the CES.

In the presidential election of 2004, Russia followed its practice in the parliamentary elections of 2002 of funding its favorites. It reportedly supplied about half the campaign expenses for Kuchma's chosen successor, Viktor Yanukovych.[15] Putin's "political technologists" gave tactical advice to both Kuchma and Yanukovych.[16] The same spin doctors helped write the illegal censorship directives for the Ukrainian media.[17] Russian television campaigned on behalf of Yanukovych, and

Putin himself visited Ukraine twice during the campaign to show his support. Finally, the Russian government may have been involved in at least two of the three or four assassination attempts against the opposition candidate, Viktor Yushchenko.[18]

The Implications of the Orange Revolution for Russian-Ukrainian Relations

For Russia, shock at the victory of the Orange Revolution went beyond the apparent loss of any early prospect for increasing Russian influence in Ukraine: The Orange Revolution gave a fillip to political turmoil elsewhere in the former Soviet Union—the Tulip Revolution in Kyrgyzstan in March 2005 and the uprising in Uzbekistan in May 2005—and awakened fears in the Kremlin that the Ukrainian experience might serve as a model for political change in Russia itself.

The growing gap between Russian and Western interests and understanding also contributed to the threat perception that the Orange Revolution had inspired in Moscow. The revolution was regarded by leading Russian politicians as the result of a Western coup.[19] It strengthened the trend in Russian foreign policy to adopt a defensive posture toward the West, strengthen ties with other former Soviet republics, and develop closer relations with other countries, such as China.

The policies of the reformers strengthened this threat perception. Besides blocking full Ukrainian membership in the CES, the reformers actively sought to join the WTO, the EU, and NATO. The Orange Coalition also gave new life to GUAM, the regional alliance of Georgia, Ukraine, Azerbaijan, and Moldova, which the Russians regard as anti-Russian. In the same vein, Ukraine worked with Georgia in December 2005 to create the Community of Democratic Choice, uniting Ukraine, Georgia, Lithuania, Latvia, Estonia, Romania, Moldova, Slovenia, and Macedonia for the purpose of spreading democracy and human rights in the area.

The Russian National Security Concept of 2000 determined the main security threats to Russia to be:

- the possible establishment of foreign military bases and large military contingents along Russia's borders;
- any weakening of Russia's political, economic, and military influence in the world;
- any strengthening of foreign military blocs and unions, above all the eastward extension/expansion of NATO; and

- any weakening of the integration processes within the
  Commonwealth of Independent States (CIS).[20]

For Russia, Ukraine's membership in NATO would put Russian control of its Black Sea naval base at Sevastopol in jeopardy and make the defense of European Russia difficult. According to Dmitrii Trenin, a senior associate of the Carnegie Moscow Center, writing in an article in *Nezavisimaia gazeta*, Moscow's principal goal is to stop the "conveyor belt" moving Kyiv toward NATO. To this end, Russia is willing to risk a "real conflict" with Ukraine.[21]

Following Yushchenko's victory in the presidential election of 2004, the Russian government, therefore, renewed its efforts to bring about a government in Ukraine favorable to Russian interests. The return of Yanukovych as prime minister is not likely to lessen Russian concern at the future direction of Ukraine. The political situation in Ukraine remains unstable; the president and the prime minister are locked in a bitter struggle for power.

To apply pressure on the Orange coalition, Russia brought charges in the Parliamentary Assembly of the Council of Europe alleging acts of repression by the new government against members of the opposition. It granted Russian citizenship to officials of the previous regime who had been criminally charged and were living in exile in Russia, thus protecting them from extradition to Ukraine.

Russia's most significant move against the reformers, however, was to set off the gas crisis at the end of 2005, by seeking a steep increase in the price of gas supplied to Ukraine. Statements by the Russian government and officials, together with the manner in which the price increase was handled, suggest that the main aim of the increase was political: the 2003 Energy Strategy of the Russian Federation to 2020 states that the country's fuel and energy complex is "an instrument for the conduct of internal and external policy. The role of a country in world energy markets largely determines its geopolitical influence."[22] Gleb Pavlovskii, one of Putin's leading political technologists, declared: "I think that the most important outcome of the gas conflict is not the additional $3 billion or so that Gazprom intends to earn from the deal with Ukraine, but the experience we have gained of conducting a policy aimed at becoming a great energy power."[23]

Just after his resignation, Andrei Illiaronov, a former economic adviser to President Putin, described, in an interview with *Time* magazine in December 2005, the price hike as a political weapon. The price was discriminatory, and the way in which it had been proposed was deliberately provocative, so as to prevent the dispute from being settled before the parliamentary elections of March 2006. One of the other aims of the increase was to take over the Ukrainian gas transit pipeline.[24]

Russia had torn up its existing gas agreement with Ukraine, concluded in 2004 and valid until 2009, which established a gas price of $50 per 1,000 cubic meters. Instead, Russia insisted on increasing the price with no transitional period to $230 per 1,000 cubic meters on January 1, 2006. To pressure Ukraine into yielding to its demands, Russia blocked not only gas shipments that were payment to Ukraine for providing the transit for Russian gas bound for Western Europe, but also the shipments of gas from Turkmenistan that the Ukrainians had bought directly from the Turkmenis.

When the Ukrainians continued to take the gas they regarded as theirs from the common pipeline supplying both Ukraine and Western Europe, there was an outcry from West Europeans at the loss of gas. The protests of the West Europeans led Russia eventually to agree to a compromise price.

Russia associated its new price, however, with conditions that, according to the leading weekly newspaper in Ukraine, *Dzerkalo tyzhnia*, and other sources, were likely to bring Russia closer to its apparent goal of taking over the pipeline to Western Europe. The gas shipments were to be handled by a Russian-controlled intermediary, Rosukrenergo, which, through a further controlled intermediary, was to take over the distribution to one-half of the Ukrainian market, thus depriving Naftohaz, the Ukrainian company that also owns the transit line to Western Europe, of half of its domestic market and threatening it with bankruptcy.

The Russians achieved one of their apparent aims. The terms of settlement of the gas crisis damaged considerably the reputation of Yushchenko's government and may have contributed to his party, Our Ukraine, taking third place in the March 2006 parliamentary elections, with only 13.95 percent of the vote, behind the Yulia Tymoshenko Bloc at 22.28 percent and Yanukovych's Party of the Regions at 32.14 percent.

In the autumn of 2006, Russia negotiated a gentler agreement with its favorite prime minister, Yanukovych, setting the gas price at $130, well below the rising world price. It continued to maintain pressure, however, to take over the pipeline to Western Europe.

Russia could, in theory at least, use other weapons against Ukraine. One of these weapons could be military pressure. On January 11, 2006, in an article in the *Wall Street Journal*, Russian Deputy Prime Minister and Minister of Defence Sergei Ivanov described the tasks of the Russian armed forces, stating, "Our top concern is the internal situation in some members of the Commonwealth of Independent States ... and the regions around them."[25]

Another tactic could be to make moves to annex the Crimea. In response to the gas crisis, Ukraine warned that it might seek a revision of the treaty regulating the rent paid for the Black Sea Base in Sevastopol; the Russian defense minister responded with an indirect threat to take Crimea away from Ukraine. A revision of the treaty, he stated, might lead to a revocation of the 1997 Ukrainian-Russian friendship treaty, by which Russia recognized the 1954 boundaries of Ukraine, which had made the Crimea part of Ukraine for the first time in modern history.[26] It has also been intimated that Russia might also revoke the 1997 treaty if Ukraine joined NATO.

In theory, Russia could accompany any revocation of the 1997 treaty with the promotion of a separatist movement in the Crimea. In the 1990s, a public opinion poll showed 70 percent of the Crimean population was in favor of joining Russia. Both President Putin and an analyst close to the Kremlin have recently indicated that, if the West grants Kosovo independence, the precedent of Kosovo's independence should also apply to the secessionist movements in the post-Soviet space—a group that presumably includes separatist movements such as those that Russia protects and supports in Georgia and Moldova.[27]

Under present circumstances, however, we doubt whether Russia would consider using force against Ukraine or promoting a secessionist movement in, for example, the Crimea: The importance to Russia of its relations with the West continues to act as a restraint on Russian behavior toward Ukraine. This element of Russian foreign policy was apparent when, in response to Western criticism, Russia backed down on its suspension of gas shipments to Ukraine. In spite of existing tensions, we believe that further development of Russia's relations with the West, especially in the economic field, remains one of the country's primary goals. Nevertheless, even within certain limitations on its behavior, Russia can still do serious harm to Ukraine.

How the West Might Support Ukraine

In his article in *Nezavisimaia gazeta*, Dmitrii Trenin noted, "The accelerated transformation of the countries of the CIS in the direction of political democracy, the free market and civil society is possible only with the support and serious assistance of the West."[28] The return of Yanukovych as prime minister in August 2006 shows how long the road to a stable democracy and a genuine independence is likely to be for Ukraine.

To help the reformers in Ukraine achieve their goals, Western policy toward Ukraine might be guided by two principles:

- First, since reforms in Ukraine will not come quickly, and Russian hostility toward reform and increased Ukrainian independence will not disappear easily, Ukraine needs from its friends a long-term, but critical, commitment.
- Second, the West should be flexible and forthcoming in its diplomacy toward Ukraine.

The vertiginous increase in the price of energy has increased Ukrainian dependence on Moscow's good graces. Since Ukraine is one of the most inefficient consumers of energy in Europe, the West might support Ukrainian independence by helping Ukraine bring its energy consumption in relation to its GDP down to the levels of more advanced economies.

The Ukrainian reformers have sought membership in the EU and NATO. NATO has generally been more forthcoming toward Ukraine than has the EU. The provocative nature for Russia of Ukrainian membership in NATO, coupled with the reluctant attitude toward NATO of the current prime minister, strongly suggests that the EU should become the leading Western organization in efforts to build closer relations with Ukraine.

In his article in *Nezavisimaia gazeta*, Trenin commented that a readiness on the part of the EU to offer Ukraine membership would change the course of the country's history.[29] The EU, however, deals with Ukraine within the framework of its European Neighbourhood Policy, a program intended for the former Soviet republics and Middle Eastern and North African states that are not expected to become EU members.[30] As a result, the EU does not give to Ukraine the generous credits and advice it offers to candidate countries to help them bring their legislation and regulations in line with EU requirements, even though Ukraine is expected to carry out largely the same reforms.

The Deputy Commission President Guenter von Heugen, in an interview in *Die Welt* on February 20, 2006, predicted that in twenty years, all European states would be members of the EU, except for the successor states of the Soviet Union not already in the EU, such as the Baltic countries. In other words, Ukraine would remain excluded.[31] Other EU officials have declared that the EU will neither offer membership prospects to the ex-Soviet republics nor rule them out forever.

One reason for the EU's reserved attitude toward Ukraine can perhaps be discerned in the remarks made by German Foreign Minister Frank-Walter Steinmeier to the German-Russian Forum on March 21, 2006: "In the EU-Russia-Ukraine triangle, the three sides must be as equal as possible. Disturbed relations between two of these partners destabilize the region. However, the precondition for regional stability is that all sides stop thinking in terms of traditional spheres of influence and in categories of geopolitical rivalry." Such remarks tend to confirm the Ukrainians' view that some members of the EU, and especially Germany and France, seek to make the EU's policy toward Ukraine dependent on Moscow's views.[32]

Although it can be argued that if the EU wants an independent Ukraine, it has to treat it as such, it is understandable that, with the present unclear political circumstances in Ukraine, there is no pressure on the EU to change its reluctant attitude toward Ukrainian membership. While President Yushchenko continues to support early Ukrainian membership, Prime Minister Yanukovych favors a slow approach.

Apart from the question of Ukraine's membership, the EU might be more forthcoming with its assistance to the country, since it is in the interest of the EU to have a stable and prosperous democracy on its doorstep. The negotiation of a free-trade zone is included in the current EU-Ukraine Action Plan. In December 2005, EU External Commissioner Benita Ferrero-Waldner announced that the EU would negotiate such an agreement as soon as Ukraine becomes a member of the WTO, which President Yushchenko now hopes will happen in 2007. The EU might consider helping Ukraine prepare for free trade by being as generous in its support for the required economic and legal reforms as it is for membership applicant countries.[33]

There is another reason for the EU being more forthcoming toward Ukraine—to support the reform movement in Ukraine in its efforts to develop the country's ties with the West. The reformers' task of winning over Ukrainian public opinion is not an easy one. According to a poll conducted by the Democratic Initiatives Fund in January 2006, 56.8 percent of Ukrainians support Ukrainian membership in the CES, while only 42.6 percent back membership in the

EU.[34] Another poll held in December 2005 by the Razumkov Center for Economic and Political Studies in Kyiv found that 42.2 percent of the population considers that ties with Russia should have priority, while only 25.4 percent would give the same importance to ties with the EU. Only 16 percent of the Ukrainian population was in favor of NATO membership, while 61.4 percent was opposed.[35]

While President Yushchenko maintains his support for Ukraine's early entry into NATO, Prime Minister Yanukovych has insisted that Ukraine is not ready to join, although he does not rule out eventual membership. He does favor continuing cooperation with the alliance. He nevertheless has echoed Russian calls for an early referendum on Ukrainian membership, apparently so as to kill the idea for the foreseeable future. He has disbanded the Interdepartmental Committee on Euro-Atlantic Integration. He has cut funds for the government's two NATO information programs by 40 percent and has reduced the budget for the NATO-sponsored reform of the armed Forces by 50 percent.[36]

When he was previously prime minister under President Kuchma, Yanukovych recognized the need for cooperation with both NATO and the EU so as to maintain Ukraine's multivectoral foreign policy. Without it, Ukraine would be more dependent on its relations with Russia.

Because Yanukovych is likely still working out his policy toward NATO, it is important that NATO keep the door open to Ukraine, not to promote membership at this time, but to maintain existing networks and programs on the condition that Ukraine practice the democratic values that it professes, such as free elections, freedom of the media, and rule of law.

The West has a strong interest in seeing Ukraine succeed in its reforms—the fate of democracy and free market in this part of Europe is at stake. The West has also a vested interest in preventing the emergence of a more powerful Russia once again exerting pressure on its neighbors. The increased assertiveness of Russia as a result of the rise in energy prices, including its willingness to use its gas as a political weapon, suggests that an independent and democratic Ukraine is increasingly important as an obstacle to the expansion of Russia's power. If Ukraine can preserve the gains of the Orange Revolution, its example may even eventually assist in the development of a democratic Russia. The question is, of course, whether the West can maintain a long-term critical commitment to Ukraine in spite of the vicissitudes of Ukrainian politics.

Notes

1. Taras Kuzio, "Revisiting the Orange Revolution, Considerable Gains Made," *Eurasia Daily Monitor* (Washington, DC), vol. 2, issue 217, November 21, 2005.
2. James Sherr, "The New Coordinates of Ukrainian Politics," *Nezavisimaia gazeta* (Moscow), April 10, 2006.
3. "Ukrainian Media Ownership Still a Concern," Associated Press (Kyiv), May 3, 2006.
4. Press Freedom Index, Reporters Without Borders, Paris, http://www .rsf.org/rubrique.php3?id_rubrique=554.
5. Corruption Perceptions Index 2005, Transparency International, Berlin, http://www.transparency.org/policy_research/surveys_indices/ cpi/2005.
6. Freedom in the World 2006, Freedom House, New York, http://www .freedomhouse.org/uploads/pdf/Charts2006.pdf.
7. Ukraine Risk: Risk Overview, Economist Intelligence Unit, New York, February 2, 2006.
8. Index of Economic Freedom 2006, Heritage House/*Wall Street Journal* (New York), http://www.heritage.org/research/features/index/coutries .cfm.
9. Yuliia Mostova et al., "A Fairy Tale Born, A Myth Destroyed," *Dzerkalo tyzhnia* 10, September 16, 2005, http://www.mirrorweekly.com/ie/ show/563/51196.
10. See Andrey Zorin, "Why We Don't Like Ukraine" *Kommersant* (Moscow), January 25, 2006.
11. Taras Kuzio, "Russia still gets it wrong in Ukraine," *Eurasian Daily Monitor* (Washington, DC), vol. 2, issue 185, October 5, 2005.
12. Varvara Zhluktenko, "Pundit says Putin's remarks on Ukraine counterproductive," *Den* (Kyiv), April 13, 2005, pp. 1, 3; Taras Kuzio, "Ukraine asks Russia to begin preparations for withdrawing Black Sea Fleet," *Eurasia Daily Monitor* (Washington, DC), vol. 2, issue 77, April 20, 2005.
13. Aleksandr Palii, "Our Answer to Chernomyrdin" (in Russian), *Ukrainska pravda* (Kyiv), February 20, 2006.
14. Ibid.
15. Andrew Wilson, *Ukraine's Orange Revolution* (New Haven, CT: Yale University Press, 2005), 118–21.
16. Wilson, *Ukraine's Orange Revolution*, 86–89.
17. Ibid.
18. Taras Kuzio, "Former security chief reveals extent of threats to Yushchenko's presidential bid," *Eurasian Daily Monitor* (Washington, DC), June 1, 2005, pp. 2, 106; Wilson, *Ukraine's Orange Revolution*, 97–103.

19. Dmitrii Trenin, "The Post-Imperial Project," *Nezavisimaia gazeta* (Moscow), February 15, 2006.
20. Dmitrii Trenin, *Reading Russia Right*, Carnegie Endowment for International Peace (Moscow), Special Edition 42, October 2005.
21. "2003 Energy Strategy of the Russian Federation to 2020" (in Russian), *Minpromenergo Rosii* (Moscow), September 27, 2005, p. 1.
22. "2003 Energy Strategy of the Russian Federation to 2020" (in Russian), *Minpromenergo Rosii* (Moscow), September 27, 2005, p. 1.
23. Gleb Pavlovskii, "Ukrainian Export of Spokes in Wheels," *Izvestiia* (Moscow), January 24, 2006.
24. Yuri Zarakhovich, "Q&A: Putin's Critical Adviser," *Time.com* (New York) December 31, 2005.
25. Sergei Ivanov, "Russia Must Be Strong," *Wall Street Journal* (New York), January 11, 2006, p. A14.
26. Masha Lipman, "Risking Another Slavic War," *Washington Post* (Washington, DC), January 30, 2006.
27. Vladimir Socor, "Putin on Kosovo and Post-Soviet Conflicts—Destructive Ambiguity," *Eurasian Daily Monitor* (Washington, DC), February 2, 2006, pp. 3, 23; Vladimir Socor, "Moscow on Kosovo: Having Its Cake and Eating It Too," *Eurasian Daily Monitor* (Washington, DC), February 6, 2006, pp. 3, 25.
28. Dmitrii Trenin, "The Post-Imperial Project," *Nezavisimaia gazeta* (Moscow), February 15, 2006.
29. Ibid.
30. "European Neighbourhood Policy, Strategy Paper," Commission of the European Communities, Brussels, 12.5.2004, COM(2004), 373 final, 31, http://europa.eu.int/comm/world/enp/pdf/strategy/strategy_paper_en.pdf (accessed February 28, 2006).
31. Eberhard Schneider, "Ukraine and the European Union," *Ukraine-Analysen* 5, April 11, 2006.
32. Ibid.
33. James Sherr, "Ukraine's Scissors: Between Internal Weakness and External Dependence," in *Russie.Nei.Visions 2006: Understanding Russia and the New Independent States*, ed. Thomas Gomart and Tatiana Kastueva-Jean (Paris: Institut français de relations internationales [IFRI], 2006).
34. "Poll shows Ukrainians favour CIS economic bloc ahead of EU," Ukrainian News Agency, UNIAN, Kyiv, February 15, 2006.
35. "Ukrainians favour ties with Russia over EU," Interfax-Ukraine, Kyiv, February 22, 2006.
36. James Sherr, "Ukraine Prospects and Risks," *Action Ukraine Report* 780, October 25, 2006.

9

The Failed Revolution: Reflections on the 2006 Elections in Belarus

David R. Marples[1]

Introduction: Uniting the Opposition

The success of "color revolutions" in Serbia, Georgia, and Ukraine, together with the success of the opposition movement in Kyrgyszstan, fueled hopes for change in Belarus, particularly among opposition circles, European Union (EU) countries, and the Bush-Rice administration in Washington. Though prospects for the removal of President Aliaksandr Lukashenka were limited (he successfully engineered a referendum in October 2004 that gave him the right to run for additional terms as president), there is no question that the situation for the opposition during the 2006 presidential elections was considerably better than it was in 2001. In that year, with the support of several key figures and institutions, including the Organization for Security and Co-operation in Europe (OSCE) Advisory and Monitoring Group in Belarus, the opposition belatedly came up with a compromise candidate from the trade union movement, Uladzimir Hancharyk. But the move came too late to have a significant impact on the campaign.[2] This time, after a difficult series of meetings across the country, the opposition managed to unite its efforts under Aliaksandr Milinkevich, a nonparty man and professional academic from the Hrodna region. Surprisingly, given past opposition politics, most parties managed to shelve political differences to enable the success of this process. Thus the key figures in what was to be the Milinkevich election campaign were Siarhei Kaliakin, leader of the Party of Communists and a fellow candidate for selection as the united choice; Aliaksandr Bukhvostau, leader of the now defunct Labor Party; and Vintsuk Viachorka, leader of the Belarusian Popular Front.

The odds against electoral success for the opposition were formidable, however. According to opinion polls conducted by the National Institute of Socio-Economic and Political Research (NISEPI), directed by Aleh Manaieu, in recent years, no individual political party in Belarus has been able to gain the support of more than 10 percent of the electorate. Instead, the various parties are often split into several factions. There are two branches of the Popular Front, there have been three wings of the Social Democrats in recent times, and there are two registered Communist Parties, as well as a Liberal Democratic Party, a Women's Party, and various others. Since 1995, when it failed to prevent the first of three referendums that altered fundamentally the 1994 Belarus Constitution in favor of presidential powers, the opposition has fought an increasingly desperate rearguard action against the Lukashenka regime. The government took control over the media from the mid-1990s, arrested or persecuted opposition activists, and eliminated or undermined nongovernmental organizations through processes of auditing and enforced re-registration. It has also shut down independent entities such as the European Humanities University and the Yakub Kolas Belarusian Humanitarian Lycee, as well as cracking down on public demonstrations through the use of the militia, Special Forces, and the KGB. Most prominent figures in the opposition from the early years of the Lukashenka government are in exile; several have been kidnapped and not seen since. Among those in exile are Zianon Pazniak, founder of the Belarusian Popular Front, and Siamon Sharetsky, former head of parliament (13th session); those who have "disappeared" include former deputy speaker Viktar Hanchar and former Minister of Defense Yuri Zakharenka.[3]

Lukashenka Prepares the Groundwork

On November 23, 2005, with an election scheduled to take place no later than July 2006, the Lukashenka government proposed several amendments to the Criminal Code and the Code of Criminal Procedure. Two days later, the lower house of parliament met to discuss the new draft law "On addenda and changes to some legislative acts of the republic of Belarus to increase responsibility for actions directed against an individual and public safety." Described as an urgent matter when it was introduced by KGB chairman Stsiapan Sukharenka, the draft nevertheless came as a surprise to most of the sitting Members of Parliament. It was accepted by 94 votes to 1 (of 110 MPs), and its passage into law was a mere formality.[4] The new law has increased the number of activities subject to criminal charges, which can be applied to any activities alleged to threaten the national security of the country. These activities relate to actions involving weapons and explosives, but also to those against the ruling order that might lead to foreign pressure on the state, and to crimes against constitutional rights and freedoms of citizens. Organizations that have been ordered to stop functioning or else face liquidation, but that continue to operate, face fines, while their leaders can be imprisoned for a period of six months to two years. Those convicted for preparing or funding "mass disorders" face up to three years in prison. The same punishment as that for preparing mass disorders applies to those who call for seizure of state power or changes to the Constitution (ironically, given the way the Constitution has been handled by the Lukashenka government). If these appeals are disseminated through the mass media, the punishment is two to five years in prison.

A significant article in the revised Criminal Code is titled "Defamation of the Republic of Belarus," which pertains to "providing a foreign state or international organization with 'false materials' on the political, social, military, or international situation." The punishment for such actions is imprisonment from six months to two years. Those suspected of terrorist activities or hooliganism can be detained for up to 10 days under the same proposals. In theory, it would now be possible for political activists who appealed to European structures such as the OSCE, the Parliamentary Assembly of the Council of Europe (PACE), or the Strasbourg Court to receive a prison sentence of between six months and two years. The definition of "false materials" could also, in theory, be interpreted very narrowly. The new law appeared to infringe further upon the human rights of citizens of Belarus, while opposition candidates in the election faced the prospect of seeing their supporters jailed for the simple act of distributing their electoral platforms. Evidently the Lukashenka regime recognized the appeal of the EU and its influence on recent elections in Georgia and Ukraine and was taking pre-emptive measures to forestall any prospects of a color revolution in Belarus. Such actions ensured that no candidate other than President Lukashenka would have a mandate to make policy announcements and the government would be the sole arbiter of how the newly revised Criminal Code would be interpreted. Arrests seemed inevitable, as later proved to be the case.

The United Democratic Candidate

Under these circumstances, Milinkevich's election as a single candidate from the Democratic opposition was a triumph for the policy of compromise among many disparate groups and potential leaders. On October 2, 2005, more than eight hundred delegates from the opposition met at the Palace of Culture of the Minsk Automobile Factory. This location was chosen because the authorities denied the organizers access to major assembly halls in the capital, and there was speculation that the election may have to take place outside the country, possibly in Kyiv (Ukraine) or Smolensk (Russia). Initially, four candidates sought the position of united leader: Milinkevich, Kaliakin, Anatol Liabedzka, chairman of the United Civic Party, and Stanislau Shushkevich, leader of one of the branches of the Social Democratic Hramada. Shushkevich, Belarus' first post-independence leader, withdrew from the election before the voting stage. Kaliakin was defeated in the first round. In the decisive contest, Milinkevich received 399 votes to Liabedzka's 391.[5] The narrow victory was perhaps a reflection of the political acumen of Liabedzka, as Milinkevich had been well ahead after the first round.

The initial question for many observers was: Who is Milinkevich? A native of Hrodna, the new leader had headed a public association called Ratusha, but had no political affiliations. Born in 1947, he was a professor of physics for twenty years at the Hrodna State University. He had been a visiting professor in the United States and Germany[6] and spoke five languages. His ancestors reportedly took part in revolts against the Russian Empire. Through his interest in ethnography, Milinkevich was oriented toward Poland, a country with which Belarus had hostile relations. The Hrodna region is home to most of the almost four hundred thousand ethnic Poles living in Belarus, and is the main center of the Roman Catholic Church in the country.

The Political Council of the Democratic opposition soon began to develop Milinkevich's election strategy based on four goals. The first was the election of a single candidate with the support of at least 50 percent of the electorate (a task that Milinkevich, who favored street demonstrations, never considered feasible or realistic). The second goal was to mobilize the public and put strong pressure on the authorities (especially the Central Election Commission chaired by Lidziia Yarmoshyna) not to falsify the election results. Third was to create a broad movement of "the majority." Finally, the fourth aim was to involve public associations and youth groups (the so-called "third sector") within this coalition.[7]

How united was the opposition following the election of Milinkevich? Two political parties did not participate in the United Democratic campaign. Zianon Pazniak, leader of the Conservative Christian Party of the Belarusian Popular Front and now living in exile and operating mainly from Warsaw, denounced the Democratic convention as a "noisy display of the anti-Belarusian pseudo-opposition."[8] The description was in reference to the contacts between the United Democrats and Russia. Pazniak accused the leaders of the convention of making frequent trips to Russia to discuss their situation with Russian secret services. One of the convention's goals, it was alleged, was the elimination of the "revival movement" (*Adradzhenne*) initiated by Pazniak a decade earlier. The rival Social Democrats (excepting the Shushkevich branch of the party) had intended to advance their own candidate for the presidency and declined to take part in the Democratic convention. Matters were simplified with the arrest and imprisonment of Mikola Statkevich, leader of the Social Democrats Narodnaia Hramada, and Paval Seviarynets, former leader of the Young Front, on May 31, 2005. Each received a three-year sentence of "personal restraint" (i.e., corrective labor) on the grounds that they had organized mass protests against falsified results of the 2004 referendum and parliamentary election.[9] Subsequently, Aliaksandr Kazulin (b. 1955), the former rector of the Belarusian State University, was elected leader of the United Democrats and agreed to serve as a presidential candidate in the forthcoming campaign.

Opinion Polls

The personal popularity of the president has always been a matter for debate among analysts of Belarus. On the one hand, Lukashenka is a populist who can communicate well with people, particularly those of the older generation who recall the Soviet era and tend to venerate Soviet symbols. On the other hand, it is not difficult to sway the public when government control of the media is 90 percent and the opposition has to rely on a few regularly persecuted media outlets. Television, the key communications medium in Belarus, is controlled completely by the government. It has also been suggested that those being polled are fearful of offering what could be construed as antigovernment opinions. In October 2004, an exit poll issued by the Baltic Gallup branch indicated that support for Lukashenka's request to extend his mandate was approximately 48 percent, thus giving rise to statements that the official result of over 82 percent had been falsified.[10]

Traditionally, the most reliable polling organization within the country has been the NISEPI, headed by Dr. Aleh Manaieu. In 2005 it was forced to "reregister" its office by moving its official headquarters from Minsk to Vilnius, an indicator of the regime's dissatisfaction with the poll's results. The Lukashenka administration has also produced its own polling agency, called EKOOM, though whether it ever functioned as a polling agency in actuality (other than issuing reported findings in the media) is unclear. This chapter will focus mainly on the findings of NISEPI, while considering the difficulties inherent in compiling accurate information in the intimidating political atmosphere of Belarus. Whatever their limitations, opinion polls are the most significant indicator during an election campaign of the difference between officially reported totals and popular opinion. In Ukraine's Orange Revolution, this discrepancy was a key element in sparking street protests.

In a poll of October 2005, before the official announcement of a new presidential election and prior to the election of United Democratic candidate Milinkevich, NISEPI reported that during a presidential election, 47.5 percent of those polled intended to vote for Lukashenka and 25.5 percent for an opposition leader. The personal popularity of the president had risen through 2005 and had been at just over 41 percent in May. In general, those who opposed the president tended to be more affluent and better educated than those who supported him. Over 70 percent of those polled felt that Lukashenka would win an election, 15 percent thought that he might be removed by a color revolution, and 15.5 percent declared themselves ready to take to the streets in protest if the results were clearly falsified. Only 13 percent favored the integration of Belarus into the Russian Federation (one of the possible scenarios of the expanded Russia-Belarus Union), a drop from the 20 percent that had supported the idea in 2002.[11] Less than three weeks later, Lukashenka declared that he expected to win 90 percent of the vote in the 2006 elections.[12] By late December, NISEPI reported that Lukashenka's rating had risen to 52 percent and support for Milinkevich—now clearly the main opposition candidate—was only 6.6 percent. At the same time, an opposition newspaper declared that Milinkevich's rating had already reached 18.1 percent.[13] In December 2005, Milinkevich was still largely unknown to the Belarusian public, so the figure seems inflated. In mid-February, just one month prior to the vote, the official media cited an opinion poll conducted by the Institute of Sociology, Belarusian Academy of Sciences, under the direction of Hryhory Evelkin, based on more than nine thousand responses from all regions of the country. The poll results purported to show a significant increase in people's satisfaction with the political situation in the country (from 29.02 percent in 2002 to 55.45 percent at the end of 2005). Over 76 percent reportedly expressed their intention to support Lukashenka in the election; approximately 3–4 percent expressed support for the opposition candidates.[14] Lukashenka began with a large and virtually unassailable lead; however, there are serious doubts as to whether the lead was as large as the authorities maintained.

The Initial Stages of the Campaign

On December 15, 2005, Lukashenka met Russian president Vladimir Putin at Sochi on the Black Sea. The following day, the Belarusian parliament agreed unanimously that the date of the presidential elections in Belarus would be March 19, 2006. The earlier-than-anticipated date was calculated to create problems for the united opposition campaign. There were also several other possible reasons for the government's choice of an early date. Conceivably, Russia expected to be occupied with chairing the meeting of the G-8 countries in St. Petersburg in July; Putin would not have wished to face embarrassing questions about the nature of the election campaign in Belarus. Liabedzka commented that the date was chosen to coincide closely with the parliamentary elections in Ukraine (March 26), which would monopolize international attention.[15] Supporters of the various candidates had one week to provide a list of members of initiative groups for delivery to the Central Commission for Elections and Republican Referendums (CEC).

Belarus has a complex procedure for elections. Initially, initiative groups for each candidate are established, and over the period of a month, the authorities can examine the validity of each candidate. According to the Constitution, candidates for president must be at least thirty-five years of age, must have been born in the country, and must have lived in the country continuously without interruption for the ten years prior to the election. Initiative groups must gather a minimum of one hundred thousand signatures for their candidate. The signatures are then scrutinized, and if more than 15 percent are declared invalid, then the candidate is obliged to withdraw from the campaign. After this process, the candidates for the 2006 election then went through a period of registration from February 12 to 21. The timing meant that less than one month could be devoted to the election campaign. Prior to February 21, no candidate could issue any form of manifesto that could be construed as campaigning. These restrictions meant that the incumbent president (who declined to resign for the period of the elections) had a significant advantage, as he appeared daily on television, usually in the context of conducting public works.

The CEC had registered eight initiative groups by December 28, 2005, and had publicized the number of members within each. The names and totals were as follows:

Aliaksandr Lukashenka, 6,212 members
Aliaksandr Milinkevich, 5,136 members
Aliaksandr Kazulin, 3,347 members
Siarhey Haidukevich, 3,073 members
Zianon Pazniak, 2,405 members
Aliaksandr Voytovich, 1,314 members
Valery Fralou, 1,152 members
Siarhey Skrebets, 130 members

Of these candidates, Haidukevich was the most familiar to voters. He was the leader of the Liberal-Democratic Party of Belarus and had been a candidate in the 2001 election, finishing third behind Lukashenka and Uladzimir Hancharyk. Since that time, he had become a supporter of the president from within the lower house of the parliament. It was suggested that his candidacy assisted Lukashenka by legitimizing the election in the event of an opposition boycott. (It is also possible that Haidukevich has ambitions to be the eventual successor to Lukashenka.) All the other candidates could be termed members of the political opposition. Aside from Pazniak, Fralou and Skrebets had been members of the opposition group Respublika in the pre-October 2004 parliament. Voytovich, like Milinkevich and Kazulin, is a former academic, in this case the former president of the Belarusian Academy of Sciences. He had been appointed chairman of the upper house of parliament but was removed in 2003 upon reaching retirement age. Voytovich was the first to drop out of the election. Skrebets was on trial for alleged bribery in January, and clearly the small size of his initiative group suggested that he would have had difficulty mounting a campaign. Pazniak, as a nonresident of Belarus for the past decade, may have eventually been declared ineligible, but he also withdrew himself from the election. Fralou opted to join the campaign of Kazulin.

As the election grew closer, the government launched a propaganda campaign that warned the electorate that the West was supporting a program of color revolution that would entail the overthrowing of President Lukashenka. Writing in the main government daily, Uladzimir Hurin, a political scientist affiliated with the Institute of Social Political Research with the Presidential Administration, wrote that the "orange virus" had brought chaos to Western European countries such as Germany, France, and Belgium, as well as to Ukraine and Georgia, albeit with some differences. To bring about such chaos, control over the media was required. In the case of Serbia, Ukraine, and Georgia, wrote Hurin, there were two sorts of intervention. On the one hand were the leaders of the United States and European "bureaucracies" (implicitly Hurin was referring to the EU); on the other hand were sponsors such as George Soros, interested in overthrowing the governments in question for personal reasons. In the case of Belarus, however, added Hurin, there could be no question of a Democratic revolution because the majority of the population supported Lukashenka.[16] The image of outside forces seeking to change the government of Belarus has been deployed frequently by the Lukashenka administration. Lukashenka has frequently referred to the United States and NATO as his enemies; he has consistently supported and offered asylum to dictators who are under pressure from the West, including the late Slobodan Milosevic and the late Saddam Hussein.

Several measures were applied to complicate opposition candidates' efforts to gather the necessary number of signatures. One of Milinkevich's campaign workers, Uladzimir Lavkovich, stated that on a daily basis the militia arrested about ten members from initiative groups. Another reported that many voters were afraid to sign the list for Milinkevich because they did not wish to get into trouble with the authorities. In Hrodna, a member of the Kazulin team was unable to enter student dormitories to collect signatures as the staff on duty maintained that they were unable to open the doors to anyone not specifically invited by a resident. In such a case, the invitee would be obliged to remain in the room of that resident and not knock on other doors.[17] The newspaper *Narodnaia volia*, the largest circulating newspaper of the opposition, received a number of telephone calls from people who declared that they were being forced to provide signatures on the list for Lukashenka. At one store, employees had been given two lists to sign: one confirming that they supported Lukashenka, and another to acknowledge that they had received their salaries. They were warned that if they refused to sign the first list, they may not be paid. When one voter visited a medical clinic, his doctor requested that he sign the list for Lukashenka. The doctor informed the patient that she was under instructions to collect signatures in this way. Students at the Belarus Institute of Law were asked to provide signatures in order to acquire credits for their courses. The Lukashenka team also informed voters, falsely, that they could sign the lists of only one candidate.[18] In the Vitsebsk region, according to the account of Miacheslau Hryb, head of the initiative group for Kazulin (and former chairman of the parliament of the 12th session), the authorities obtained the list of those people supporting Kazulin and threatened to dismiss them from their jobs. In the Brest region, a woman collecting signatures for Milinkevich was arrested and her lists confiscated. The lists were returned to her after several days.[19] There are dozens of similar examples demonstrating how the initial stage of the campaign was heavily weighted in favor of the incumbent president. At the same time, the opposition found it very difficult to get supporters into the CEC and the territorial commissions. Lavkovich, cited above, declared that these commissions embodied the gravest of violations, especially in terms of their composition. The United Civic Party had nominated more than eight hundred people for membership, many of whom had experience as state officials, either in parliament or in local government. Only one member was accepted, however. In some areas, representatives of this party were informed that commissions had been formed prior to the submission of names.[20]

The Campaigns

On February 17, the CEC announced that four candidates would be registered officially for the election of March 19. These were Lukashenka, Haidukevich, Milinkevich, and Kazulin. Lidziia Yarmoshyna also reported that Lukashenka had received 1,903,069 valid signatures (i.e., more than one-third of the electorate had expressed its willingness to support him). More than 180,000 valid signatures (of more than 226,000 submitted) had been accepted in support of Milinkevich. Each of the other two candidates had slightly lower totals.[21] The Lukashenka team, made up of prominent members of the government, adopted a four-point strategy: first it focused on the stability, economic prosperity, and general contentment of the population. Belarusians, it was alleged, would face potential chaos with any change of leadership, and much was made of the new agreement with the Russian conglomerate Gazprom that low prices for Russian gas would remain the same for Belarus as in 2005: $46.68 per 1,000 cubic meters.[22] Close friendship and partnership with Russia, through the structure of the Russia-Belarus Union, were considered the linchpin of this stability. Second, the team strived to maintain very close control over all aspects of the election campaign, including exerting pressure regularly on the opposition camps. Third, in conjunction with this pressure, individual activists were to be detained regularly. Fourth, although it was reported officially that the president would not campaign actively as he was preoccupied with state business, there was almost blanket coverage of the president's activities on television and radio and in the press.

Neither opposition candidate offered radical proposals. Milinkevich denounced the Russia-Belarus Union as impractical and vowed to return Belarus to the status of a neutral and nonaligned state that would maintain close relations with Russia and develop closer ties with the West. Most important in his view were close relations with immediate neighbors (i.e., Russia, Ukraine, Poland, Lithuania, and Latvia). He also suggested that the notion of a common currency with Russia should be abandoned. The long-term goal, maintained Milinkevich, should be entry into the EU. Belarus needed to put an end to its gross infringements of human rights, and Milinkevich demanded an end to the plethora of petty laws restricting foreign investment and more privatization of mid-sized companies.[23] Kazulin's proposals were similar but rather more fully elaborated as they constituted part of the Social Democratic Party's platform "Conception," which would return Belarus in stages to the status of a parliamentary republic, reducing the power of the president, and offering incentives for investment and privatization, while allowing workers' collectives more control on the factory floor. They focused on the "presidential vertical," that is, the centralization of all power in the hands of the president.[24] In terms of distribution, it is fair to say that Kazulin's public speeches were more widely available to the electorate (outside the country,

Milinkevich's statements were more publicized). Both Kazulin's television interviews and his radio interview of March 6 were available on the Web page of the Belarusian Social Democratic Party.[25]

Harsh measures were imposed from the day candidates were registered. On February 17, there was a violent confrontation at the National Press Center when guards refused to allow Kazulin entry to the building. A lawyer associated with the Kazulin campaign, Aleh Volchak, was temporarily blinded when one of the guards sprayed a substance into his face. As in 2001, Lukashenka had announced an "all-Belarusian People's Assembly," at which he would outline his policies for the future—an incongruent development unless the election was a formality. Delegates to this assembly, which was held at the main Palace of Culture in Minsk, were prescreened. On March 2, however, the day before the assembly convened, Kazulin tried to register for the assembly at the Palace of Railway Workers. He was prevented from entering the building and then beaten by militia, who were acting under the orders of the head of the Belarusian Special Forces, Dzmitry Paulichenka.[26] He was then detained for several hours, though he was released by the evening and made his way to Liberty Square to join a rally called by Milinkevich. The rally, attended by an estimated twenty thousand people according to opposition sources, constituted a defiant rejoinder to the closed People's Assembly, and was the largest public gathering seen in Belarus for many years.[27] It exemplified the opposition's policy of using street demonstrations to counter Lukashenka's overwhelming control over the media.

The government permitted each of the opposition candidates two television and radio slots, each thirty minutes in duration. (Milinkevich had already been seen by some viewers on the Russian edition of *Euronews*.) On these occasions, the most polished performance was provided by Kazulin, an excellent public speaker, who wasted no opportunity to denounce the Lukashenka government for low living standards and corruption, and even focused on the president's unusual private life, alleging that he had mistresses in Minsk, and that the capital had yet to see his wife, the "first lady," who had remained in the same village where the president had once been a state farm chairman. The theme of Kazulin's second television broadcast, released in a slightly censored version on March 2 at 6:00 p.m., was: "Better to leave as the first president of Belarus than as the last dictator of Europe." These broadcasts were received by the public with such astonishment that some viewers wondered if there had been a coup in Belarus. By comparison, Milinkevich was more restrained and careful and focused on a campaign "to win the hearts and minds of the people." He spent the early part of the year visiting several capitals of Europe and many leaders of the EU, where he was embraced as the Democratic candidate. His campaign was also marked by symbols reminiscent of the Orange Revolution in Ukraine. His emblem was blue denim, which could be symbolized simply by his wearing jeans. He held a series of meetings in various parts of the country, though the brevity of the campaign did not permit him to visit all areas. His young supporters, particularly those from *Zubr* (Bison) and the Young Front, daubed graffiti in various places in the cities, including phrases such as "Long live Belarus!" and "Dostal!" ("We are fed up!").

The government responded to Milinkevich's campaign by increasing pressure. Most notably, it declared that the opposition was planning a coup d'etat on March 19, the day that both opposition candidates had encouraged their supporters to assemble at Kastrychnitska (October) Square. KGB chief Sukharenka cited a false exit poll, allegedly prepared by the *Partnerstva* group, indicating a victory for Milinkevich, as well as the participation of Georgian activists in an anticipated uprising. He declared that any public demonstrations would be regarded as acts of terrorism, carrying a punishment for participants of a twenty-five-year prison term, life in jail, or the death penalty. Belarusian television also revealed that a large supply of tents, military goods, and clothing, which originated in the United States and was to be used for a color revolution in the Belarusian capital, had been confiscated at the Latvian border. By March 15, the Belarusian police had set up an emergency headquarters, placed its personnel on high alert, and begun monitoring all polling stations (by this date, early voting had already begun). Lukashenka added fuel to the situation by claiming that "hooligans" from Georgia, Ukraine, and Russia were preparing to enter Belarus to help unseat his government.[28] At the same time, all three major leaders of the Milinkevich campaign—Vintsuk Viachorka, Anatol Liabedzka, and Siarhei Kaliakin—together with hundreds of local supporters, had been arrested. Most commonly, those arrested were sentenced to 15 days in prison for "petty hooliganism" for violating article 156 of the Code of Administrative Offenses.

The "Results" and the Aftermath

On March 19, 2006, all independent sources of media were suspended. Even Web and blog pages based in Belarus were inaccessible.

About 70 percent of the voting took place on the day of the election, the remainder having been completed through advance polls. Independent pollsters were unable to take exit polls, thus making it difficult to ascertain the accuracy of the results. By the evening, about fifteen thousand people had gathered in October Square, close to the House of Trade Unions. By 3:00 a.m. on March 20, Lidziia Yarmoshyna had announced that Lukashenka had acquired a convincing majority of over 82 percent. As in past elections, the statement clearly preceded the completion of vote counting—if indeed the process had even reached the initial stages. The figure was also considerably higher than most observers had predicted. The "denim protest" continued for several days in October Square, with a small tent city watched by riot police. The protest consisted mainly of young people prepared to defy the authorities and Lukashenka, who had declared that he would "wring their necks" as he would the neck of a chicken should they take such an action. The protests increased in size as people finished the working day (the usual assembly time was 6:30 p.m.); however, a small group remained in the square throughout in order to avoid dispersal. Both Milinkevich and Kazulin attended these gatherings, though Kazulin wished to abandon the protests after the second day. The goal of Milinkevich was to continue protests until the Independence Day demonstration of March 25 (commemorating the declaration of the independence of Belarus in 1918). The protests received widespread publicity in the international media, and clearly revived memories of what had occurred in central Kyiv some 16 months earlier, albeit in modified form and with fewer people.

The reaction of the authorities was a combination of caution and fury. On Belarusian Television, the protesters were denounced as a small group of hooligans in the pay of foreign powers. Emphasis was placed on the futility and weakness of the opposition movement, and its lack of relevance to an election that had demonstrated the popularity of Lukashenka. At the same time, the regime was angered by the lack of international recognition of the election results (with the exception of Russia and some countries of the CIS), particularly by the EU, the OSCE, and the United States. *Sovetskaia Belorussiia* editorialized that "there was no basis for a revolution," while citing the president's remarks that the "Georgian authorities" were trying to foment problems in Belarus. Curiously, it also berated Russian Duma deputy Ryzhkov for declaring that Lukashenka had received only 4 percent of the vote.[29] At 3:00 a.m. on March 24, riot police stormed the sparsely manned protest camp and removed demonstrators from the square. Nevertheless, a large protest occurred on March 25, ending in a violent confrontation when hundreds of demonstrators led by Kazulin clashed with police as they tried to move to the prison where many protestors were being held. Kazulin received a prison sentence of five and a half years for his part in the protests of March 25. At the time of writing, he was on an extended hunger strike in prison, and there were concerns about his health. According to a fellow prisoner, he has suffered a catastrophic loss in weight. Hundreds of people, most of them young, were injured in the clash, at which police used tear gas and stun guns to subdue the crowd. The event effectively ended the period of protests until the Chernobyl March on April 26, at which Milinkevich was arrested and given a fifteen-day sentence, along with other leaders of his movement.[30]

The official election results were published in the media on March 24, and provided the following results:[31]

Number of people voting: 6,630,653
Total turnout: 92.9 percent
Totals for individual candidates:

Lukashenka, A. G.: 5,501,249; 83 percent
Milinkevich, A. V.: 405,486; 6.1 percent
Haidukevich, S. V.: 230,664; 3.5 percent
Kazulin, A. V.: 147,402; 2.2 percent

Both the size of the turnout and the proportion of the votes for Lukashenka appear considerably inflated. Conversely, the totals for Milinkevich and Kazulin appear to have been reduced. The return for Haidukevich is possibly accurate. Why the authorities felt the need to inflate totals, given that Lukashenka had a clean majority in the first round, is not clear. (Manaieu, for example, calculated that the "real" total for Lukashenka was around 63.6 percent, with Milinkevich at 20.6 percent, though it is unclear how he gathered his results since it had proved impossible to obtain exit polls.[32]) Subsequently, Lukashenka disappeared from public view for several days, and his inauguration ceremony was delayed from the anticipated date of March 31 until April 8. Starting his third term in office, the president was pale and subdued, clearly showing the strains of a campaign in which the authorities appeared to overreact to the threat of regime change and dealt rigorously with those who opposed the government.

During the period of the election, civic society re-emerged briefly in Belarus, but from a political perspective, several crucial issues need yet to be addressed. The first pertains to the reasons behind the sustained popularity of Lukashenka, along with the apparent gullibility of the electorate. After 2006, there seems to be little hope of removing the president via the ballot box since control over the electoral processes has been honed to perfection over twelve years of campaigns and referendums. But the regime faces several significant problems, including its relations with Russia. Thus, the second issue is the status of the Russia-Belarus Union and the attitude of the Putin government toward Minsk. In contrast to his behavior during the 2004 presidential election in Ukraine, Vladimir Putin notably refrained from active participation in the Belarus campaign, offering instead quiet support for the incumbent government. Since the election, Russia has acted more belligerently, with Gazprom demanding "more realistic" prices for gas exported to Belarus, and with the Russian government issuing a decree on May 9 on fundamental changes in Russia's trade-economic and credit-financial policies toward Belarus.[33] Possibly Putin wished to be seen as taking a firmer line on Belarus prior to the G-8 summit in St. Petersburg in July 2006. On the other hand, Russia may be more determined to establish a more credible foundation for the Russia-Belarus Union, which could conceivably include the direct annexation of Belarus, or its relegation to a role as secondary partner in the Union. In either case, the Lukashenka administration faces a potentially difficult situation. A threefold rise in gas prices would in one sweep undermine the economic stability that was the main factor in Lukashenka's electoral success. Following talks between Russia and Belarus in late November, Russian president Vladimir Putin announced that by the end of 2007, the Belarusian transit company Beltransgaz would be transformed into a joint venture in which Russia's Gazprom would obtain a 50 percent share. Such a turn of events would likely satisfy Gazprom's ambitions and allow Belarus to continue to receive Russian gas at subsidized prices. The Russians may also demand a more precise formulation of the terms of the Russia-Belarus Union. In turn, Lukashenka and the chairman of the National Academy of Sciences, Mikhail Miasnikovich, announced on December 1, 2006, that Belarus intends to build a nuclear power station in the Mahileu region, based on two VVER-1000 reactors, and to come on stream in 2013–15. The station, which is opposed widely by the public, would supply up to 25 percent of the energy needs currently satisfied by Russia.[34]

The third issue is the sustainability of the United Democratic opposition beyond the period of the elections. The unity was always somewhat fragile, particularly given the narrowness of Milinkevich's victory over Liabedzka, and the more direct and confrontational tactics adopted by Kazulin, whose activities at times made Milinkevich appear pedestrian by comparison. The government has imposed relatively mild sentences on the Milinkevich team but has been thorough and vindictive in the way it has dealt with youth activists. The EU and the United States have responded to the election by expanding the travel ban on thirty-five Belarusian leaders and freezing their financial assets abroad.[35] Such actions are more symbolic than practical since it is unlikely that these leaders—including Lukashenka—have significant holdings in foreign bank accounts. What is not clear is how far the West is prepared to maintain its support for the united opposition in the event that it can hold together and whether it will extend sanctions beyond travel bans to include international trade. It is also uncertain if the G-8 will opt to focus on Belarus rather than on more pressing concerns, such as the nuclear power program in Iran, the war in Iraq, and the situation in the Middle East. During the election campaign, the opposition made significant progress in several respects, particularly in the mobilization of young people for regime change. Yet its situation is highly vulnerable, and the government is now in a strong position to consolidate its new authority further. But the fourth factor to be considered is the government's overreaction to civic protests and its fear of a color revolution, even when such responses were hardly warranted by prevailing conditions at the time. How does one account for the regime's anxieties?

Here the president's personality must be taken into consideration. Belarus is notable for its single center of power (i.e., the residence of President Lukashenka). Though he has a team of officials, none has any real authority and any official can be removed at the president's whim. Lukashenka is an isolated figure, not only in terms of the outside world, but also within the ruling circle—a factor that only Kazulin really exploited during the campaign. The frenetic propaganda campaign, which echoed Soviet examples, demonstrated also the president's fear of being overthrown. Lukashenka has no exit strategy for leaving his presidential post, he distrusts most people (especially those members of his former cabinets who have departed on bad terms), and his most meaningful dialogues are with television viewers or public audiences, especially in the countryside. His physical decline, while not especially marked, is nonetheless evident. More frequently in recent years he has exhibited a wish to be on a broader stage—hence the widespread local publicity for his appearance and speech at the United Nations, when he took along his own media crew who interviewed him *ad nauseam* for Belarusian Television. To an increasing degree, the policies of official Minsk are merged with the personality of Lukashenka, with his fluctuating moods and idiosyncrasies. It is no longer credible to suggest that the president reflects the wishes of the Belarusian people; rather, he seeks to mold the people to his own, very limited, personality and perspectives. Such maneuvers are reflected in the obsequious tributes to Lukashenka in the media, the sale of his photograph in stores, and the appearance of Lukashenka icons in the villages.

In theory, the situation in Belarus has not changed significantly as a result of the 2006 election. But the election has weakened rather than strengthened the president. It exposed his fears and prejudices and alienated most of the younger generation, many of whom were exposed for the first time to the blatant repression of the Special Forces, the militia, and the KGB, and were detained and imprisoned on the flimsiest of pretexts. The election also highlighted Lukashenka's astonishing lack of vision for Belarus: After twelve years, it is difficult to point to any major policy initiatives, and the president's regular references to past Soviet glories inculcate only a limited nostalgia. Interestingly, after fifteen years of independence, and whatever its electoral proclivities, the Belarusian population is satisfied with its independence status, has no wish to be appended in any form to the Russian Federation, and is evenly split on the benefits of joining the EU.[36] Lukashenka has been successful in the accumulation of power and the removal or belittlement of real and alleged enemies. Yet he has not outlined any conception for the future. He merely reacts to events, such as the statements of Putin, the leaders of Gazprom or Lukoil, or the activities of the opposition and its international supporters. Ultimately (and ironically, given his political attitude), his departure may be hastened by the impatience of Russia toward the protracted debate on the structure of the Russia-Belarus Union and the need to continue what are in effect subsidies to bolster the Belarusian economy. Under such circumstances, a power-hungry dictator can at best "muddle through," while his fears, his neuroses, and even his paranoia continue to increase with each passing month.

Notes

1. The author expresses his thanks to Minsk residents Uladzimir Padhol and Liuba Pervushina for assistance with materials used in this chapter. He would also like to acknowledge the use of information provided at

two conferences in 2006, in Warsaw and Bratislava by Aleh Manaieu and Andrei Sannikau.

2. For an analysis of the 2001 campaign, see Uladzimir Padhol and David R. Marples, "The Dynamics of the 2001 Presidential Election," in *Postcommunist Belarus*, ed. Stephen White, Elena Korostoleva, and John Loewenhardt (Lanham, MD: Rowman and Littlefield, 2005), 79–96.

3. See, for example, the press release issued by the Belarusian Helsinki Committee on April 19, 2001, http://bhc.unibel.by/arhiv/2001/2001_apr.htm.

4. *Belarusy i rynok*, November 28, 2005. After the referendum of November 1996, parliament was reduced from 260 seats to 110. The parliamentary election of 2004, which coincided with another contrived referendum on whether or not the president should be allowed to serve for additional terms in office upon the expiry of his second term, was notable for the exclusion of numerous candidates on various grounds. In the current parliament, there are no opposition MPs and only one MP (Olha Abramova of Belarusian Yabloko) who can be described as independent.

5. http://www.charter97.org, October 2, 2005.

6. http://www.charter97.org, February 14, 2006.

7. *Belarusy i rynok*, October 31, 2005.

8. *Belarusy i rynok*, October 24, 2005.

9. http://www.belarusindependent.com/english/news3.html.

10. See, for example, BBC News, October 18, 2004: http://news.bbc.co.uk/2/hi/europe/3736312.stm.

11. The results of the poll were reported in *Narodnaia volia*, October 26, 2005.

12. http://www.pravda.ru, November 17, 2005.

13. *Nasha niva*, December 23, 2005.

14. Igor Melnikov, "76% izbirateley gotovy progolosovat za Aleksandra Lukashenko," *Sovetskaia Belorussiia*, February 18, 2006.

15. See *Sovetskaia Belorussiia*, December 29, 2005, and January 4, 2006; and *Narodnaia volia*, December 29, 2005.

16. Vladimir Gurin, "Samolikvidatsiia 'oranzhevogo virusa,'" *Sovetskaia Belorussiia*, January 18, 2006.

17. *Belarusy i rynok*, January 9, 2006.

18. *Narodnaia volia*, January 16, 2006.

19. *Belarusy i rynok*, January 16, 2006.

20. *Narodnaia volia*, February 13–14, 2006; http://www.charter97.org, February 15, 2006.

21. *Itar-TASS*, February 17, 2006.

22. *RIA Novosti*, December 26, 2005.

23. *Narodnaia volia*, December 18, 2005.

24. Ibid., January 4, 2006.

25. http://bsdp.org.

26. *Narodnaia volia* prepared to issue a special edition of 250,000 copies containing photographs of the assault on Kazulin. But the issue, which was printed in Smolensk, was confiscated by the authorities once trucks transporting it crossed the border from Russia.
27. *Narodnaia volia*, March 4–5, 2006.
28. Belarusian Television, March 15–16, 2006.
29. Dmitriy Kryat, "Narod izbirat bez podskazki," *Sovetskaia Belorussiia*, March 21, 2006.
30. *Narodnaia volia*, May 3, 2006.
31. From *Sovetskaia Belorussiia*, March 24, 2006.
32. See Jan Maksymiuk, "Pollster Questions Size of Lukashenka's Victory," *Radio Free Europe/Radio Liberty*, April 21, 2006.
33. *Kommersant*, May 12, 2006.
34. Belorusskoe Telegrafnoe Agenstvo, November 27–28, 2006, December 1 and 4, 2006.
35. Associated Press, May 19, 2006.
36. On May 15, 2006, *Radio Svaboda* (Minsk) cited the results of a recent survey by NISEPI, which revealed that respondents were divided evenly on whether they considered themselves Soviet people or European people. Only 20 percent wish to restore the Soviet Union, with 63 percent opposed. Only 14.8 percent would wish to see Belarus incorporated into Russia as a province. If there were a referendum on whether Belarus should join the EU, 32.4 percent would vote in favor, 33.8 percent would be opposed, and 30 percent are undecided.

10

EU-Russia Relations and the Repercussions on the "In-Betweens"

Stefan Gänzle

Introduction

After the end of the Cold War in 1989, the European Union (EU) was compelled to redefine its relationship with the countries of the former Eastern bloc. It was only in 1988 that the European Community (EC)[1] agreed upon granting financial assistance to support Poland and Hungary on their difficult paths toward market economies and democracy. Concomitantly, the EU was engaged in negotiations with the Soviet Union about a new Trade and Cooperation Agreement, which entered into force in April 1990. While at that time the EC considered a unified approach toward Eastern Europe, the dismantlement of the Soviet Union provided yet another incentive for the Central and Eastern European countries (CEECs) to realign themselves with Western institutions. Hence, these states[2] of the former Soviet sphere of influence started demanding a membership perspective within both the EC/EU and the North Atlantic Treaty Organization (NATO). Cooperation with and integration into the EU and NATO subsequently became the central foreign policy objectives of most of the CEECs. As a consequence, the "integration divide" between the "West" and the "East" of Eastern Europe came into existence. The scope of political and economic cooperation between the West and the New Independent States (NIS) of the former Soviet Union (excluding the Baltic States) remained much more modest; in particular, it did not investigate any kind of future affiliation or membership in the EC or EU and NATO. The EU's enlargement and the Common Foreign and Security Policy had been fleshed out simultaneously at the beginning of the 1990s; whereas the CEECs aspiring for EU accession were dealt with from the more domestic-policy perspective of enlargement, the NIS were much more targeted as objects of the EU's emerging foreign policy. Thus, the EU's "dual track approach"[3] in dealing with Eastern Europe was gradually implemented. The twofold approach *vis-à-vis* Eastern Europe not only entailed a different scope in terms of objectives and methods but also put different EC actors on the stage. As much as the enlargement process was "Commission-driven," the EU's approach toward the NIS remained more in the domain of the Council and Common Foreign and Security Policy (CFSP) institutions.

Subsequently, the EU's relations with the NIS evolved on the basis of Partnership and Cooperation Agreements (PCAs) signed with Russia, Ukraine, Belarus, Moldova, and other NIS in the mid-1990s. Ultimately, the PCAs entered into force in 1997–98. As ratification of the non-Community aspects of these mixed agreements took much longer than anticipated, those parts of the agreements that covered commerce and trade and fell under Community competence entered into force immediately. Thus, one may argue that until the end of the 1990s, the European Commission had a prominent role in shaping the EU's stance toward the whole of Europe. At the same time, the EU concluded Europe Agreements with all CEECs aspiring to future membership. Although both sets of (mixed) agreements[4] were similar in terms of scope and institutional set-up, the PCAs did not entail a membership perspective.[5] At best, they provided evolutionary clauses that recognized the need to further improve the agreements and ultimately provide for a free market in the long term. While the membership carrot would become the EU's main foreign policy instrument geared toward the candidate countries, the looming of a free trade area should account for dynamism in bilateral relations between the EU and the Western NIS.

Throughout this process, Russia has remained a pace- and frame-setter for the EU's overall relations with the NIS. Even in the case of the EU's eastern enlargement toward the Baltic States, some member states were willing to account for geopolitical concerns leveled by various Russian governments. Due to Russia's role in the process of German reunification, as well as the legacies of "Eastern policy," both the Kohl and Schröder governments tended to be rather permissive in this respect. Moreover, in 1997, Chancellor Helmut Kohl, French President Jacques Chirac, and Russian President Boris Yeltsin decided to establish regular tripartite meetings of heads of state and government (later enlarged to encompass Spain[6]). The mere fact that some member states claimed to pursue their own foreign policy triggered three major consequences: First, Russia was singled out as the primary partner of the EU's Eastern policy in the context of enlargement. Second, it became much more difficult to conduct a common foreign policy *vis-à-vis* Eastern Europe given the solo efforts of individual countries. Third, the EU subscribed to the idea that the Commonwealth of Independent States (CIS) would form a regional unit—with Russia as its regional center, destined to lead this alliance both economically and politically. It was only in the second half of the 1990s that the EU acknowledged "the initial expectation that the CIS states would remain a cohesive group"[7] to be wrong.

Since then, bilateral approaches toward those countries have prevailed. Clearly, Russia remained "special," as it was prioritized as the EU's strategic partner (similar to the United States, India, China, Japan, and Canada[8]) in terms of overall political and economic importance to the EU. The "in-betweens"—Belarus, Ukraine, and Moldova—were increasingly perceived as individual countries of a highly sensitive geopolitical subregion in Europe. As Belarus had developed into Europe's last dictatorship, and was put under EU sanctions, there was no immediate need to flesh out a long-term plan for relations with Minsk.[9] Any form of closer association was not likely to be pursued in the aftermath of the November 1996 referendum, which had substantially limited the powers of the Belarusian Parliament and halted the ratification of the PCA between the EU and Belarus. At the same time, Ukraine and—to some extent—Moldova sought to keep the option for future EU membership open.

The dialogue with the in-betweens and Russia has been framed by focusing on soft security issues, such as secure borders, organized crime, and environmental degradation. While the official discourse has emphasized the need for avoiding the emergence of new dividing lines in Europe, the EU has also been very much concerned about the lack of progress in terms of transition of Russia and the in-betweens to market economy, democracy, and rule of law. Thus, the relationship developed paternalistic characteristics, in particular with regards to Ukraine. Overall, developments not only left the NIS countries frustrated, but also exhausted the EU, which was much less inclined to financially support those countries in light of the enlargements. Consequently, the Western NIS for a long time was not very high up on the EU's foreign policy agenda. This became evident upon comparison of the amount of financial support set aside for the Balkan and Ukraine, Belarus, and Moldova. Hence, "EU policy towards the NIS was, and remains, a work in progress"[10] and today still needs to bridge the "Capability-Expectations-Gap"[11] that had become a main characteristic of the relationship between the NIS and the EU by the end of the last decade.

This chapter examines the development of the EU's policy toward Russia and the three in-betweens: Ukraine, Belarus, and Moldova. It briefly reviews the general framework enshrined in the EU's policy, focusing on the PCAs and the European Neighbourhood Policy (ENP) Action Plans concluded between the EU and individual countries. Then it analyzes the bilateral approach toward each of these countries. The conclusion considers best practices and lessons learned, as well as future challenges in the EU's relations with the new Eastern Europe.

The General Framework of the EU's Eastern Policy in Transition: From Financial Assistance to the European Neighbourhood Policy

After the disintegration of the USSR, the EU ultimately opted for a dual-track approach toward Eastern Europe. The countries outside the NIS were covered by Europe Agreements or Stabilization and Association Agreements enshrining the prospect of future membership, whereas the NIS countries themselves were offered PCAs devoid of any membership promise. The PCA subsequently replaced the 1989 Trade and Cooperation Agreement concluded between the EC and the USSR. Ukraine was the first NIS country to sign a PCA in 1994, followed by Russia and Moldova. In 1995, Belarus signed its PCA, which was later suspended due to various human rights infringements committed by the Aliaksandr Lukashenka regime. PCAs with all other NIS countries were concluded from 1996 onwards. The PCAs were negotiated on a bilateral basis, for an initial period of 10 years. Despite minor variations in terms of scope and objectives, the basic objectives of the PCAs were similar.

First, the PCAs established a new trade regime between the EU and the NIS countries by providing the latter with the EU's Generalized System of Preferences, similar to the most-favored nation status; for various sensitive trade sectors (such as steel and textiles), however, special sectoral arrangements were concluded. Second, the PCAs institutionalized the political dialogue between the EU and each NIS. The PCAs laid the legal groundwork for establishing the Cooperation Councils, the Cooperation Committees, and the Parliamentary Cooperation Committee, institutions that reflect the EU's general approach in terms of dealing with "third countries" in any associational agreement. The committees, serving as the work horses of the cooperative relationship, are composed of senior civil servants and chaired alternately by the European Commission and a representative from the NIS. Furthermore, several specialized subcommittees at the expert level support the work of the Cooperation Committee. Third, the PCAs introduced the principle of conditionality,[12] which, since the 1980s, has been an integral part of all development and associational agreements concluded between the EU and third countries, and which makes further support and technical assistance conditional upon compliance with the rules set out in the agreements. An additional "carrot" was added by introducing an evolutionary clause proposing that the midterm objective of bilateral relations would be the establishment of a free market area. In a nutshell, the "PCA offered neither prospective membership, nor any sort of association with the EU."[13]

Trade

The process of EU enlargement has set the stage for a significant diversion of trade in Central and Eastern Europe. After enlargement, the EU is not only the most important trading partner for the CEECs, but also for the Western NIS. From the EU's perspective, as will be demonstrated, the trade relationship between all partners is extremely unbalanced. Furthermore, NIS exports to the EU are dominated by textiles, agricultural products, and—most importantly—energy products. This reflects the low competitiveness and output decline of the NIS countries' manufacturing industry over the past decade, leading to the predominance of primary-production, work-intensive goods in export trade to the EU.

In 2006, Russia was the EU's third largest trading partner (after the United States and China). The EU's share of Russia's total external trade has risen from approximately one-third to more than one-half. EU-Russia trade more than quadrupled between 1995 and 2005: in 1995, EU trade with Russia amounted to €38 billion (the EU had a trade deficit of €6 billion); in 2005, EU trade amounted to €166 billion (the EU had a trade deficit of approximately €53 billion). In terms of trade patterns, Russia's trade continues to be biased toward raw materials over manufactured goods. In 2003, energy and fuels accounted for approximately 65 percent of Russian exports to the EU.[14]

Since the 2004 enlargement, the EU has become Ukraine's largest trading partner, accounting for about 35 percent of Ukraine's total trade. In contrast, Ukraine represents less than 1 percent of the EU's imports. Ukraine is an important transit country for energy products from Russia and the Caucasus. Without a PCA or interim agreement in force, bilateral trade between the EU and Belarus is still covered by the provisions of the Generalized System of Preferences (GSP) enshrined in the 1989 agreement between the EC and the former Soviet Union. The GSP is one of the EU's key instruments to respond to the needs of developing countries and to promote sustainable development and good governance. In December 2003, the EU decided to initiate an investigation into violation of freedom of association in Belarus as the first step toward a possible temporary withdrawal of the GSP from Belarus. Following a 2005 Commission report presented to the GSP committee regarding the alleged violations, the EU member states decided on December 21, 2006, to adopt the decision on the temporary withdrawal of GSP preferences from the Republic of Belarus. However, the decision was delayed six months after its adoption by the council. Finally, as of June 21, 2007, the EU has temporarily withdrawn Belarus from its Generalized System of Preferences.[15] While the EU is still Belarus' main trading partner outside the NIS, trade flows with Belarus are marginal for the EU, accounting for 0.1 percent of EU trade. The structure of bilateral trade has remained unchanged compared to previous years, with Belarusian exports consisting mainly of agricultural products (€172 million) and textiles and clothing (€112 million), and EU exports consisting primarily of machinery and transport material (€673 million). In addition, the bulk of Belarusian exports to the EU is composed of Russian energy resale, which is not covered by the GSP.[16] In 2004, the EU was Moldova's largest trading partner, with Russia and Ukraine second and third, representing 22 percent and 17 percent (respectively) of Moldova's overall trade. Agricultural products, textiles, and clothing were the major EU imports from Moldova, making the country the EU's 95th trading partner in 2003 in rank. When compared to that of neighboring countries, Moldova's transition process proved to be extremely difficult for both political and economic reasons. The *de facto* secession of

Transnistria left the bulk of Moldovan industry outside Chișinău's control. Growth rates rose only modestly after 2000, leaving the country's per capita real GDP the lowest in Europe. Yet trade between Moldova and the EU increased significantly during 2004, with EU exports to Moldova up 14 percent and EU imports from Moldova up 29 percent.[17]

European Union Technical and Financial Assistance

The EU is the world's largest provider of technical and financial assistance to the NIS. All NIS countries have been recipients of EU assistance under the TACIS (Technical Assistance to the Commonwealth of Independent States) program throughout the past 15 years. The program's main aims are to promote the transition to market economy and to support democracy, the rule of law, and good governance. From 1991 to 2005, more than €2.6 billion was allocated to Russia, approximately €220 million to Belarus, and more than €2 billion to Ukraine; from 1991 to 2003, Moldova received more than €250 million in EU assistance.[18]

The Common Foreign and Security Policy

In 1999, the EU issued Common Strategies on Russia and Ukraine aimed at developing a more comprehensive approach to the EU's relationship with key countries in Eastern Europe. Furthermore, the Common Strategies were intended to offer some sort of framework orientation for the individual member states in order to better coordinate the members' foreign policies toward Ukraine and Russia. It was the German government, under the newly elected Gerhard Schröder, that initiated the common strategy toward the East—a new policy instrument created in the Treaty of Amsterdam—in efforts to forge a more common EU foreign policy. Thus, the German presidency of the EU was instrumental in devising the Common Strategy of the EU on Russia, launched in June 1999; this initiative was followed by the EU's Common Strategy on Ukraine later the same year. In 2001, the High Representative of the CFSP, Javier Solana, criticized the Common Strategies as being devoid of detailed proposals, and hence useless foreign policy tools.[19] In December 2001, the EU put together a Country Strategy Paper on Russia, specifying the objectives and priorities in EU policy for 2002–6. When the EU was working on similar policy documents *vis-à-vis* Ukraine, Belarus, and Moldova, it became clear that the strategy papers would eventually become the instruments of the emerging ENP.

Against this backdrop, Javier Solana presented the European Security Strategy in December 2003, declaring that "building security in our neighbourhood"[20] is one of the three strategic objectives[21] of the EU, and singling out Russia as one of the most important countries. With regards to Eastern Europe, the strategy notes, "It is not in our interest that enlargement should create new dividing lines in Europe. We need to extend the benefits of economic and political cooperation to our neighbours in the East while tackling political problems there. We should now take a stronger and more active interest in the problems of the Southern Caucasus, which will in due course also be a neighbouring region."[22]

The European Neighbourhood Policy—A New Approach?

The first steps toward the making of the ENP were taken in January 2002, when British Foreign Minister Jack Straw suggested offering Ukraine, Belarus, and Moldova "clear and practical incentives" for proceeding with political and economic reform.[23] Furthermore, his proposal included granting these countries the status of "special neighbor," based on a firm commitment to democratic governance and free market principles. In December 2002, the European Council of Copenhagen approved the idea in principle: "The enlargement will strengthen relations with Russia. The EU also wishes to enhance its relations with Ukraine, Moldova, Belarus and the southern Mediterranean countries, based on a long-term approach promoting democratic and economic reforms, sustainable developments and trade and is developing new initiatives for this purpose."[24]

At a conference in December 2002, Commission President Romano Prodi declared: "We have to be prepared to offer more than partnership and less than membership, without precluding the latter."[25] The ENP offers its partner countries the opportunity to take part in a number of EU activities through greater political, security, economic, and cultural cooperation, albeit below the membership level. Prodi emphasized that the "aim is to extend to this neighbouring region a set of principles, values and standards which define the very essence of the European Union."[26] In March 2003, the European Commission explained that the EU's neighbors should be offered the prospect of "a stake in the EU's Internal Market."[27]

In March 2003, the European Commission released the document titled "Wider Europe—Neighbourhood: A New Framework for Relations with Our Eastern and Southern Neighbours." At that time, following pressure from the southern member states, it became clear that this proximity policy had to encompass the non-EU countries of the Mediterranean rim as well as the Western NIS, thus establishing a "ring of friends,"[28] as Prodi put it. Furthermore, the Commission was still confident in including Russia in this new policy.

In the meantime, however, Russia had declared that it did not wish to be included in this policy, instead opting for a strategic partnership approach in its own right. The Russian decision needs to be interpreted in light of a rather general foreign policy change undertaken by Moscow in the wake of EU enlargement. Russia is increasingly uneasy with the status of its relationship with the EU. The "(self-)exclusion of Russia"[29] in terms of the ENP membership may, indeed, have helped the Central Caucasian countries accept entering the orbit of the ENP. But it has given the neighborhood approach an additional enlargement twist,[30] as practically all countries of the new East are likely to consider future EU membership. Thus, it is probably the fate of the ENP not to fully realize its potential as a policy stabilizing the Western NIS below the EU membership line evoked by the European Constitution.[31]

In May 2004, the European Commission published a strategy paper on the ENP. In this document, the Commission laid down the principles and objectives that would govern all future ENP partnerships. The ENP aims at "sharing the benefits of the EU's enlargement in 2004 with neighbouring countries in strengthening stability, security and well-being for all concerned" in order to "prevent the emergence of new dividing lines in Europe."[32] The ENP aims to address these concerns and, ultimately, to contribute toward greater security. One month after the Commission decided to make this initiative a top priority, the General Affairs Council decided to extend the ENP to the Caucasian republics of Georgia, Azerbaijan, and Armenia. This decision clearly adds to the political weight of the initiative.

The ENP builds upon several key principles. First, the ENP subscribes to a conservative institutional approach as it is built into the existing framework of the EU's bilateral relations with a respective ENP partner country. Thus, the EU avoids any duplication of existing institutional structures. Ultimately, this is also a commitment to a strict and differentiated bilateralism in terms of interinstitutional relations, despite the fact that the ENP also encourages its neighboring countries to engage in subregional cooperation.[33] Second, the Commission has declared that the ENP constitutes a case for "joint ownership" of the institutions and of the process in general—albeit one "based on the awareness of shared values and common interests."[34] Although the EU does not argue explicitly that the normative model is to be taken from the EU itself, it is clear that ENP countries are expected to move toward the normative model of the EU. Third, the ENP establishes a procedure for monitoring the success as well as the shortcomings of agreements made under the ENP.

Following this comprehensive step toward achieving the overarching policy goals of ENP, the European Commission refined the existing country strategies that were based either on TACIS or on MEDA (the assistance program for Mediterranean countries) regulations. Thus, the ENP is being reshaped in order to be compatible with the existing framework of relationships between the EU and its neighbors. Each country strategy paper subsequently supplies a strategic framework for the period of 2002–6. Furthermore, these strategy papers set out EU cooperation goals and policy responses, as well as those areas for cooperation defined as key priorities. In addition, the country strategy papers provide an assessment of the partner countries' policy agendas and political and socioeconomic situations.

While the primary objective of the strategy papers was to define the scope and modes of cooperation, underpinned by financial aspects, the European Commission drew up concomitantly a first set of country reports. Country reports were published in May 2004 on the first seven of the ENP countries that have association or partnership agreements with the EU in force; an additional five country reports were published in March 2005 on the next countries to be included in the policy (Georgia, Azerbaijan, and Armenia) and those countries whose agreements had already come into force (Egypt and Lebanon). The reports provide an outline of the political, economic, and social situation of the ENP countries. They will provide the space for future assessments on the achievements of each of the EU's partner countries. The European Commission released its first assessment in 2006; another round of country reports followed in 2007.

The next stage in the development of the ENP saw the conclusion of the Action Plans with each of the countries.[35] Action Plans were negotiated with each country individually. The Action Plans lay out a number of core priorities at the beginning of each policy document; subsequently, a wide range of other areas is emphasized. They jointly define an agenda of political and economic reform by means of short- and medium-term (between three and five years) priorities. They cover political dialogue and reform, economic and social cooperation and development, trade-related issues, market and regulatory reform, cooperation in justice and home affairs, and cooperation in particular sectors (such as transport, energy, information society, environment, research and development), as well as a human dimension (people-to-people contacts, civil society, education, public health). The incentives that the EU offers in return for progress on relevant reforms are greater integration into European programs and networks, increased assistance, and enhanced market access.

Until the end of 2006, EU assistance to countries covered by the ENP was channeled through various geographical programs.[36] For the budgetary period of 2007–13, approximately €12 billion in EC funding will be available to support these partner countries, an increase of 32 percent in real terms. This is conceived as a part of the reform of EU assistance instruments, primarily the MEDA and TACIS programs, which will be replaced by a simplified structure and a single instrument—the European Neighbourhood and Partnership Instrument (ENPI). This will be a much more flexible and "policy-driven instrument,"[37] designed to target sustainable development and approximation to EU policies and standards and to support the priorities outlined in the ENP Action Plans. One of the most innovative features of the ENPI is that it entails "a radical simplification to the current situation where cross-border cooperation at the external EU border is hampered by interfaces between internal and external funding instruments operating through different rules."[38] This means that cross-border cooperation with non-EU countries will be eased considerably along the EU's external land and sea borders in the east and in the south, putting partners under the same funding regime and instruments.

The ENPI also envisages extending to partner countries forms of technical assistance that had previously been used in the process of the CEECs' *rapprochement* toward the EU, such as Technical Assistance and Information Exchange (TAIEX), long-term twinning arrangements with EU member states' administrations (national, regional, and local), as well as participation in EC programs and agencies. Moreover, the European Commission expects that the priorities identified in the Action Plans, which are agreed to by the authorities of each country, will have a lighthouse effect in terms of guiding the programming development of assistance programs from other donor countries and institutions.

The past 15 years have revealed a number of deficiencies of the EU's policy toward the NIS. First, the EU assumed Russia would become the other regionalizing center of Europe, building on the establishment of a fully fledged CIS. Consequently, Russia enjoyed a privileged relationship as a *primus inter pares* with regards to the other NIS. Second, the PCAs as such did not serve as blueprints for managing domestic transformation. Throughout the process of EU enlargement in the 1990s, it became obvious that the prospect of joining the EU would provide the decisive incentive for CEECs to unilaterally comply with the *acquis communautaire.* Without this perspective, the PCAs have clearly failed to set the tone for those countries to accelerate their domestic reform processes. Moreover, the TACIS program fell short of unfolding sustainable systemic change in the countries concerned. At the domestic level, many NIS remained uncertain about their foreign policy preference for various reasons. Third, the EU itself exhibited many difficulties when it came to dealing with the NIS, given its cumbersome internal decision- and policymaking structures.

Against this particular backdrop, the instruments of EU conditionality have generally proved to be insufficient. The linkage among democratization, human rights, and financial support from the EU has been demonstrated to be weak. Furthermore, the energy-rich NIS, such as Russia, are increasingly independent from EU-spurred assistance programs. As a result, starting with the introduction of the ENP, the EU is increasingly ready to revise the content and scope of its policies and to develop more country-focused approaches.

EU-Russia Relations

The EU's immediate response to the dismantlement of the Soviet Union was to set up a financial assistance program (TACIS) in 1991–92 in order to support the NIS, in particular Russia, in their transition toward democracy and market economies. In general, approximately 60 percent of all foreign aid to Russia comes from European countries. Since 1991, over €2.5 billion has been channeled to Russia via TACIS, making it the main target of this program. It is worth mentioning, however, that despite being an absolute leader with regards to overall TACIS funding received, the Russian Federation is far behind the in-between states in terms of per-capita amounts. While TACIS has been aiming at the promotion of privatization and emergence of a market economy in conjunction with support for democracy (the so-called Washington consensus), its post-1991 reforms put more emphasis on the principle of rule of law, and most recently the support of civil society in Russia. In addition,

TACIS is increasingly being used to support the implementation of the PCA that Russia and the EU signed in 1994, which came into force in December 1997.

Although the EU might have hoped for more, this agreement, covering matters that fall both within the EC's purview and within the jurisdiction of its member states, is essentially not a political agreement, but rather an economic and commercial one. Like all EU agreements with third countries since 1992, this PCA contains a suspension clause that may be invoked if a partner does not comply with the agreed-upon rules. After long debate, a protocol extending the provisions to cover the ten new member states was signed in April 2004. The PCA grants the GSP and suppresses most qualitative restrictions (with the significant exceptions of steel, which accounts for 5 percent of Russian exports to the EU, and nuclear materials), aims to contribute to the creation of a free trade area (1998), and supports Russia's accession to WTO. Central issues of the EU-Russia partnership are transport, energy, environment, education, science, technology, and the fight against organized crime.

The Common Strategy on Russia, which was adopted by the Cologne European Council in June 1999, remained in force until 2004. It was the first of its kind since the creation of this instrument by the Treaty of Amsterdam, representing a further attempt in the realm of EU foreign policy to establish greater consistency and coordination between the EU's member states in terms of foreign policy. Whereas the PCA attached greater importance to economic relations, the strategy placed more emphasis on political action concerning consolidation of democracy, respect for the rule of law and public institutions, stability and security in Europe (management of crises and regional conflicts on Europe's doorstep in particular), and challenges common to the whole continent (environmental problems, organized crime). The main instruments for implementing strategy goals remain the PCA, the member states' assistance programs, and the TACIS program.

Semiannual summits of heads of state and governments between the EU and Russia provide opportunities for strengthening relations and determining the direction to be given to the PCA. At the St. Petersburg summit in May 2003, it was decided to strengthen the Cooperation Council by transforming it into the Permanent Partnership Council (PPC). The first meeting of the PPC took place on April 27, 2004, with meetings to be held more frequently and in different council formations. The EU and Russia also used the occasion of the summit to launch a more strategic vision for relations, with the aim of creating a series of common spaces—for external security; freedom, security, and justice; economic cooperation; and science and education, including culture.

The EU-Russia summit on May 10, 2005, in Moscow adopted a comprehensive package of road maps for the development of the four common spaces. These road maps, which set out shared objectives for EU-Russia relations, as well as the actions necessary to make these objectives a reality, determine the agenda for cooperation between the EU and Russia for the medium term. Throughout the negotiations, Russia has focused primarily on the economic and internal security side of the agreement.[39] While the PCA set out to ultimately achieve a free trade area between the EU and Russia,[40] a first reference to a "Common European Economic and Social Space" was made in the EU's Common Strategy on Russia in 1999; the St. Petersburg EU-Russia summit in 2002 renamed it the Common Economic Space (CES). Although the PCA clearly asked Russia to ensure "the approximation of legislation"[41] along the lines of the EC's *acquis communautaire* in order to strengthen economic links, the agreements that followed were less explicit in terms of Russia's commitment to adapt unilaterally to the EU's accumulated rules.

With a backdrop of sluggish World Trade Organization (WTO) talks, Russia and the EU decided in 2001 to establish a high-level working group to study the potential scope of a CES. Yet negotiations within the expert group were difficult. When the high-level group reported to the EU-Russia summit in Rome in November 2003, it had still not come up with detailed suggestions. Originally, the intention was to present a concrete CES Action Plan to the summit meeting in The Hague in November 2004; however, in light of the events in Ukraine, the EU and Russia were unable to converge their expectations with regard to the creation of a CES. It was not until the Moscow EU-Russia summit that the high-level group was able to present an outline of the CES as the most prominent part of the road maps toward common spaces. This was primarily the result of two factors: First, in the aftermath of the disputes over the Kaliningrad transit, relations between the EU and Russia had cooled considerably; second, Russia does not have enough skilled trade specialists to negotiate a WTO deal and the CES at the same time.[42]

Within the road maps package, the CES is the most detailed element. Interestingly, it "proceeds through the standard agenda of all EU negotiations with its accession candidates and other neighbours and association partners"[43]; hence, it covers industrial standards, competition, and public procurement policies; investment climate and enterprise policy; cross-border cooperation; financial services, accounting standards, and statistics; agriculture and forestry; customs procedures; transport and telecommunications networks; and energy, space, and the environment. The CES encourages cooperation and dialogue between both partners in almost every policy area. In terms of substance, there are two remarkable features; first, the long-term objective of establishing a free trade area is not mentioned once. This might be attributed to the fact that the creation of a free trade area, as spelled out in the PCA, does not properly serve Russian interests since Russian exports to the EU are mainly tariff-free goods such as gas and oil. Some economists are convinced that it would only be beneficial for Russia to implement smaller parts of the *acquis communautaire*—notably in the area of the "four freedoms" in terms of a free movement of goods, services, capital, and persons (which is why Russia shows such a profound interest in achieving visa-free travel with the EU and its member states). In contrast, higher standards in environmental and social issues may hamper Russia's socio-economic development. Although Russia has been assured that it is not necessary to take over the whole *acquis*, it is clear that especially the new member states will not allow Russia any sort of cherry-picking of those parts of the *acquis* she likes. The new EU members are very much aware of the difficulties in adopting and implementing the *acquis*; furthermore, they are, for historical and political reasons, less willing to foster a privileged role for Russia in the context of European integration. Second, the road map for the CES does not explicitly call on Russia to bring its legislation in line with EU norms and standards; instead, the language of the agreement emphasizes the need for two-sided convergence and harmonization of both Russia and the EU without indicating who is converging or harmonizing with whom. Russia's insistence on the principle of equal partnership has made it almost impossible to refer to EU legislation and the *acquis communautaire*.

Ultimately, this raises the question of which cooperative blueprint or model of integration and adaptation is most valid in EU-Russia relations. A fully-fledged CES would require Russia to adopt large parts of the EU's *acquis*, similar to the states that are part of the European Economic Area (EEA). While countries such as Norway and Iceland are obliged to implement the *acquis* in all relevant areas, the EEA gives full access to the single market and denies EEA members a stake in the law-making process. In contrast, Russia favors a somewhat more balanced approach to the approximation of legislation.

Because of the embryonic state of the EU's Common Foreign and Security Policy (CFSP), Russia did not regard the EU as a credible actor in the field of foreign and security policy.[44] This attitude changed when France and the UK decided in 1998 at a bilateral summit in St. Malo to add a defense component to CFSP, titled the European Security and Defence Policy (ESDP). With the backdrop of NATO's campaign in Kosovo in 1999, Russia started to reassess its European security policy, shifting its emphasis on cooperation with the EU in the framework of ESDP.[45] Thus, Russia hoped to further reduce the role of NATO and the United States in Europe. With this move, EU-Russia cooperation under the umbrella of ESDP gained an anti-American flavor. During its EU presidency in 2000, France launched a security dialogue with Russia. Since then, and especially after the terrorist attacks of September 11, 2001, the number of meetings and agreements in the political and security area has increased substantially. A Russian officer cooperates closely with the EU military staff in Brussels; the head of the Russian mission to the EU meets regularly with representatives from the EU's Political and Security Committee. Furthermore, Russian and EU experts exchange views on topics such as antiterrorism, the proliferation of weapons of mass destruction (WMD), and so on. In early 2003, Russia sent a small number of officers to the first EU police mission in Bosnia and Herzegovina.

Russia has clearly sought to exert influence on the development of ESDP. Thus, Russia stresses the need for the EU to operate only within a UN mandate. Furthermore, Russia attempted to achieve a stake in the decision-making process of ESDP. While the EU is ready to accept Russian involvement in military planning and in operations, it does not want to blur the institutional boundary in a way that would allow Russia to shape ESDP. In particular, the EU has resisted Russia's suggestion to create a distinct EU-Russia Council similar to the NATO-Russia Council.

Since 2002, because of the lack of progress in ESDP in general, and Russia's limited role as an equally footed partner[46] of ESDP in particular, Russia has increasingly lost enthusiasm for ESDP. Furthermore, divergences amongst EU members on the war in Iraq, as well as the controversial plan to deploy U.S. anti-ballistic missile defense components in Eastern Europe, clearly demonstrated the structural impediments of ESDP. The road map for a Common Space of External Security does not address the issue of ESDP. Instead, it outlines an agenda for cooperation over terrorism, crisis management, nonproliferation, and civil protection. The road map is not very detailed as far as it concerns "the settlement of regional conflicts, *inter alia* in regions adjacent to EU and Russian borders."[47] In this respect, Russia was not ready to engage in a more concrete plan for common action in Russia's troubled neighborhoods, such as the Caucasus.

Contrary to the field of external security, the Common Space of Freedom, Security and Justice (CSFSJ) exhibits a wide range of common commitments made concerning combating international crime, drug and human trafficking, and terrorism. Measures for concrete cooperation involve various Russian security agencies and a number of EU bodies, such as Europol and Eurojust.

It is striking that the CSFSJ contains a preamble referring to the relevance of common interests and equal partnership, as well as common values such as democracy, rule of law, and the respect of human rights. This mirrors to some extent the provision concerning these core values as they are outlined in the Action Plans launched under the umbrella of the ENP. It can be assumed that the EU is in a position to get this reference only because Russia, in general, is a *demandeur* under the provisions governing the second common space, as it was trying to get visa-free travel for its citizens. This led to difficult negotiations, as the EU was demanding, for its part, a strengthening of Russian border control, including the proper demarcation of its external borders as well as the conclusion of readmission agreements. The latter presents huge difficulties for Russia, as its eastern borders are lengthy and porous. The Russian government, however, accepted the link between readmission and further talks on visa-free travel. Thus, President Putin declared at a press conference following the EU-Russia summit in Moscow: "It is Russia's responsibility to settle the readmission issue with its neighbours, and resolve our own problems in this area. It is our responsibility to properly equip our borders and to reach agreements with our closest neighbours on these questions."[48] Finally, two agreements were signed on visa facilitation and readmission at the EU-Russia summit in Sotchi, on May 25, 2006.[49] This is just one more recent example of the *quid pro quo* approach in EU-Russia relations. Another trend should be noted as well: Both the EU and Russia rely increasingly on sectoral approaches to issues of common interest, such as energy, for example.

Today, the EU-25 imports 30 percent of its oil and 50 percent of its gas from Russia, and is thus the final destination for two-thirds of Russia's oil and gas exports. Aware of its own limited energy resources, the EU anticipates a shift of consumption toward gas, and thus fosters its reliance on Russian gas supplies. Consequently, Russia is likely to play a vital role in the future of the EU's energy policy. Hence, the EU-Russia energy dialogue serves as an institutional clearinghouse, focused on the "resolution of problems."[50] In this respect, the Commissioners for External Relations and Trade, Patten and Lamy, have suggested using the dialogue as a "pioneer for wider relations."[51] Briefly put, the main purpose of the energy dialogue was to establish and to maintain durable links of a particular aspect in EU-Russia relations. Ultimately, in terms of mutual perceptions, the energy dialogue should contribute to the conversion of mutual dependency to interdependence.

The impulse for an energy dialogue was driven by Russian president Putin, French president Chirac, and head of the European Commission Prodi during the EU-Russia summit of October 2000. After the EU's Common Strategy had called for "enabling Russia to integrate into a common economic and social space in Europe"[52] the year before, the presidents of Russia, France, and the European Commission wanted to set a new dynamic in EU-Russia relations. Hence, the energy dialogue was to "provide an opportunity to address all questions of common interest relating to the sector, including the introduction of cooperation on energy saving, rationalization of production and transport infrastructures, European investment possibilities, and relations between producer and consumer countries."[53] Although the energy dialogue was put under the umbrella of the PCA, the energy partnership soon revealed some distinct features. Involving regular meetings of experts, as well as high-level political discussions during the EU-Russia summits, the energy dialogue was highly personalized from the outset. Both Putin and Prodi promoted career bureaucrats as sole interlocutors to preside over the energy dialogue: Vice Prime Minister Khristenko and the Director-General of DG Energy and Transport, Lamoureux, respectively. Thus, the institutional format converts the dialogue into a "sui generis bilateral initiative,"[54] focusing on issues of common interest.

The progress that both partners have (not) made is regularly monitored by so-called "progress reports." The name clearly mirrors the enlargement jargon of the EU, though the reports are drafted and presented jointly by the administrative heads of the energy dialogue. From the outset of the energy dialogue, industrial representatives were invited to take part in bilateral thematic groups on energy strategies, technology transfer, investments, environmental questions, and energy efficiency. These groups, composed of Russian and EU experts from the private and public sector, examined areas of common interest and recommended priorities for the dialogue. Furthermore, the EU-Russia industrialists' round table created a pilot group on energy in 2003, composed of senior representatives of major European and Russian companies.

Progress since 2000 has been mixed. There have been notable successes, such as the establishment of a joint Energy Technology Centre in Moscow in November 2002, discussions on an investment guarantee scheme funded by the EU, and the launch of several pilot projects for energy-saving measures. Yet, as Barysch observes, the EU and Russia remain divided on a number of central issues, such as pipelines, gas supply contracts, the restructuring of the electricity sector, and nuclear fuel supply.[55] The EU's acceptance in May 2004 of Gazprom's monopoly on gas pipelines proved to be a watershed. While EU countries have been committing themselves to further liberalize their energy markets for industrial and household users, the Russian supplier is allowed to sell gas to various EU countries at different prices. It is clear that such an arrangement is not favorable to the development of an EU-wide gas market. Most importantly, the energy dialogue has yet to decrease opposition to the European Energy Charter in the Russian energy market. Eventually, the strategic goal of the Commission is to incorporate the Energy Charter with its Transit Protocol into the new PCA between the EU and Russia.

Taking into account that the EU is to a large extent a *demandeur* in this particular policy field, the energy dialogue is not easily dismissed. The recently signed road map document emphasizes the dialogue's importance in the overall framework of EU-Russia relations. Yet the EU is not in a position to shape Russia's energy policies unilaterally. While the European Commission[56] called for the *acquis communautaire* to "become a reference framework for a reform of the energy sector to be implemented in Russia," the road maps emphasize the promotion of "regulatory convergence."[57]

Throughout its five-year existence, the energy dialogue has clearly been shaped in a multiactor environment comprising public and private actors from Russia, the EU, and various member states. To what extent the EU has actually had an impact on Russian law making remains to be seen. Yet, in turn, Russia has been able to trigger some transformative effects on the institutions of the EU; the format of the energy dialogue has served as a model for promoting flexibility in EU-Russia relations. As Russia is a net *demandeur* in this particular area, the EU is, for various reasons, ready to accept the *exception russe* as demonstrated above and to abide by its rules. Still, it is clear that this leverage cannot easily be transferred to other sectors of EU-Russia relations.

Ukraine

In the realm of the EU's Eastern policy, Ukraine stands out as the most challenging partner given its vested interest in EU membership. Similar to the case of Russia, Ukraine has been labeled a strategic partner of the EU. Consequently, the same institutional procedures and mechanisms used for strategic partners have been implemented for Ukraine, including biannual summit meetings between the EU Council presidency and the Ukrainian president and government representatives. The EU's major strategy *vis-à-vis* Ukraine consists in ensuring the development of good governance, a stable democracy, rule of law, and a sound market economy. These objectives are ultimately designed to make Ukraine's independence and geopolitical position sandwiched between Europe's key regional players, durable and sustainable.

Since 1998–99, both sides have made efforts to clarify their position toward each other by outlining political strategies. For the EU, the basic approach to relations with Ukraine was laid down in the Common Strategy of 1999 as a response to the Ukrainian president's 1998 Strategy for European Integration. Still today, this repeatedly confirmed document initiated by former President Leonid Kuchma and supported by the parliament serves as one of Ukraine's baselines for dealing with the EU. Furthermore, in 2002, Ukraine initialed a road map for the period of 2002–11. A joint statement of the Yalta EU-Ukraine summit on September 11, 2002, reinforced the "strategic partnership between Ukraine and the EU."[58] Until 2004, one may have been right in saying that EU-Ukraine "cooperation can hardly be seen as a success story."[59] Until then, the EU did not recognize any systemic change brought to Ukraine based on the commitments outlined in the PCA or in the Common Strategy. The EU attempted to cope with Ukraine's demands by inviting the country to join the Europe conferences bringing together, since 1998, the applicant countries of Central and Eastern Europe and Turkey. At the Göteborg European Council of June 2001, the EU member states decided to invite Ukraine and Moldova to join the European Conference.[60] The conference involved regular meetings of heads of state and government to discuss a wide range of policy issues of mutual interest.[61] Without any political decision-making capacity, the European conference remained largely an exercise in symbolic politics that did not yield any major tangible successes.

After the 2004 presidential elections, President Victor Yushchenko declared European integration to be a strategic top priority of Ukraine, a course reflected by the creation of the post of Deputy Prime Minister for European Integration in the new government. The presidential elections of November 2004 seem to have been a decisive landmark in EU-Ukraine relations. Although many initiatives, including the negotiations of the ENP Action Plan for Ukraine, had been strongly supported by the former government, Yushchenko made it clear that his foreign policy would not consist of shifting between Europe and Russia but, instead, of playing Ukraine's European card. In his February 2005 speech at the European Parliament, Yushchenko declared, "Ukraine still has much to do to become a full member of the European family, but we are all now united by values, history and aspirations. . . . Like making bread, you need the right ingredients and a lot of work. European integration is the only path open for Ukraine. It is time to move beyond words and take action to develop democracy, the rule of law, freedom of the media and to tackle corruption. We must not lose this unique opportunity to bring the EU and Ukraine closer."[62] On March 6, 2006, Ukrainian Foreign Minister Borys Tarasiuk declared Ukraine "an inseparable part of Europe," and thus it was "unfair" and "unwise" for the EU to keep the country outside its framework. He was the first high-ranking Ukrainian official to set a timeline, announcing that his country aims to join the EU as a full member by 2015. Tarasiuk added that he would press for a formal application by Kyiv for EU membership. In addition, Ukraine also aims to join NATO by 2008.[63] While then Commissioner for Enlargement Günter Verheugen ruled out Ukraine's accession to the EU in principle,[64] the present-day EU is increasingly reluctant to shut the door on prospective EU membership for Ukraine. Yet the EU is still very hesitant to commit in terms of a new association agreement or a timeline.

The new Ukrainian government made it clear from the beginning that it was worried by the multilateralization of its foreign policy goals—first, by being lumped together with other states from Eastern Europe, including Russia, which did not have any interest in joining the EU; and second, by the foreign policy focus on soft security matters framed as common interests. Despite these concerns, Ukraine used the ENP platform to present itself as a solid and reliable partner of the EU. Even during the gas dispute in the winter of 2005/6, Ukraine expressed a strong commitment to the European dimension of its foreign policy, despite significant economic pressure from Russia. Amongst other topics, the EU-Ukraine Action Plan sets up closer cooperation based on people-to-people contacts. With regards to education, training, and youth, for instance, the EU-Ukraine Action Plan strives to enhance "a policy dialogue between EU and Ukrainian authorities in the field of education and training."[65] Furthermore, it sets out to include Ukraine in a number of higher-education and university programs, such as Tempus III, the Erasmus Mundus, and the youth programs. It also encourages Ukraine to subscribe fully to the objectives of the Bologna process in higher education, ensuring that the Ukrainian university system is compatible with that of EU member states. Together with the other Eastern ENP countries Armenia, Azerbaijan, Georgia, and Moldova, Ukraine joined the Bologna process in May 2005.[66] Furthermore, the Ukraine-EU partnership has been extended to cover Europe's satellite radio navigation system (Galileo), which sets the framework for cooperation in satellite navigation in a wide range of sectors, particularly in science and technology; industrial manufacturing; service and market development; and standardization, frequency, and certification. According to the European Commissioner for External Relations and the ENP, Ukraine is the "avant-garde country"[67] in terms of complying with ENP standards and furthering its market economy status, necessary for Ukraine's bid for WTO membership, visa facilitation, and energy solutions.

Moldova

Amongst the three in-betweens, Moldova (the only country of the four under examination to have joined the WTO in 2001) holds a very special place: Europe's poorest country was interested in joining the Balkan Stability Pact from its very inception in 1999. Yet it was only after the landslide April 2001 victory of the Party of Communists and the election of Vladimir Voronin as Moldova's president that EU-Moldova relations became dynamic. For economic and ideological reasons, Voronin had expressed interest in bringing his country into the Russia-Belarus Union formed in December 1999. But the Balkan Stability Pact coordinator's special envoy, Romanian diplomat Mihai Razvan Ungureanu, came to a rather surprising assessment in June 2001, declaring that Moldova was ripe for joining the EU-sponsored pact. For Ungureanu, Moldova's entry into the pact was a clear signal to other former Soviet republics that Europe's door, and ultimately the door to the EU, was open to them: "Moldova's admission in the Stability Pact should make the European members of the Commonwealth of Independent States understand that there is a clear alternative—European integration."[68] It is right to assume that, at least theoretically, Moldova's admission to the Stability Pact also implies the country's eligibility to sign a Stabilization and Association Agreement with the EU and hence to become an EU member in the long term.[69]

The PCA constitutes the legal basis for the EU's relations with Moldova. Following the adoption of the EU-Moldova Action Plan on February 22, 2005, the EU and Moldova have further reinforced their bilateral relationship, providing a new tool for implementing the PCA and laying out the strategic objectives for cooperation. The agreement's implementation will significantly further Moldovan efforts to bring into line its legislation, norms, and standards with those of the EU. According to the European Commission, the priorities of the Action Plan are to strengthen administrative and judicial capacity, to ensure respect for freedom of expression and freedom of the media, and to address economic and regulatory issues with the aim of improving the business climate and enhancing the long-term sustainability of economic policy. Further collaboration on a number of related issues (such as border management, management of migration and the fight against the trafficking of drugs and human beings, organized crime, and money laundering) is also identified as a priority for the enhanced EU-Moldova cooperation. It is interesting to note that the new Moldovan government has put this priority at the center of Moldova's reform program.

In March 2005, the council appointed as EU Special Representative Jacobovits de Szeged, who, for the Transnistrian conflict, had been a special envoy of the Organization for Security and Co-operation in Europe (OSCE) Chairman in Office under the Netherlands' OSCE presidency in 2003. The EU is increasingly involved in the solution of this particular frozen conflict, thus adding significant political clout to the ENP. Since 1995, Moldova and Transnistria, which split from the country in 1992, have engaged in discussions focusing on a settlement using the so-called "five-sided mediation process" (the other "sides" being Russia, Ukraine, and the OSCE). President Yushchenko, who previously declared his willingness to increase Ukraine's engagement in order to find a solution to the crisis, launched a set of proposals for a negotiated settlement based upon democratic elections in Transnistria at the summit of GUAM in Chişinău on April 22, 2005. On June 2, 2005, the Ukrainian and Moldovan presidents sent a joint letter to Commission president Barroso and High Representative of the CFSP Solana, requesting the international monitoring of the Transnistria section of their common border under the leadership of the EU. Hence, the Border Assistance Mission was launched in November 2005. Furthermore, during the five-sided mediation process in Odesa on September 26 and 27, 2005, the EU and the United States were invited to join in future discussions as observers. At the same time, recent developments in Moldova were quite discouraging for Western observers—in a declaration signed jointly by Moldovan president Vladimir Voronin and Transnistrian leader Igor Smirnov in April 2007, Moldova for the first time recognized the political leadership of the breakaway province as a legitimate entity.[70] Moreover, Russia tends to consider Kosovo's potential independence as a precedent for other breakaway regions, including Transnistria.[71]

So far, the EU has honored the Moldovan government's attempts to comply with the many priorities set out in the Action Plan. As a result, in January 2006, Moldova became the beneficiary of a modified GSP, under which it is eligible to apply for the "special incentive for sustainable development and good governance" (new GSP Plus). According to EU External Relations Commissioner Benita Ferrero-Waldner, this "scheme offers indeed some better access to the European market, and it has improved also the certification and the control of origin rules, which opens the way also to a possible granting of additional autonomous trade preferences."[72] Given the reluctance of the EU to upgrade the bilateral relationship by offering a membership perspective, Moldova may also hope to find an advocate once Romania joins the EU in 2007.[73]

Belarus

Relations between the EU and Belarus began to deteriorate in the mid-1990s. Although Aliaksandr Lukashenka was democratically elected in 1994, he soon tried to establish an authoritarian rule. Both sides negotiated a PCA in 1995, yet the agreement's ratification process was frozen and the interim agreement never enacted due to the worsening domestic situation in Belarus. In 1996, Lukashenka started to concentrate powers around the presidential office by modifying the

constitution of 1994. His measures aimed at undermining the democratic conditions, putting the opposition, the media, and the judiciary under pressure. Ultimately, the EU responded by freezing the
bilateral relationship. With the exception of humanitarian aid,
regional programs, and support to civil society, the EU's technical
assistance to Belarus was suspended.

In 1998, the EU adopted the policy of conditional engagement[74]:
with some signs of moderate changes in the Belarusian regime at
hand, the EU attempted to resume a major role in the upcoming parliamentary and presidential elections of 2000 and 2001. The EU
joined the Council of Europe and the OSCE in recommending that
Belarus comply with a set of four criteria for the parliamentary elections: the return of substantial powers to the parliament; opposition
representation in electoral commissions; fair access to the state media
for the opposition; and electoral legislation in line with international
standards.[75] Ultimately, during both elections, the Lukashenka
regime did not conform to international standards of fair and democratic elections. In a declaration of the EU presidency, the EU pointed
out that "the development of [the EU's] relations with Belarus is
essentially dependent on respect for human rights and the progress of
democracy in that country. In that context, the European Union wel-
comes the emergence in Belarus of a degree of pluralism and of a civil
society which is aware of the challenges of democracy . . . . The
European Union regrets that the Belarus authorities have not seized
the opportunity afforded by these presidential elections to engage
their country fully on the path of democracy."[76] Starting in 2002, the
EU subscribed to a gradual normalization of its relations with
Belarus (a "benchmarks" approach) "in response to improvements in
the protection of democratic principles and rights."[77] Conducted by
the EU Heads of Mission in Minsk, the benchmarks talks did not produce any tangible results. Since 2003, the European Parliament has
stressed the need to develop a strategy within the ENP framework
that will provide greater financial support to those nongovernmental
organizations working in the field of civil society and fostering the
role of independent media. The council attempted to use the development of ENP, which was initially welcomed by the Belarusian government, as a yardstick to induce change within the Lukashenka
regime. Hence, in the run-up to the parliamentary elections of 2004,
the council emphasized "its hope that Belarus will take its rightful
place among European democratic countries. In this case, the EU
would be able to further develop the relations between the EU and

Belarus, including in the context of the European Neighbourhood Policy. If, however, the parliamentary elections and the announced referendum do not take place under free and fair conditions, this cannot remain without its consequences for the relations."[78] In December 2004, the EU imposed visa restrictions on "persons who are directly responsible for the fraudulent elections and referendum in Belarus on October 17, 2004, and those who are responsible for severe human rights violations in the repression of peaceful demonstrators in the aftermath of the elections and referendum in Belarus."[79] Although members of the Belarusian opposition (such as Aliaksandr Milinkevich) called the EU visa ban insufficient, the EU reiterated this position following the presidential election on March 19, 2006.[80]

Following the elections, which were considered by various international organizations to be flawed, the European Commission is likely to propose lifting the GSP on trade from Belarus. Exempting EU imports of petrol and gas, the "suspension would see higher EU import tariffs on Belarusian minerals, textiles, clothes and wood products worth €390 million a year."[81] Belarus would join Burma as the second country in history to be banned from the EU's GSP.

The case of Belarus is very special, indeed, as the credibility of the EU's foreign policy is at stake. On the overall development of EU-Belarusian relations, two conclusions may be drawn. First, the EU has significantly upgraded its conditional engagement approach by actually focusing on sanctions *vis-à-vis* the Lukashenka regime. At the same time, the EU wants to ensure that a minimum of assistance reaches various NGOs and representatives of civil society. Second, in the aftermath of increasingly strained relations with Russia, Lukashenka faces limited foreign policy choices. Any substantiation of the Russian-Belarusian union is likely to diminish the role of any Belarusian government, albeit recent years have proved that this union is essentially an ephemeral structure similar to the CIS. Ironically, the preservation of Belarusian identity is likely to lie with some form of closer relationship with the EU.

Conclusion

The analysis of the EU's policy toward Russia and the in-betweens—Belarus, Moldova, and Ukraine—over the past fifteen years reveals four increasingly divergent versions of a policy that once set out to support a unifying NIS approach. Although to this day Russia is constantly singled out as a strategic partner of utmost importance to the

EU, the EU no longer subscribes unequivocally to an uncritical "Russia first" approach in the Eastern European region, as it did throughout the 1990s. The EU's new member states—in particular the Baltic States and Poland—are keen on bringing the European states on Russia's periphery as close to the EU as possible, creating a belt of states that stretches from Belarus to the Caucasus.

The EU's Eastern policy exhibits many features of a highly differentiated foreign policy; while Belarus is increasingly isolated (with the help of various other diplomatic instruments), Ukraine and Moldova are amongst the beneficiaries of the EU's ENP approach. Although ENP does not entail any automatism leading toward EU accession, it does embrace dynamics that may ultimately push these countries further toward membership. Moldova's situation is unique, given its inclusion into the EU's Balkan Stability Pact. Furthermore, the Moldovan government is likely to receive strong support from Romania as an EU member.

What does this imply for the future of the EU's Eastern policy? First, there is a correlation between cohesiveness in the EU's approach and the effectiveness of the policies on the ground. The EU has been most successful in those areas where it was relying on common interest and where the Commission has been granted room for action, in particular the field of ENP. The scope of bilateral relations fostered by ENP is astonishing in the case of Ukraine and Moldova. Given the accession of some new member states with vested interests in maintaining the in-betweens, the old members—in particular Germany—are compelled to revise their traditional stances in the EU's Eastern policy. Poland and Lithuania, for instance, are actively committed in Belarus and Ukraine; Latvia is strongly engaged in Belarus, Estonia in Georgia. Possibly the Polish publicist Adam Krzeminski is right to state that the EU's Common Foreign and Security Policy will be forged in the East[82]—by, ultimately, CEECs.

Second, the EU's foreign policy in its immediate vicinity is stronger the more it can rely on instruments equal to (or, at least, similar in value to) the promise of membership. In the case of ENP, the key for success is dependent on the policy takers' acceptance of carrots of lesser value than the membership promise—such as the EU's support of the country's bid for WTO membership, increased market access based on a GSP Plus, and so on. Yet it should be clear that the potential of membership remains a significant part of the game.

Third, the EU needs to ensure that Russia does not perceive the ENP as a major vehicle for sidelining or decreasing Russian influence in its periphery. Thus, the EU must invest in keeping Russia on board without accepting a Russian *droit de regard* as the last word. This has become increasingly difficult, since Russia seems to define its relationship with the EU in terms of a zero-sum game: an EU-Russia Kaliningrad transit agreement in exchange for Russia extending the PCA toward new member states; the EU's support for Russia's bid for WTO membership in exchange for the Kremlin's guarantee to ratify the Kyoto Protocol; and, most recently, Russia's readiness to sign a readmission with the EU in exchange for the EU's willingness to accept a facilitated bilateral visa regime. Thus, the EU is compelled to reshape its relationship with a partner that does not subscribe to the same principles of postnational behavior in international politics.[83] The ongoing discussion about a follow-up to the PCA, which must be renewed or replaced in 2007, is a good occasion to hammer out a compromise.

Notes

1. I use the term EC to refer to both the first pillar of the EU and the period prior to the introduction of the Maastricht Treaty.
2. The term "CEECs" includes the Baltic States, which acquired independence during the course of 1990–91.
3. The concept was coined by Heinz Timmermann in the first half of the 1990s; see, for instance, Heinz Timmermann and Stefan Gänzle, "The European Union's Policy towards Russia," in *EU Enlargement and Beyond: The Baltic States and Russia*, ed. Helmut Hubel (Berlin: Spitz, 2002), 145–71.
4. Mixed agreements are based on articles 113 and 235 of the EC treaty. They cover areas of exclusive EC competence as well as areas where the community is exclusively competent. Hence, their entry into force requires ratification by each member state. Interim agreements were signed between the EC and various NIS in the framework of the EC's Common Commercial Policy (Art. 113) in order to implement trade and trade-related parts of the PCAs.
5. See Christophe Hillion, "Partnership and Cooperation Agreements between the European Union and the New Independent States of the Ex-Soviet Union," *European Foreign Affairs Review* 3 (1998): 399–420.
6. Spain joined the format on a summit meeting on March 18, 2005.
7. Andrei Zagorski, "Policies towards Russia, Ukraine, Moldova and Belarus," in *European Union Foreign and Security Policy: Towards a Neighbourhood Strategy*, ed. Roland Dannreuther (London: Routledge, 2004), 80.

8. Similar to Canada, Russia is the only strategic partner to meet twice each year at the level of heads of state and government.
9. Zagorski, "Policies," 92.
10. Zagorski, "Policies," 80.
11. Cf. Christopher Hill, "The 'Capability-Expectations-Gap' or Conceptualizing Europe's International Role," *Journal of Common Market Studies* 32, no. 3 (1993): 305–28.
12. Cf. Karen E. Smith, "The Use of Political Conditionality in the EU's Relations with Third Countries: How Effective?" *European Foreign Affairs Review* 3 (2001): 256, which states, "Political conditionality entails the linking, by a state or international organization, of perceived benefits to another state (such as aid), to the fulfillment of conditions relating to the protection of human rights and the advancement of democratic principles. Positive conditionality involves promising the benefit(s) to a state if it fulfills the conditions; negative conditionality involves reducing, suspending, or terminating those benefits if the state in question violates the conditions. Political conditionality differs from the cold war practice of 'linkage' in that it is broader in its objectives (general political reform) and is not applied only to a certain group of (communist) states."
13. Zagorski, "Policies," 81.
14. For the EU's trade relations with Russia, see European Commission External Trade Issues, http://ec.europa.eu/trade/issues/bilateral/countries/russia/index_en.htm (accessed May 7, 2007).
15. See European Parliament, Parliamentary questions, January 30, 2007, H-0058/07, Oral question for Question Time at the part-session in February 2007 pursuant to Rule 109 of the Rules of Procedure by Justas Vincas Paleckis to the Commission, Subject: Sanctions against Belarus, http://www.europarl.europa.eu/omk/sipade3?OBJID=135955&L=EN&NAV=X&LSTDOC=N (accessed April 4, 2007).
16. For the EU's trade statistics on Belarus, see http://trade.ec.europa.eu/doclib/docs/2006/september/tradoc_113351.pdf (accessed May 7, 2007).
17. For the EU's trade relations with Moldova and Ukraine, see http://ec.europa.eu/comm/trade/issues/bilateral/countries/moldova/index_en.htm and http://ec.europa.eu/comm/trade/issues/bilateral/coutries/ukraine/index_en.htm (accessed June 20, 2006); for EU trade with Belarus, see Directorate General for External Relations and European Neighbourhood Policy, http://ec.europa.eu/comm/external_reations/belarus/intro/index.htm#comm (accessed June 20, 2006).
18. Cf. Directorate General for External Relations and European Neighbourhood Policy (ENP), the EU's relations with Belarus at http://ec.europa.eu/comm/external_relations/belarus/intro/index.htm#comm); Moldova at http://ec.europa.eu/comm/external_relations/

moldova/intro/index.htm#comm; Ukraine at http://ec.europa.eu/comm/ external_relations/ukraine/intro/index.htm#comm; and Russia at http:// ec.europa.eu/comm/external_relations/russia/intro/index.htm #comm (all accessed June 20, 2006).

19. Dov Lynch, Russia faces Europe, Chaillot Paper No. 60 (Paris: Institute for Security Studies, 2003), 85.

20. European Union, European Security Strategy 2003, Brussels, December 12, 2003, p. 7.

21. The other objectives are (1) to address the new threats to security, such as nuclear proliferation, terrorism, and organized crime, and (2) to help create "an international order based on effective multilateralism." See European Union, European Security Strategy, Brussels, December 12, 2003, p. 9.

22. European Union, European Security Strategy, Brussels, December 12, 2003, p. 8.

23. For a comprehensive overview, see Stefan Gänzle, "The EU's Neighbourhood Policy. A Strategy for Security in Europe?" in *Europe Alone: Transatlantic Relations and European Security*, ed. Stefan Gänzle and Allen Sens (London: Palgrave, 2007), 110–34.

24. European Council, Presidency Conclusions, Copenhagen, December 12–13, 2002, p. 8.

25. Romano Prodi, "A Wider Europe—A Proximity Policy as the Key to Stability," Peace, Security and Stability International Dialogue and the Role of the EU, Sixth ECSA-World Conference, Brussels, December 5–6, 2002.

26. Prodi, "A Wider Europe."

27. European Commission, Paving the Way for a New Neighbourhood Instrument, COM (2003) 393 final, Brussels, July 1, 2003, p. 4.

28. Prodi, "A Wider Europe."

29. Cf. Karen E. Smith, "The Outsiders: The European Neighbourhood Policy," *International Affairs* 81, no. 4 (2005): 759; and Dimitri Danilov, "Russia and the ESDP: Partnership Strategy versus Strategic Partnership," in *Europe Alone: Transatlantic Relations and European Security*, ed. Stefan Gänzle and Allen Sens (London: Palgrave, 2007).

30. Stefan Gänzle, "Externalizing EU Governance: The Case of the European Neighbourhood Policy" (unpublished manuscript).

31. "1. The Union shall develop a special relationship with neighbouring countries, aiming to establish an area of prosperity and good neigh-bourliness, founded on the values of the Union and characterised by close and peaceful relations based on cooperation. 2. For the purposes of paragraph 1, the Union may conclude specific agreements with the countries concerned. These agreements may contain reciprocal rights and obligations as well as the possibility of undertaking activities

jointly. Their implementation shall be the subject of periodic consultation." (Art. I-57)

32. European Commission, Communication from the Commission, European Neighbourhood Policy, Strategy Paper, COM (2004) 373 final, Brussels, May 12, 2004, 3.

33. "The European Union is not seeking to establish new bodies or organisations, but rather to support existing entities and encourage their further development; the importance of local ownership is one of the most pertinent lessons that can be drawn from the Northern Dimension" (European Commission, Communication from the Commission, European Neighbourhood Policy, Strategy Paper, COM (2004) 373 final, Brussels, May 12, 2004, 21).

34. European Commission, Communication from the Commission, European Neighbourhood Policy, Strategy Paper, COM (2004) 373 final, Brussels, May 12, 2004, 8.

35. In June 2004, the Council of the EU endorsed the Commission's proposal: "Action plans should be comprehensive but at the same time identify clearly a limited number of key priorities and offer real incentives for reform. Action plans should also contribute, where possible, to regional cooperation" (Council of the European Union, General Affairs and External Relations, 2590th Council Meeting, 10189/04 [Presse 195], Luxembourg, June 14, 2004, 12).

36. These programs include TACIS for the eastern neighbors and MEDA for the southern Mediterranean neighbors of the European Union, as well as thematic programs such as EIDHR (the European Initiative for Democracy and Human Rights). The budgetary period covering 2000–2006) released funds of approximately €5.3 billion for MEDA and €3.1 billion for TACIS; in addition, the European Investment Bank lent approximately €2 billion to MEDA beneficiary countries and €500 million to TACIS beneficiary countries.

37. European Commission, Proposal for a Regulation of the European Parliament and of the Council Laying Down General Provisions Establishing a European Neighbourhood and Partnership Instrument, COM (2004) 628 final, 2004/0219 (COD), Brussels, September 29, 2004, p. 4.

38. European Commission, Proposal for a Regulation of the European Parliament and of the Council Laying Down General Provisions Establishing a European Neighbourhood and Partnership Instrument, COM (2004) 628 final, 2004/0219 (COD), Brussels, September 29, 2004, 3.

39. Author's interview with a member of the European Commission, May 26, 2005.

40. Article 1 of the PCA: "The objectives of this Partnership are: . . . the necessary conditions for the future establishment of a free trade area

between the Community and Russia covering substantially all trade in goods between them, as well as conditions for bringing about freedom of establishment of companies, of cross-border trade in services and of capital movements."

41. Article 55 of the PCA.

42. Katinka Barysch, "The EU and Russia. Strategic Partners or Squabbling Neighbours?" Centre for European Reform, May 2004, 26.

43. Michael Emerson, "EU-Russia. Four Common Spaces and the Proliferation of the Fuzzy," CEPS Policy Brief No. 71, May 2005, 2.

44. Dieter Mahncke, "Russia's Attitude to the European Security and Defence Policy," *European Foreign Policy Review* 6 (2001): 428.

45. Tuomas Forsberg, "The EU-Russia Security Partnership: Why the Opportunity Was Missed," *European Foreign Policy Review* 9 (2004): 251f.

46. At the Russian Mission to the EC, some complained that "Russia had no voice in the process of ESDP" (author's interview, June 1, 2005).

47. EU-Russia Summit, Road map for the 4 Common Spaces, Luxembourg, May 10, 2005, 39.

48. Vladimir Putin, Press Statement and Responses to Questions Following the Russia-European Union Summit, May 10, 2005, at http://kremlin.ru/eng/speeches/2005/05/10/2030_type82914type8291 5_88025.html (accessed June 12, 2005).

49. Council of the EU, 17th EU-Russia Summit, Sotchi, 9850/06 (Presse 157), May 25, 2006, 2.

50. European Commission, Communication from the Commission to the Council and the European Parliament, Energy Dialogue between the European Union and the Russian Federation between 2000 and 2004, COM (2004) 777 final, Brussels, December 13, 2004, 2.

51. *Financial Times 2001*, quoted in Barysch, "Strategic Partners," 31.

52. Council of the European Union, Common Strategy on Russia, Brussels, June 1999, 2.

53. Joint Declaration of the President of the European Council, Jacques Chirac (assisted by the Secretary-General of the Council/High Representative for the Common Foreign and Security Policy of the EU, Javier Solana), of the President of the Commission of the European Communities, Romano Prodi, and of the President of the Russian Federation, Vladimir V. Putin, Paris, October 30, 2000, at http://ec .europa.eu/comm/external_relations/russia/summit_30_10_00/statement _en.htm (accessed May 3, 2007).

54. European Commission, Communication from the Commission to the Council and the European Parliament. The Energy Dialogue between the European Union and the Russian Federation between 2000 and 2004, COM (2004) 777 final, Brussels, December 13, 2004, 2.

55. See Barysch, "Strategic Partners," 32.
56. European Commission, Communication from the Commission to the Council and the European Parliament. The Energy Dialogue between the European Union and the Russian Federation between 2000 and 2004, COM (2004) 777 final, Brussels, December 13, 2004, 14.
57. EU-Russia Summit, EU-Russia: Road map for the 4 Common Spaces, Luxembourg, May 10, 2005, p. 14, at http://www.eu2005.lu/en/actalites/documents_travail/2005/05/10-4spaces/4spaces.pdf (accessed June 15, 2006).
58. See European Commission's Delegation to Ukraine, at http://www.delukr.ec.europa.eu/page4824.html (accessed June 15, 2006).
59. Zagorski, "Policies," 87.
60. Cf. European Council, Presidency Conclusion, SN 200/1/01 REV 1, June 15–16, 2001, 3.
61. The European Council Presidency Conclusions state: "The members of the Conference must share a common commitment to peace, security and good neighbourliness, respect for other countries' sovereignty, the principles upon which the European Union is founded, the integrity and inviolability of external borders and the principles of international law and a commitment to the settlement of territorial disputes by peaceful means, in particular through the jurisdiction of the International Court of Justice in The Hague. Countries which endorse these principles and respect the right of any European country fulfilling the required criteria to accede to the European Union and sharing the Union's commitment to building a Europe free of the divisions and difficulties of the past will be invited to take part in the Conference." See Bulletin EU 12-1997, Conclusions of the Presidency (4/27), http://europa.eu/bulletin/en/9712/i1004.htm.
62. European Parliament, "Ukraine's future is in the EU." Address by President of Ukraine Viktor Yushchenko, EP05-022EN, Brussels, February 23, 2005.
63. See "EU refused to consider Ukraine for membership," *Pravda* online, March 3, 2006.
64. Derek Fraser, "Taking Ukraine Seriously: The Western and Russian Responses to the Orange Revolution, 10 (unpublished manuscript).
65. EU-Ukraine, Action Plan, 2004, 39, at http://ec.europa.eu/comm/world/enp/pdf/action_plans/Proposed_Action_Plan_EU-Ukraine.pdf (accessed June 10, 2006).
66. Communiqué of the Conference of European Ministers Responsible for Higher Education, The European Higher Education Area—Achieving the Goals, Bergen, May 19–20, 2005, 1.
67. Benita Ferrero-Waldner, "Die Europäische Nachbarschaftspolitik als Wohlstands- und Sicherheitsanker [The European Neighborhood Policy

as an Anchor for Prosperity and Security]," Meeting of COSAC (Conférence des Organes Spécialisés dans les Affaires Communautaires), Vienna, May 22, 2006, at http://europa.eu/rapid/pressReleasesAction .do?reference=SPEECH/06/325&format=HTML&aged=0&language=DE&guiLanguage=en (accessed June 4, 2006).

68. The Balkan Stability Pact coordinator's special envoy, Romanian diplomat Mihai Razvan Ungureanu Moldova, quoted in Eugen Tomiuc, "Envoy Says Nation Is Ready to Join Balkan Stability Pact," *Radio Free Europe/Radio Liberty*, Prague, June 15, 2001.

69. Andrei Zagorski, "Policies," 90.

70. *The Economist*, April 21, 2007, 61.

71. See U.S. Department of State Web site at http://usinfo.state.gov/ xarchives/display.html?p=washfile-english&y=2007&m=March &x=20070321142711MVyelwarC0.6473047 (accessed May 7, 2007).

72. Ahto Lobjakas, "Moldova: EU Officials Say Union Membership Hopes Are Premature," *Radio Free Europe/Radio Liberty*, Brussels, April 11, 2006.

73. Andrew Rettman, "Moldova's EU hopes piggyback on Romanian accession," *EUobserver*, March 30, 2006.

74. Charles Grant and Mark Leonard, "The EU's awkward neighbour: time for a new policy on Belarus," policy brief (London: Centre for European Reform, 2006), 2.

75. See the European Commission's Web site at http://ec.europa.eu/ comm/external_relations/belarus/intro/index.htm (accessed June 16, 2006).

76. Council of the European Union, Declaration by the Presidency on behalf of the European Union on the holding of presidential elections in Belarus, 11812/01 (Presse 320), p. 152/01, Brussels, September 14, 2001.

77. See the European Commission's Web site at http://ec.europa.eu/ comm/external_relations/belarus/intro/index.htm (accessed June 16, 2006).

78. Ibid.

79. Council Common Position 2004/848/CFSP of December 13, 2004, amending Common Position 2004/661/CFSP concerning restrictive measures against certain officials of Belarus, Official Journal of the European Union L 367 (December 14, 2004), 35.

80. See Mark Beunderman, "Belarus opposition leader calls EU visa ban insufficient," *EUobserver*, April 10, 2006.

81. See Andrew Rettman, "Belarus likely to join Burma as EU trade pariah," *EUobserver*, June 14, 2006.

82. Quoted in Martin Kremer, "Towards an EU Baltic Eastern Policy," in *Russia, the EU and the Baltic States: Enhancing the Potential for*

Cooperation, ed. Matthes Buhbe and Iris Kempe, 23–37 (Moscow: Friedrich Ebert Stiftung, 2005), 25.

83. See Stefan Gänzle, "Externalizing Governance and Europeanization in EU-Russian Relations," in *The External Relations of the EU*, ed. Joan DeBardeleben (London: Palgrave, 2007).

Selected Bibliography

Abrahamson, Kjell-Albin. 1999. *Vitryssland—89 millimeter från Europa.* Stockholm: Fischer.

Anderson, Benedict. 1991 (1983). *Imagined Communities.* London: Verso.

Andrukhovych, Yurii. 2006. "Atlas. Medytatsii." *Krytyka* (1–2): 10–11.

———. 2005. "Shukaiuchy Dreamland." *Krytyka* (1–2): 2.

Arel, Dominique. 2005. "Paradoksy Pomaranchevoi revoliutsii," *Krytyka* (4): 2–4.

Armstrong, John A. 1990. *Ukrainian Nationalism.* 3rd ed. Englewood, CO: Ukrainian Academic Press.

Assemblée Nationale. 2004. Rapport d'information déposé en application de l'article 145 du Règlement par la Commission des Affaires Etrangères sur les relations entre l'Union Européenne et la Russie et présenté par MM. René André et Jean-Louis Bianco, députés. No. 1989, December 14, 2004, Paris.

Barysch, Katinka. 2004. *The EU and Russia. Strategic Partners or Squabbling Neighbours,* Centre for European Reform, May.

Bilinsky, Yaroslav. 1978. "Mykola Skrypnyk and Petro Shelest: An Essay on the Persistence and Limits of Ukrainian National Communism." In *Soviet Nationality Policies and Practices,* edited by Jeremy R. Azrael, 105–43. New York: Praeger.

Blacker, Coit, and Condaleezza Rice. 2001. "Belarus and the Flight from Sovereignty." In *Problematic Sovereignty: Contested Rules and Political Possibilities,* edited by Stephen D. Krasner, 224–51. New York: Columbia University Press.

Brubaker, Rogers. 1996. *Nationalism Reframed: Nationhood and the National Question in the New Europe.* New York: Cambridge University Press.

Brzozovska, Anna. 2004. "Discourses of Empowerment: Understanding Belarus' International Orientation." In *Contemporary Change in Belarus, Baltic and East European Studies,* vol. 2, edited by Egle Rindzeviciute, 73–108. Huddinge, Sweden: Baltic and East European Graduate School.

Cernovodeanu, Paul, Nicolae Edroiu, and Constantin Bălan, eds. 2002. *Istoria Românilor.* Vol. 6. *Românii între Europa clasică și Europa luminilor (1711–1821).* Academia Română Secția de Științe Istorice și Arheologie, București: Editura Enciclopedică.

Checkel, Jeffrey. 1998. "The Constructivist Turn in International Relations Theory." *World Politics* 50:324–48.

———. 2001. "Why Comply? Social Learning and European Identity Change." *International Organization* 55 (3): 553–88.

Chirică, Codrin Valentin. 2004. *Republica Moldova între Romania si Rusia.* Iași: Helios.

Ciobanu, Ștefan. 1992. *Basarabia. Populatia, istoria, cultura.* Chișinău: Editura Știința; București: Editura Clio.

Comaroff, Jean, and John Comaroff. 1992. *Ethnography and the Historical Imagination.* Boulder, CO: Westview.

Commission of the European Communities. 2004. Communication from the Commission. European Neighbourhood Policy. Strategy Paper. COM (2004) 373 final. Brussels, May 12, 2004.

Commission of the European Communities. 2003. "Wider Europe Neighbourhood: New Framework for Relations with our Eastern and Southern Neighbours." Strategy Paper by the European Commission. March 2003.

Constitutia Republicii Moldova, adoptata la 29 iulie 1994 Monitorul Oficial al R.Moldova nr.1 din 12.08.1994.

Council of the European Union. 1999. *Common Strategy on Russia.* Brussels.

———. 2004. *Council Common Position 2004/848/CFSP of 13 December 2004 amending Common Position 2004/661/CFSP concerning restrictive measures against certain officials of Belarus.* Official Journal of the European Union L 367 (December 14, 2004).

———. 2004. General Affairs and External Relations. *2590th Council Meeting,* 10189/04 (Presse 195), Luxembourg, June 14, 2004.

———. 2001. *Declaration by the Presidency on behalf of the European Union on the holding of presidential elections in Belarus,* 11812/01 (Presse 320), P. 152/01 Brussels, September 14, 2001.

———. *17th EU-Russia Summit,* 9850/06 (Presse 157), Sotchi, May 25, 2006.

Cowles, Maria, James Caporaso, and Thomas Risse. 2001. *Transforming Europe: Europeanization and Domestic Change.* Ithaca, NY: Cornell University Press.

Crowther, William. 1997. "The Politics of Democratisation in Post-Communist Moldova." In *Democratic Changes and Authoritarian Reactions in Russia, Ukraine, Belarus and Moldova,* edited by Karen Dawisha and Bruce Parrot. Cambridge: Cambridge University Press.

———. 1991. "The Politics of Ethnic-National Mobilization: Nationalism and Reform in Soviet Moldavia." *The Russian Review* 50:183–203.

Danilov, Dimitri. 2007. "Russia and the ESDP: Partnership Strategy versus Strategic Partnership" In *Europe Alone: Transatlantic Relations and*

European Security. Edited by Stefan Gänzle and Allen Sens. London: Palgrave.

Demirdirek, Hülya. 2001. *(Re)making of a Place and Nation: Gagauzia in Moldova.* PhD diss. Department of Social Anthropology, University of Oslo.

———. 2000. "Living in the present: The Gagauz in Moldova." *The Anthropology of East Europe Review: Central Europe, Eastern Europe, Eastern Europe and Eurasia* 178 (1): 67–71.

———. 1993. *Dimensions of Identification: Intellectuals in Baku, 1990–1992.* PhD diss. Oslo: University of Oslo.

Demirdirek, H., and Claus Neukirch. 2001. "Moldova." In *Countries and Their Cultures,* edited by M. Ember and C. R. Ember, 1477–88. New York: Macmillan Reference.

Dima, Nicholas. 1982. *Bessarabia and Bukovina: the Soviet-Romanian Territorial Dispute.* New York: East European Monographs.

———. 2001. *Moldova and the Transdnestr Republic.* New York: East European Monographs.

Dziuba, Ivan. 2004. "Spohady i rozdumy na finishnii priamii." In *Rukopys.* Vol. 1. Kyiv: Vyd-vo Krynytsia.

———. 1968. *Internationalism or Russification?* Trans. M. Davies. London: Weidenfeld and Nicolson.

Easton, David. 1953. *The Political System.* New York: Alfred A. Knopf.

Eke, Steven M., and Taras Kuzio. 2000. "Sultanism in Europe: The Socio-Political Roots of Authoritarian Populism in Belarus." *Europe-Asia Studies* 52 (3): 523–47.

Eley, Geoff. 1988. "Remapping the Nation: War, Revolutionary Upheaval, and State Formation in Eastern Europe, 1914–1923." In *Ukrainian-Jewish Relations in Historical Perspective,* edited by Howard Aster and Peter J. Potichnyj, 205–46. Edmonton, AB: Canadian Institute of Ukrainian Studies Press.

Emerson, Michael. 2005. *EU-Russia. Four Common Spaces and the Proliferation of the Fuzzy.* CEPS Policy Brief No. 71, May 2005.

Enciu, Nicolae, and Ion Pavelescu. 1998. "Un miracol istoric: Renaşterea romanismului in Basarabia." In *Istoria Basarabiei: De la inceputuri pînă in 1998,* edited by Ioan Scurtu. Bucharest: Semne.

European Commission. 2006. *Green Paper.* A European Strategy for Sustainable, Competitive and Secure Energy, COM (2006) 105 final, Brussels, March 8, 2006.

———. 2004. *Communication from the Commission to the Council and the European Parliament. The Energy Dialogue between the European Union and the Russian Federation between 2000 and 2004.* COM (2004) 777 final, Brussels, December 13, 2004.

———. 2004. *Communication from the Commission, European Neighbourhood Policy. Strategy Paper.* COM (2004) 373 final, Brussels, May 12, 2004.

————. 2003. *Paving the Way for a New Neighbourhood Instrument.* COM (2003) 393 final, Brussels, July 1, 2003.

European Council. 2000. *Presidency Conclusions.* Nice, December.

European Union. 2003. *European Security Strategy.* Brussels, December 13, 2003.

EU-Russia Energy Dialogue. 2004. *Fifth Progress Report.* Presented by Russian Minister of Energy and Industry Victor Khristenko and European Commission Director-General François Lamoureux, Moscow/Brussels, November.

EU-Russia Summit. 2005. *Road Map for the Four Common Spaces.* Luxembourg, May 10, 2005.

Fane, Daria. 1993. "Moldova: Breaking Loose from Moscow." In *Nations & Politics in the Soviet Successor States,* edited by Ian Bremmer and Ray Taras, 121–53. Cambridge: Cambridge University Press.

Featherstone, K., and C. Radaelli, eds. 2003. *The Politics of Europeanization.* Oxford: Oxford University Press.

Fedor, Helen, ed. 1995. *Belarus and Moldova: Country Studies.* Washington, DC: Federal Research Division, Library of Congress.

Feduta, Aleksandr. 2005. *Lukashenko: politicheskaia biografiia.* Moscow: Referendum.

Filtenborg, Mette Sicard, Stefan Gänzle, and Elisabeth Johansson. 2002. "An Alternative Theoretical Approach to EU Foreign Policy. 'Network Governance' and the Case of the Northern Dimension Initiative." *Cooperation and Conflict* 37 (4): 387–407.

Forsberg, Tuomas. 2004. "The EU-Russia Security Partnership: Why the Opportunity Was Missed." *European Foreign Policy Review* 9:247–67.

Gabani, Anneli. 2005. "Die Perspektive einer Perspektive. Moldova und die Neue Nachbarschaftspolitik der EU." *Ostpolitik* 55 (2): 24–39.

Gänzle, Stefan. 2007. "Externalizing Governance and Europeanization in EU-Russian Relations." In *The External Relations of the EU,* edited by Joan DeBardeleben. London: Palgrave.

————. 2007. "The EU's Neighbourhood Policy. A Strategy for Security in Europe?" In *Europe Alone: Transatlantic Relations and European Security,* edited by Stefan Gänzle and Allen Sens, 110–34. London: Palgrave.

————. 2006. "Externalizing EU Governance: The Case of the European Neighbourhood Policy." Unpublished manuscript.

————. 2006. "The EU's Policy towards Russia: Extending Governance beyond Borders?" Paper prepared for "Europe—Our Common Home?" Seventh World Congress of the International Council for Central and East European Studies, Berlin, July 25–30, 2005.

Gänzle, Stefan, and Allen Sens, eds. 2007. *Europe Alone: Transatlantic Relations and European Security.* London: Palgrave.

Garnett, Sherman W., and Robert Legvold, eds. 1999. *Belarus at the Crossroads.* Washington, DC: Carnegie Endowment for International Peace.

Grant, Bruce. 1995. *In the Soviet House of Culture: A Century of Perestroikas.* Princeton, NJ: Princeton University Press.

Grant, Charles, and Mark Leonard. 2006. The EU's Awkward Neighbour: Time for a New Policy on Belarus. Policy brief. London: Centre for European Reform.

Guthier, Stephen L. 1977. *The Belorussians: National Identification and Assimilation, 1897–1970*. Ann Arbor: University of Michigan Press.

Handler, Richard. 1988. *Nationalism and the Politics of Culture in Quebec*. Madison: University of Wisconsin Press.

Herzfeld, Michael. 1997. *Cultural Intimacy: Social Poetics in the Nation-State*. London: Routledge.

Hill, Christopher. 1993. "The 'Capability-Expectations-Gap' or Conceptualizing Europe's International Role." *Journal of Common Market Studies* 32 (3): 305–28.

Hillion, Christophe. 1998. "Partnership and Cooperation Agreements between the European Union and the New Independent States of the Ex-Soviet Union." *European Foreign Affairs Review* 3:399–420.

Himka, John-Paul. 1988. *Galician Villagers and the Ukrainian National Movement in the Nineteenth Century*. Edmonton, AB: Canadian Institute of Ukrainian Studies Press.

Hirschman, Albert O. 1970. *Exit, Voice, and Loyalty: Responses to Decline in Firms, Organizations, and States*. Cambridge, MA: Harvard University Press.

Holovakha, Yevhen. 2004. "Pora ukrainskoho vyboru: mizh revolintsiieiu ta reformoiu." *Krytyka* (12): 7.

Hopf, Ted. 1998. "The Promise of Constructivism in International Relations Theory." *International Security* 23, no. 1 (Summer): 171–200.

Hroch, Miroslav. 1985. *Social Preconditions of National Revival in Europe*. Trans. Ben Fowkes. Cambridge: Cambridge University Press.

Hubel, Helmut. 2004. "The EU's Three-Level Game in Dealing with Neighbours." *European Foreign Affairs Review* 9:347–62.

Human Rights Watch. 1999. *Republic of Belarus: Violations of Academic Freedom* 11, no. 7 (July). Washington, DC: Human Rights Watch.

———. 1998. *Republic of Belarus: Turning Back the Clock* 10, no. 7 (July). Washington, DC: Human Rights Watch.

Huntington, Samuel P. 1996. *The Clash of Civilizations and the Remaking of World Order*. New York: Simon and Schuster.

Ioffe, Grigory. 2003. "Understanding Belarus: Belarusian Identity." Part 2. *Europe-Asia Studies* 55 (8): 1241–72.

Jewsbury, George F. 1976. *The Russian Annexation of Bessarabia, 1774–1828: A Study of Imperial Expansion*. New York: East European Quarterly.

Joint Statement. 2005. *Road Map for the Common Economic Space—Building Blocks for Sustained Economic Growth*. Moscow, May.

Kapferer, Bruce. 1988. *Legends of People, Myths of State: Violence, Intolerance, and Political Culture in Sri Lanka and Australia*. Washington, DC: Smithsonian Institution Press.

Kappeler, Andreas. 2001. *The Russian Empire: A Multiethnic History*. Trans. Alfred Clayton. Harlow: Longman.

Kaufman, Stuart. 1996. "Spiraling to Ethnic War: Elites, Masses, and Moscow in Moldova's Civil War." *International Security* 21:108–38.

Kelley, Judith. 2004. *Ethnic Politics in Europe: The Power of Norms and Incentives.* Princeton, NJ: Princeton University Press.

Kenney, Padraic. 2002. *A Carnival of Revolution: Central Europe 1989.* Princeton, NJ: Princeton University Press.

Khazanov, Anatoly M. 1995. *After the USSR. Ethnicity, Nationalism, and Politics in the Commonwealth of Independent States.* Madison: University of Wisconsin Press.

King, Charles. 2000. *The Moldovans: Romania, Russia, and the Politics of Culture.* Stanford, CA: Hoover Institution Press.

———. 1998. "Ethnicity and Institutional Reform: The Dynamics of 'Indigenization' in the Moldovan ASSR." *Nationalities Papers* 26:57–72.

———. 1999. "The Ambivalence of Authenticity, or How the Moldovan Language Was Made." *Slavic Review* 58 (1): 117–42.

———. 1994. "Moldovan Identity and the Politics of Pan-Romanism." *Slavic Review* 53 (2): 345–68.

Klier, John Doyle. 1986. *Russia Gathers Her Jews: The Origins of the "Jewish Question" in Russia, 1772–1825.* DeKalb: Northern Illinois University Press.

Kolstø, Pål, Andrei Edemsky, and Natalya Kalashnikova. 1993. "The Dniester Conflict: Between Irredentism and Separatism." *Europe-Asia Studies* 45:973–1000.

Kolstø, Pål, and Andrei Malgin. 1998. "The Transnistrian Republic: A Case of Politicized Regionalism." *Nationalities Papers* 26 (1): 103–27.

Kotljarchuk, Andrej. 2004. "The Tradition of Belarusian Statehood: Conflicts about the Past of Belarus." In *Contemporary Change in Belarus, Baltic and East European Studies*, vol. 2, edited by Egle Rindzeviciute. Huddinge, Sweden:Baltic and East European Graduate School.

Kovkel, I. I., and E. S. Iarmusik. 2000. *Istoriia Belarusi: S drevneishikh vremen do nashego vremeni.* Minsk: Aversev.

Krasner, Stephen D., ed. 2001. *Problematic Sovereignty: Contested Rules and Political Possibilities.* New York: Columbia University Press.

Krause, Kevin Deegan. 2003. "The Ambivalent Influence of the European Union on Democratization in Slovakia." In *The European Union and Democratization*, edited by Paul J. Kubicek, 56–86. London: Routledge.

Kremer, Martin. 2005. "Towards an EU Baltic Eastern Policy." In *Russia, the EU and the Baltic States. Enhancing the Potential for Cooperation*, edited by Matthes Buhbe and Iris Kempe, 23–27. Moscow: Friedrich Ebert Stiftung.

Kubicek, Paul J., ed. 2003. *The European Union and Democratization.* London: Routledge.

Kuromiya, Hiroaki. 1998. *Freedom and Terror in the Donbas: A Ukrainian-Russian Borderland, 1870s–1990s.* Cambridge: Cambridge University Press.

Kuzio, Taras, and Andrew Wilson. 1994. *Ukraine: Perestroika to Independence.* Edmonton, AB: CIUS Press.

Ladislav, Holy. 1996. *The Little Czech and the Great Czech Nation: National Identity and the Post-Communist Social Transformation.* Cambridge: Cambridge University Press.

Lavanex, Sandra. 2004. "EU External Governance in 'Wider Europe.'" *Journal for European Public Policy* 11 (4): 680–700.

Legea Parlamentului Republicii Moldova cu privire la funcţionarea limbilor vorbite pe teritoriul RSS Moldoveneşti, Nr.3465-XI din 01.09.89, Veştile nr.9/217, 1989.

Lewis, Ann, ed. 2004. *The EU & Moldova: On a Fault-Line of Europe.* London: Federal Trust for Education and Research.

Liber, George O. 1998. "Imagining Ukraine: Regional Differences and the Emergence of an Integrated State Identity, 1926–1994." *Nations and Nationalism* 4 (2): 187–206.

Lindner, Rainer, and Boris Meissner, eds. 2001. *Die Ukraine und Belarus' in der Transformation: Eine Zwischenbilanz.* Köln: Wissenschaft und Politik.

Liska, J. 1991. "The Human Dimension in the Helsinki Process." In *International Security and Humanitarian Co-operation in the ReUnited Europe*, edited by Wolfgang Kleinwachter and Kaarle Nordenstreng. Tampere, Finland: University of Tampere.

Livezeanu, Irina. 1995. *Cultural Politics in Greater Romania: Regionalism, Nation Building, and Ethnic Struggle, 1918–1930.* Ithaca, NY: Cornell University Press.

———. 1981a. "Urbanization in a Low Key and Linguistic Change in Soviet Moldavia." Part 1. *Soviet Studies* 32 (3): 327–51.

———. 1981b. "Urbanization in a Low Key and Linguistic Change in Soviet Moldavia." Part 2. *Soviet Studies* 32 (4): 573–92.

Ljungvall, Tobias. 2003. *Kontroll: Rapport från Vitryssland.* Stockholm: Svenskt Internationellt Liberalt Centrums förlag.

Lubachko, Ivan S. 1972. *Belorussia under Soviet Rule, 1917–1957.* Lexington: University Press of Kentucky.

Lynch, Dov. 2003. *Russia Faces Europe.* Chaillot Paper No. 60. Paris: Institute for Security Studies.

Magocsi, Paul Robert. 1996. *A History of Ukraine.* Toronto: University of Toronto Press.

Mahncke, Dieter. 2001. "Russia's Attitude to the European Security and Defence Policy." *European Foreign Policy Review* 6:427–36.

Manners, Ian. 2002. "Normative Power Europe: A Contradiction in Terms?" *Journal of Common Market Studies* 40 (2): 235–58.

Maresca, John. 1987. *To Helsinki: The Conference on Security and Co-operation in Europe, 1973–1975.* Durham, NC: Duke University Press.

Markus, Ustina. 1996. "The Bilingualism Question in Belarus and Ukraine." *Transition* 2, November 29.

Marples, David R. 2005. "Europe's Last Dictatorship: The Roots and Perspectives of Authoritarianism in 'White Russia.'" *Europe-Asia Studies* 57 (6): 895–908.

———. 2002. "Belarus: The Last European Dictatorship?" In *The EU and Belarus: Between Moscow and Brussels*, edited by Ann Lewis, 31–44. London: Federal Trust.

———. 1999. *Belarus: A Denationalized Nation*. Amsterdam: Harwood Academic.

———. 1996. *Belarus: From Soviet Rule to Nuclear Catastrophe*. New York: St. Martin's.

———. 1994. "Kuropaty: The Investigation of a Stalinist Historical Controversy." *Slavic Review* 53 (2): 513–23.

Martin, Terry. 2001. *The Affirmative Action Empire: Nations and Nationalism in the Soviet Union, 1923–1939*. Ithaca, NY: Cornell University Press.

McGoldrick, Amy. 2002. "Belarus." In *Let's Go, Eastern Europe: The World's Bestselling Budget Travel Series, Completely Updated and Revised for 2002*. New York: St. Martin's.

Mikhailov, Boris. 1999. *Case History*. Zurich and New York: Scalo.

Miller, Hugh, and Charles Fox. 2001. "The Epistemic Community." *Administration & Society* 32 (6): 668–85.

Moore, Henrietta. 1990. "Paul Ricoeur: Action, Meaning and Text." In *Reading Material Culture: Structuralism, Hermeneutics and Post-Structuralism*, edited by Christopher Tilley, 85–120. Oxford: Basil Blackwell.

Mungiu-Pippidi, Alina. 2004. "Beyond the New Borders." *Journal of Democracy* 15:48–62.

Mychajlyszyn, Natalie. 2002. "The OSCE and the Prevention of Ethnic Conflict: Lessons Learned from Field Missions and the HCNM." In *Conflict Prevention: Grand Illusion or Path to Peace?*, edited by Albrecht Schnabel and David Carment. Tokyo: United Nations University Press.

———. 2001. "The OSCE: The Impact of International Factors on Regionalism in the Former Soviet States." In *Regionalism in Post-Soviet States*, edited by James Hughes and Gwendolyn Sasse. London: Frank Cass.

———. 1997. "The OSCE and Conflict Prevention: The Case of Ukraine." In *Balancing Hegemony: The OSCE in the CIS*, edited by S. Neil MacFarlane and Oliver Thränert. Kingston, ON: Queen's Centre for International Relations.

Mykhnenko, Vlad. 2003. "State, Society and Protest under Post-Communism: Ukrainian Miners and Their Defeat." In *Uncivil Society? Contentious Politics in Post-Communist Europe*, edited by Peter Kopecký and Cas Mudde. London: Routledge.

Neukirch, Claus. 2004. "Moldova's Eastern Dimension." In *The EU and Moldova: On a Fault Line of Europe*, edited by Ann Lewis, 133–43. London: Federal Trust for Education and Research.

Nistor, Ion. 1943–44. "Localizarea numelui Basarabiei în Moldova transpruteană." *Analele Academiei Române Memoriile Secţiunii Istrice.* Academia Română, Bucureşti 3, 24 (1): 1–27.

O'Loughlin, John, Vladimir Kolossov, and Andrei Tchepalyga. 1998. "National Construction, Territorial Separatism, and Post-Soviet Geopolitics in the Transdniester Moldovan Republic." *Post-Soviet Geography and Economics* 39 (6): 332–58.

Padhol, Uladzimir, and David R. Marples. 2005. "The Dynamics of the 2001 Presidential Election." In *Postcommunist Belarus,* edited by Stephen White, Elena Korostoleva, and John Loewenhardt, 79–96. Lanham, MD: Rowman and Littlefield.

Pelenski, Jaroslaw. 1975. "Shelest and His Period in Soviet Ukraine (1963–1972): A Revival of Controlled Ukrainian Autonomism." In *Ukraine in the 1970s,* edited by Peter J. Potichnyj, 283–305. Oakville, ON: Mosaic.

Plokhy, Serhii. 2005. *Unmaking Imperial Russia: Mykhailo Hrushevsky and the Writing of Ukrainian History.* Toronto: University of Toronto Press.

Popescu, Nicu. 2005. "The EU in Moldova—Settling Conflicts in the Neighborhood." Occasional Paper No. 60. The European Union Institute for Security Studies.

Portnov, Andrii. 2005. "Svoboda ta vybir na Donbasi." *Krytyka* 3: 5–6.

Prodi, Romano. 2002. "A Wider Europe—A Proximity Policy as the Key to Stability." Peace, Security and Stability International Dialogue and the Role of the EU, Sixth ECSA-World Conference, Brussels, December 5–6, 2003.

Protsyk, Oleh. 2005. "Federalism and Democracy in Moldova." *Post-Soviet Affairs* 21:72–90.

Pursiainen, Christer, and Sergei Medvedev, eds. 2005. *Towards the Kaliningrad Partnership in EU-Russia Relations: A Road Map into the Future.* Moscow: RECEP.

Riabchuk, Mykola. 2002. "Ukraine: One State, Two Countries?" *Transit* 23.

Rindzeviciute, Egle, ed. 2004. *Contemporary Change in Belarus, Baltic and East European Studies,* 2. Huddinge, Sweden: Baltic and East European Graduate School.

Roper, Steven D. 2004. "From Frozen Conflict to Frozen Agreement: The Unrecognized State of Transnistria." In *De Facto States: The Quest for Sovereignty,* edited by Tozun Bahcheli, Barry Bartmann, and Henry Srebrnik. New York: Routledge.

Šabić, Claudia. 2004. "The Ukrainian Piedmont: Institutionalisation at the Borders of East Central Europe." In *The Making of Regions in Post-Socialist Europe—The Impact of Culture, Economic Structure and Institutions. Case Studies from Poland, Hungary, Romania and Ukraine.* Vol. 2. Edited by Melanie Tatur. Wiesbaden: VS Verlag.

Šabić, Claudia, and Kerstin Zimmer. 2004. "Ukraine: The Genesis of a Captured State." In *The Making of Regions in Post-Socialist Europe—The*

Impact of Culture, Economic Structure and Institutions. Case Studies from Poland, Hungary, Romania and Ukraine. Vol. 2. Edited by Melanie Tatur. Wiesbaden: VS Verlag.

Sahm, Astrid. 2001. "Belarus' Von der parlamentarischen Republik zum präsidentalen Regime." In *Die Ukraine und Belarus' in der Transformation: Eine Zwischenbilanz*, edited by Rainer Lindner and Boris Meissner, 125–48. Köln: Wissenschaft und Politik.

Sanford, George. 1996. "Belarus on the Road to Nationhood." *Survival* 38 (1): 131–53.

Schimmelfennig, Frank. 2001. "The Community Trap: Liberal Norms, Rhetorical Action, and the Eastern Enlargement of the European Union." *International Organization* 55 (1): 47–80.

Schimmelfennig, Frank, Stefan Engert, and Heiko Knobel. 2003. "Cost, Commitment and Compliance: The Impact of EU Democratic Conditionality on Latvia, Slovakia and Turkey." *Journal of Common Market Studies* 41 (3): 495–518.

———. 2005. "The Impact of EU Political Conditionality." In *The Europeanization of Central and Eastern Europe*, edited by Frank Schimmelfennig and Ulrich Sedelmeier, 29–50. Ithaca, NY: Cornell University Press.

Schimmelfennig, Frank, and Ulrich Sedelmeier. 2005. Introduction: Conceptualizing the Europeanization of Central and Eastern Europe. In *The Europeanization of Central and Eastern Europe*, edited by Frank Schimmelfennig and Ulrich Sedelmeier. Ithaca, NY: Cornell University Press.

Schimmelfennig, Frank, and Wolfgang Wagner. 2004. Preface: External governance in the European Union. *Journal for European Public Policy* 11 (4): 657–60.

Schmidtke, Oliver. 2006. "Immigration Policy in Europe: A Challenge to Established Forms of Multi-Level Governance." In *European Governance: Policy Making between Politicization and Control*, edited by G. Walzenbach, 127–46. Aldershot, UK: Ashgate.

Scurtu, Ion, ed. 2003. *Istoria Românilor. Vol VIII: România întregită.* Academia Română Secţia de Ştiinţe Istorice şi Arheologie. Bucureşti: Editura Enciclopedică.

Serebian, Oleg. 2004. "'Good Brothers,' Bad Neighbours: Romanian/Moldovan Relations." In *The EU and Moldova: On a Fault Line of Europe*, edited by Ann Lewis, 149–53. London: Federal Trust for Education and Research.

Sheremet, Pavel, and Svetlana Kalinkina. 2004. *Sluchainyi Prezident.* St. Petersburg: Limbus.

Sherr, James. 2006. "Ukraine's Scissors: Between Internal Weakness and External Dependence." In *Russie.Nei.Visions 2006: Understanding Russia and the New Independent States*, edited by Thomas Gomart and Tatiana Kastueva-Jean. Paris: Institut français de relations internationales.

Shushkevich, Stanislau. 2002. *Neokommunizm v Belarusi: ideologiia, praktika, perspektivy*. Smolensk, Russia: Skif.

Siegelbaum, Lewis H. 1997. "Freedom of Prices and the Price of Freedom: The Miners' Dilemma in the Soviet Union and Its Successor States." *Journal of Communist Studies and Transition Politics* 13 (4): 17–18.

Silitski, Vitali. 2002. "The Change Is Yet to Come: Opposition Strategies and Western Efforts to Promote Democracy in Belarus." In *The EU and Belarus: Between Moscow and Brussels*, edited by Ann Lewis, 351–73. London: Federal Trust for Education and Research.

Skvortsova, Alla. 2002. "The Cultural and Social Makeup of Moldova: A Bipolar or Dispersed Society?" In *National Integration and Violent Conflict in Post-Soviet Societies: The Cases of Estonia and Moldova*, edited by Pål Kolstø. Lanham, MD: Rowman and Littlefield.

Smith, Karen E. 2005. "The Outsiders: The European Neighbourhood Policy." *International Affairs* 81 (4): 757–73.

———. 2001. "The Use of Political Conditionality in the EU's Relations with Third Countries: How Effective?" *European Foreign Affairs Review* 3:253–74.

Stăvilă, Ion. 2004. Moldova between East and West: A Paradigm of Foreign Affairs." In *The EU and Moldova: On a Fault Line of Europe*, edited by Ann Lewis, 127–32. London: Federal Trust for Education and Research.

Strong, John W., ed. 1971. *The Soviet Union under Brezhnev and Kosygin*. New York: D. Van Nostrand.

Stus, Vasil. 2001. *Lysty do syna*. Ivano-Frankivsk, Ukraine: Lileia-NV.

Suny, Ronald Grigor. 1993. *The Revenge of the Past: Nationalism, Revolution, and the Collapse of the Soviet Union*. Stanford, CA: Stanford University Press.

Szporluk, Roman. 2000. "Ukraine: From an Imperial Periphery to a Sovereign State." In *Russia, Ukraine, and the Breakup of the Soviet Union*, by Roman Szporluk, 361–94. Stanford, CA: Hoover Institution Press.

Ther, Philipp, and Ana Siljak, eds. 2001. *Redrawing Nations: Ethnic Cleansing in East Central Europe, 1944–1948*. Lanham, MD: Rowman and Littlefield.

Tillett, Lowell. 1975. "Ukrainian Nationalism and the Fall of Shelest." *Slavic Review* 34 (4): 752–68.

Timmermann, Heinz. 2004. "*Koloboks* Union: Belarus und Rußland am Wendepunkt?" *Konturen und Kontraste: Belarus sucht sein Gesicht, Osteuropa* 2 (54): 218–27.

———. 2002. "The Union of Belarus and Russia in the European Context." In *The EU and Belarus: Between Moscow and Brussels*, edited by Ann Lewis, 277–302. London: Federal Trust for Education and Research.

Timmermann, Heinz, and Stefan Gänzle. 2002. "The European Union's Policy towards Russia." In *EU Enlargement and Beyond: The Baltic States and Russia*, edited by Helmut Hubel, 145–217. Berlin: Spitz.

Tishkov, Valery. 1997. *Ethnicity, Nationalism and Conflict in and after the Soviet Union: The Mind Aflame*. London: Sage.

Trebici, V. 1993. "Basarabia şi Bucovina: Aspecte demografice." In *Sub povara graniţei imperiale*, edited by A. Pop. Bucharest: Recif.

Troebst, Stefan. 2003. "'We Are Transnistrians!' Post-Soviet Identity Management in the Dniester Valley. *Ab Imperio* 1:437–66.

Upson Clark, Charles. 1927. *Bessarabia: Russia and Roumania on the Black Sea*. New York: Dodd, Mead and Company.

Vaitovich, A. P., et al., eds. 2000. *Belarus': na miazhy tysiachahoddziau*. Minsk: Belaruskaia Entsyklapedyia.

Van Meurs, Wim. 1998. "Carving a Moldavian Identity out of History." *Nationalities Papers* 26:39–56.

Van Zon, Hans. 2001. "Neo-Patrimonialism as an Impediment to Economic Development: The Case of Ukraine." *Journal of Communist Studies and Transition Politics* 17 (3): 71–95.

Verdery, Katherine. 1991. *National Ideology under Socialism, Identity and Cultural Politics in Ceausescu's Romania*. Berkeley: University of California Press.

Viţu, Liliana. 2004. "Moldova and the Baltic States: Lessons of Success and Failure." In *The EU and Moldova: On a Fault Line of Europe*, edited by Ann Lewis, 155–59. London: Federal Trust for Education and Research.

Way, Lucan A. 2002. "Pluralism by Default in Moldova." *Journal of Democracy* 13:127–41.

Webber, Mark. 2001. "Third-Party Inclusion in European Security and Defence Policy: A Case Study of Russia." *European Foreign Policy Review* 6:407–26.

Weiner, Amir. 2006. "The Empires Pay a Visit: When Gulag Returnees Encountered East European Rebellions on the Soviet Western Frontier." *Journal of Modern History* 78 (2): 333–76.

White, Stephen, and Ian McAllister. 2005. "Moldova and the Politics of Meso-Areas." In *Emerging Meso-Areas in the Former Socialist Countries: Histories Revived or Improvised?* edited by Kimitaka Matsuzato. Sapporo, Japan: Slavic Research Center, Hokkaido University.

Wieck, Hans-Georg. 2002. "The OSCE and the Council of Europe in Conflict with the Lukashenko Regime." In *The EU and Belarus: Between Moscow and Brussels*, edited by Ann Lewis, 261–75. London: Federal Trust for Education and Research.

Wilson, Andrew. 2005. *Ukraine's Orange Revolution*. New Haven, CT: Yale University Press.

Woolhiser, Curt. 2003. "Constructing National Identities in the Polish-Belarusian Borderlands, Part 1." *Ab Imperio* 1 (April): 293–345.

Yekelchyk, Serhy. 2004. *Stalin's Empire of Memory: Russian-Ukrainian Relations in the Soviet Historical Imagination*. Toronto: University of Toronto Press.

Youngs, Richard. 2001. *The European Union and the Promotion of Democracy: Europe's Mediterranean and Asian Policies*. Oxford: Oxford University Press.

Zagorski, Andrei. 2004. "Policies towards Russia, Ukraine, Moldova and Belarus." In *European Union Foreign and Security Policy: Towards a Neighbourhood Strategy*, edited by Roland Dannreuther, 79–97. London: Routledge.

Zaprudnik, Jan. 1993. *Belarus: At a Crossroads in History*. Boulder, CO: Westview.

Zenkovich, Nikolai. 2005. *Tajny ushedshego veka: Granitsy, spory, obidy*. Moscow: Olma.

Zimmer, Kerstin. 2004. "The Captured Region: Actors and Institutions in the Ukrainian Donbas." In *The Making of Regions in Post-Socialist Europe— The Impact of Culture, Economic Structure and Institutions. Case Studies from Poland, Hungary, Romania and Ukraine*. Vol. 2. Edited by Melanie Tatur. Wiesbaden: VS Verlag.

Index

Notes: CEE stands for Central and Eastern Europe; ENP, for European Neighbourhood Policy; EU, for European Union; OSCE, for Organization for Security and Co-operation in Europe; PCA, for Partnership and Cooperation Agreements; SSR, for Soviet Socialist Republic

acquis communautaire, 44–45, 145, 206, 208–10, 213
Akhmetov, Rinat, 105
Andrukhovych, Yurii, 101–2, 109–10
Austro-Hungarian Empire, 15

Bahushevich, Francishak, 15, 16
Balkan Stability Pact, 216–17, 221
Barysch, Katinka, 213
Belarus, Republic of: 2006 election, 175–76, 178–87; 2006 election pre-emptive crackdown, 176–78; 2006 election "results" and aftermath, 72–73, 187–92; civil society, weakness of, 5, 191; Communist Party de-nationalized, 60–61; constitutional reforms, 63, 65–66; declaration of independence (1991), 27, 62; "Europe's last dictatorship," 2, 55, 62–70, 197; future prospects, 70–73; history, 11–16, 19–20, 21–22, 57; independence phase (1991–94), 55, 62–64; isolation of, 67–68, 71; Lukashenka era (1994–96), 55, 64–66; nationhood, factors leading to,

10, 21–22, 24–25, 27–28, 61–62; Putin's assimilation efforts, 68–69, 71; relations with West, 7, 67–68; Stalinist massacre in Kurapaty Forest, 25, 59, 69–70. *See also* Lukashenka, Aliaksandr; *entries beginning with* Belarusian
Belarus and Russia. *See* Russia and Belarus
Belarus and the European Union. *See* European Union and Belarus
Belarusian Democratic Republic (1918), 16
Belarusian national identity: language and, 26, 56–57, 59–60, 65, 74n15; Lukashenka and, 64–70; pan-Soviet identity, 58, 59, 60–62; reluctant independence (1991–94), 62–64; rise of, 71–72; weakness of, 5, 56–58, 62
Belarusian nationalism: Belarusian Popular Front (BPF), 25, 26, 59, 62, 63–64; Belarusian the official state language (1990), 26, 60, 65; Belarusization periods, 56–57; declaration of independence (1991), 27, 62; declaration of sovereignty (1990), 60; first stage

of national movement (mid-1800s), 15; after Gorbachev's perestroika, 57; independence favored by population, 192; national identity weak, 5, 56–58, 62; nationhood, factors leading to, 10, 21–22, 24–5, 27–28, 61–62; during Soviet period, 24–26, 56–57, 59–60

Belarusian Popular Front (BPF), 25, 26, 59, 62, 63–64

Belarusian Soviet Republic (1918–19), 16

Belarusian Soviet Socialist Republic: Belarusization periods, 56–57; declaration of sovereignty (1990), 60; eastern Belarus to Soviet sphere post-WWI, 16, 19–20, 57; industrialization and assimilation (1945–91), 58–62; language issue, 26, 56–57, 59–60, 74n15; late Soviet period, 23–27; nationalism during Soviet period, 24–26, 56–57, 59–60; Soviet massacre in Kurapaty Forest, 25, 59, 69–70; Soviet role in nation building, 21–22, 24–25, 27–28

Beria, Lavrentii, 57

Bessarabia: history pre-1939, 13–14, 18–19, 23, 80–81, 139–40; multiethnic region, 116–17; part of Moldovan SSR (1939), 22–23, 81–82; Romanian connections, 1, 13, 81, 140–41. See also Moldova, Republic of; Moldovan Soviet Socialist Republic

Brubaker, Rogers, 19

Budjak. See Gagauzia; Moldova, Republic of

Bukhvostau, Aliaksandr, 176

Bukovyna, 13, 17, 18, 22, 81

Bush, George W., 67

Charles XII, King of Sweden, 13

Checkel, Jeffrey, 148

Chernobyl disaster (1986), 25

Chernomyrdin, Viktor, 163

Chior, Pavel, 22

Chirac, Jacques, 197, 212

Cold War, 2, 36–37, 134–36

Common Economic Space (CES), 32, 164, 208–10

Common Foreign and Security Policy (CFSP), 201–2, 207, 210

Common Space of Freedom, Security and Justice (CSFSJ), 211

Common Strategies, 201–2, 207, 210, 214

Commonwealth of Independent States (CIS): EU's early perception of, 197; Moldova's membership, 79, 85, 141; Ukraine's membership, 32, 45

Community of Democratic Choice, 165

Conference for Security and Co-operation in Europe (CSCE), 36, 38, 50n11

Corruption Perceptions Index, 159

Crimea, 39, 168

Cruc, Mircea, 83

Czechoslovak Republic, 20

"Defamation of the Republic of Belarus," 177–78

Democratic League of Moldovan Students, 83

Democratic Movement in Support of Restructuring, 25, 82

Dnieper (Eastern) Ukraine, 13, 16–17, 163

Domovitov, Nikolai, 111

Donbas, Ukraine: contemporary images of region, 101–3; economic situation, 97, 103–7, 110; electoral fraud and Orange Revolution, 6, 108; future prospects, 106–9, 110–11;

historical background, 6,
98–101; identity within Ukraine,
98, 108–9; miners' strikes, 104,
105, 108; political leanings,
99–101, 104–5; relationship with
western Ukraine, 104–6, 109–10;
support for independence, 103
Dontsov, Dmytro, 100
Druc, Mircea, 83–84
Dziuba, Ivan, 24

Eastern (Dnieper) Ukraine, 13,
16–17, 163
Easton, David, 148
Edemsky, Andrei, 83
Euro-Atlantic Partnership Council
(EAPC), 40, 41–42, 45, 52n19
European Commission, 195–96,
202–4
European Neighbourhood and
Partnership Instrument (ENPI),
205
European Neighbourhood Policy:
Action Plan with Moldova
(2005), 6, 92–93, 145–47,
217–18; Action Plan with
Ukraine, 170, 215, 216; Action
Plans, 137, 145, 147, 204–5;
conditionality aspect, 137–38,
145; deficiencies, 205–6;
development, 202–3;
instruments, 201, 204–5,
225n36; with Moldova, 7, 147,
221; political ideology, spread of,
144–46; principles and
objectives, 137–38, 144–45,
203–4; Russia's concern about,
203, 221–22; surrogate for EU
membership, 138, 145, 150, 221,
225n33; trade incentives,
146–47; with Ukraine, 44–45,
169, 216, 221
European Security and Defence
Policy (ESDP), 210–11

European security institutions:
CSCE/OSCE, 36, 38–40;
manifestation of collective
identity, 34; security vacuum
after collapse of Soviet Union,
37; state identity and, 34–35;
"Ukraine fatigue," 47, 48. See also
European Union; NATO;
Organization for Security and
Co-operation in Europe (OSCE)
European Security Strategy, 202
European Union and Belarus: EU
policy of conditional
engagement, 219, 220; EU
reaction to flawed elections, 73,
188, 191, 219–20; PCA, 196,
198–99, 218–19; relationship, 67,
138, 196, 200, 218–20, 221;
technical and financial
assistance, 201; trade
relationship, 200, 220
European Union and Eastern
enlargement: bilateral strategies
for CEE and NIS, 8, 136, 196–98,
203, 220–22; Common Strategies
on Russia and Ukraine, 201–2,
207, 210, 214; conditionality
principle, 136, 137–38, 145,
150–51, 154n41, 199, 223n12;
Copenhagen membership
criteria, 133, 151n1; cost to CEE
of compliance with EU, 138;
economic incentives for CEE, 3,
133, 146–47, 198–99; European
identity as draw, 149–50;
Europeanization of eastern
frontier, 3, 7, 134–36;
Generalized System of
Preferences (GSP), 200, 207, 218;
membership possibility, 7, 133,
138, 150, 169–70, 196; norms
and values, spread of, 136,
147–49, 204; partnership, not
membership, 136, 138, 145, 150,
196, 198–99, 221, 225n33; as

perceived threat to Russia's authority, 8, 203, 221–22; political ideology, expansion of, 136, 137–38, 144–46; security objective, 44, 137, 202; technical and financial assistance, 201; trade relationships, 137, 146–47, 196, 198–201, 207. *See also* European Neighbourhood Policy; *entries beginning with* European Union

European Union and Moldova: Action Plan (2005), 6, 92–93, 145–47, 217–18; Border Assistance Mission (2005), 93, 143, 218; competing East-West loyalties, 87–90, 134, 139, 142–43, 149–50; conditionality principle of EU, 136, 137–38, 145, 150–51, 154n41; dual citizenship (Moldovan-Romanian) issue, 89–90, 142–43; economic inclusion, 146–47; ENP, 7, 147, 221; EU membership goal of Moldova, 7, 94, 133–34, 145, 150–51; European identity and belonging, 149–50; foreign policies toward EU, 87–88; member of European Conference, 214–15, 227n61; normative inclusion, 147–49; orientation to West, 5–6, 79–80, 90–94, 134, 142–44, 216–18; PCA, 87, 93, 143, 152n8, 196, 217; political reforms in Moldova, 144–46, 150, 154n42; technical and financial assistance, 201; trade relationship, 85, *86*, 93, 200–201; Transnistria conflict and, 87, 93, 143, 145, 217–18

European Union and Russia: economic agreements, 207–10; energy dialogue and partnership,

211–14; EU's bilateral approaches to Eastern bloc, 8, 196–98, 203; focus on "soft" security issues, 197; individual European states' policies regarding Russia, 196–97; Russia's concern regarding EU enlargement, 8, 203, 221–22; security agreements, 201–2, 207, 210–11; TACIS program, 206–7; technical and financial assistance, 201, 206–7; trade relationship, 199–201

European Union and Ukraine: argument for inclusion of Ukraine, 169–71; ENP, 44–45, 169, 216, 221; EU's Common Strategy on Ukraine, 201–2, 214; EU's hesitancy about Ukrainian membership, 169–70, 214–15; EU-Ukraine Action Plan, 170, 215, 216; influence of EU on Ukraine's post-Soviet identity, 43–45; member of European Conference, 214–15, 227n61; NATO membership, goal of Ukraine, 42, 48, 171, 215; PCA (1998), 44, 152n8, 169, 196, 198–99; technical and financial assistance, 201; trade relationship, 199–200

Evelkin, Hryhory, 181

Ferrero-Waldner, Benita, 170, 218
Fralou, Valery, 182
France, 210. *See also* Chirac, Jacques
Freedom House, 160

Gagauzia: conflict and independence, 26–27, 83, 117–19; development of identity politics, 124–26; Kozak Memorandum and, 92; language situation, 83, 125, 126–28; nation-building process, 123–24;

Soviet ethno-national
  classification, 121–22, 128,
  130n11, 131n15
Galicia, 13, 17, 18, 20
Gamsakhurdia, Zviad, 64
Gazprom, 166, 213
Generalized System of Preferences
  (GSP), 200, 207, 218, 220
Gongadze, Heorhii, 164
Gorbachev, Mikhail, 24–25, 82–84
Grand Duchy of Lithuania, 11–12
Green World (Ukraine), 25

Haiduk, Vitalii, 105, 107
Haidukevich, Siarhey, 182, 189
Hanchar, Viktar, 176
Hancharyk, Uladzimir, 175
Helsinki Final Act (1975), 36, 50n9
Heugen, Guenter von, 169–70
Hirschman, Albert, 99
Holovakha, Yevhen, 109
Hramada, Narodnaia, 179
Hroch, Miroslav, 9–10, 15, 28
Hrushevsky, Mykhailo, 11, 18
Hryb, Miacheslau, 184
Huntington, Samuel, 2, 110
Hurin, Uladzimir, 183

Ihnatouski, Usevalad, 22
Ilaşcu, Ilie, 90–92
Illiaronov, Andrei, 166–67
Index of Economic Freedom, 160
Industrial Union of the Donbas,
  105, 107
Internationalism or Russification?
  (Dziuba), 24
Internationalist Movement for
  Unity, 83
Istanbul Declaration (OSCE), 87
Ivano, Sergei, 167–68

Kalashnikova, Natalya, 83
Kaliakin, Siarhei, 176, 178, 187
Kalinowski, Kastus, 14

Kazulin, Aliaksandr, 179, 182,
  185–86, 189
Kebich, Viacheslau, 63, 64
Kenney, Padraic, 110
Khmelnytsky, Bohdan, 12
Kiev Agreement, 91
King, Charles, 83, 84
Kohl, Helmut, 197
Kolstø, Pål, 83
Kozak, Dmitri, 91–92
Kozak Memorandum, 90–92
Kravchuk, Leonid, 45–46, 104
Krzeminski, Adam, 221
Kuchma, Leonid, 46–47, 67, 104–5,
  164, 214
Kyivan Rus, 11, 162–63

Lavkovich, Uladzimir, 184
Liabedzka, Anatol, 178, 181, 187
Lucinschi, Petru, 85, 87
Lukashenka, Aliaksandr: 2006
  election, results and reaction,
  187–92, 219; 2006 election
  campaign, 176–81, 184–87;
  authoritarian rule of Belarus,
  64–70, 176–78, 187–92, 218–19;
  election performances, 63–64,
  72–73, 176–81, 184–92; future
  prospects, 70–73, 191–92; gas
  prices and Russian pressure, 190;
  relations with Russia, 68–69,
  71–73

Maistrenko, Ivan, 99–100
Manaieu, Aleh, 176, 180, 189
Marushchenko, Viktor, 110
Masherau, Piotr, 58
Mazepa, Ivan, 13
MEDA (EU program), 204, 205
Miasnikovich, Mikhail, 190
Milinkevich, Aliaksandr: candidate
  in 2006 Belarus elections, 72,
  175–76, 178–79, 181, 182;
  electoral campaign in 2006, 185,
  186–87, 189

Moldova, Republic of:
  Commonwealth of Independent
  States, 79, 85, 141; Communist
  (PCM) government, 79, 88–90,
  93; competing East-West
  loyalties, 87–90, 134, 139,
  142–43, 149–50; declaration of
  independence (1991), 27, 116;
  history, 13–15, 18–19, 22–23,
  80–83, 139–41; language issues,
  88–89; minorities' status, 89;
  minority ethnic movements (see
  Gagauzia; Transnistria);
  multiethnic population, 116–17;
  orientation toward West, 2,
  79–80, 85, 90–94, 134, 142–44,
  216–18; Popular Front, 25, 26,
  83, 118–19. See also Bessarabia;
  Voronin, Vladimir; entries
  beginning with Moldovan
Moldova and Russia. See Russia and
  Moldova
Moldova and the European Union.
  See European Union and
  Moldova
Moldovan Autonomous Soviet
  Socialist Republic, 22–23, 81–82,
  140
Moldovan Community Party
  (PCM), 79, 88–90, 93
Moldovan Democratic Republic of
  Bessarabia (1918), 19, 81
Moldovan national identity:
  competing loyalties, 87–90, 134,
  139, 142–43, 149–50;
  confirmation in constitution
  (1994), 141; development post-
  1991, 116–17; dual citizenship
  (Moldovan-Romanian) issue,
  89–90, 142–43; European
  orientation, 5–6, 79–80, 90–94,
  134, 142–44, 216–18; language
  issues, 3, 22, 25, 81–83, 88–89,
  125; in late 1980s, 82–84;
  Moldovanization by Soviets

(1920s), 22, 140;
  Romanianization vs.
  Russification, 79–83, 139–44;
  Soviet nurturing of ethno-
  nationalist movements, 6, 27–28,
  82, 140–41
Moldovan nationalism: declaration
  of independence (1991), 27, 116;
  glasnost and (late 1980s), 24–25,
  82–84; imperial collapse as
  catalyst, 10; language issue, 22,
  25, 81–83, 88–89, 125; national
  awakening (early 1900s), 18–19,
  81; Popular Front, 25, 26, 83,
  118–19; reunification with
  Romania rejected, 116, 125–26;
  Soviet nurturing of ethno-
  nationalist movements, 6, 27–28,
  82, 140–41
Moldovan Popular Front, 25, 26, 83,
  118–19
Moldovan Soviet Socialist Republic:
  ethnic Russians in population,
  81–82; formation (1939), 22–23,
  81–82, 140–41; glasnost and rise
  of dissent, 24–25, 82–84;
  identification with Romania,
  116; language issues, 25, 82–83,
  125; late Soviet period, 23–27;
  Moldovan Popular Front, 25, 26,
  83; Soviet nurturing of ethno-
  nationalist movements, 6, 27–28,
  82, 140–41
Molotov-Ribbentrop Pact (1939),
  22–23, 81, 140–41
Mykhnenko, Vlad, 106–7, 108

national identity: external events
  and identity development,
  15–16, 17, 61–62; link with
  geopolitics, 10; link with
  language, 56; post-colonial vs.
  post-Soviet context, 119–20,
  130n8. See also Belarusian
  national identity; Moldovan

national identity; Ukrainian national identity; Ukrainian state identity

nationalism and nationhood: "nationalizing states" post-WWI, 19–23; role of intelligentsia, 15–16, 21, 24, 57, 59, 122, 124–25; state intervention and nation building, 4–5, 10, 21, 27–28; three-stage model of national movements, 4, 9–10, 28. *See also* Belarusian nationalism; Moldovan nationalism; Ukrainian nationalism

NATO (North Atlantic Treaty Organization): alleged anti-Russian bias, 7; Euro-Atlantic Partnership Council (EAPC), 40, 41–42, 45, 52n19; Individual Partnership Program, 40; Membership Action Plan (MAP), 41–42, 51n16; Partnership for Peace (PfP), 40–41, 43, 45, 51n15; Russia and, 47

NATO and Ukraine: Information and Documentation Centre (Kyiv), 42, 46; Intensified Dialogue on Ukraine's NATO membership, 42; interactions with Ukraine post-1991, 40–43; NATO-Ukraine Action Plan (2002), 42, 46, 47, 52n22; Partnership for Peace (PfP), 44, 152n8, 169, 196, 198–99; Ukraine-NATO Charter on a Distinctive Partnership (1997), 41–42, 46, 47; Ukraine's membership goal, 42, 48, 169, 171

NISEPI (National Institute of Socio-Economic and Political Research), 176, 180–81

Orange Revolution in Ukraine, 39, 50n12, 158–62, 164–68

Organization for Security and Co-operation in Europe (OSCE): CSCE's successor, 38; election monitoring in 2004 in Ukraine, 39, 50n12; on fairness of 2006 Belarus election, 73; influence on Ukrainian identity, 36, 38–40; Istanbul Declaration, 87; Ukrainian membership, 45, 46

Organization of Ukrainian Nationalists, 20

Partnership and Cooperation Agreements: with Belarus, 196, 198–99, 218–19; conditionality principle, 199, 223n12; failure to accelerate domestic reform, 206; with Moldova, 87, 93, 143, 152n8, 196, 217; objectives, 137, 196, 198–99, 207; with Russia, 207–8; with Ukraine, 44, 152n8, 169, 196, 198–99

Partnership for Peace (PfP) (NATO), 40–41, 43, 45, 51n15

Partnership for Peace (PfP) (NATO and Ukraine), 44, 152n8, 169, 196, 198–99

Pavlovskii, Gleb, 166

Pazniak, Zianon: 2006 Belarus election and, 179, 182–83; candidate in 1994 Belarus election, 64; in exile from Belarus, 176; leader of Belarus Popular Front, 25, 59, 65, 179

Pereiaslav Treaty (1654), 13, 163

"Petersberg Tasks" of European Union, 44

Poland: history, 12–13, 16, 18, 19–20; Molotov-Ribbentrop Pact (1939), 22; relations with Belarus, 67

Polish-Lithuanian Commonwealth, 12

Poltava, battle of (1709), 13
Popular Movement for Restructuring (*Rukh*), 25, 26, 100
Principality of Moldavia, 13, 139–40
Prodi, Romano, 202, 212
Putin, Vladimir: attitude toward Ukraine, 163; and Belarus, 68–69, 71, 190; EU-Russia energy dialogue, 212; interference in Ukrainian politics, 164–65; involvement in Transnistria negotiations, 91; on readmission issue, 211

Revolution of 1905, 16–18
Rice, Condoleezza, 67
Romania: assimilation efforts interwar, 20–21; Bessarabia part of historical Moldovia, 13, 140; dual citizenship (Moldovan-Romanian) issue, 89–90, 142–43; Gagauzian pan-Romanian sentiment, 118; on Moldova's education policy (2001), 89; Moldova's rejection of reunification, 116, 125–26; Moldova's Romanianization *vs.* Russification, 79–83, 139–44; relationship with Moldova, 13, 19, 80–83, 139–44; Romanian language use in Moldova, 1, 13, 81, 140–41; Transnistrian pan-Romanian sentiment, 118–19; union with Bessarabia (1918), 19, 81, 140
Rukh (Popular Movement for Restructuring, Ukraine), 25, 26, 100
Russia: concern over EU's threat to its authority, 8, 203, 221–22; East-West political divide, 2, 4; history, 13–19, 162–63
Russia and Belarus: 2006 election and, 190; Belarus identification with Russia, 27, 58, 59, 60–62, 65, 69, 71–72; gas prices and Russian pressure, 190; relations with, 68–69, 71–72, 185, 190; Russia-Belarus Union key to economic stability, 8
Russia and European Union. *See* European Union and Russia
Russia and Moldova: foreign relations, 84–87; historical ties, 3, 13–14, 27, 139; language issues, 3, 22, 88–89; Moldova's economic exclusion, 142; negotiations regarding Transnistria, 90–92, 94; Russian support for Transnistria, 84, 85, 87, 118–19; trade, 5–6, 85, *86*
Russia and Ukraine: Crimea's position in power struggle, 168; gas deal with Russia (2006), 107, 162, 166–67; historical ties, 27, 32, 162–63; impact of Russia-West relationship, 7; implications of Orange Revolution, 165–68; pro-Russian government in Ukraine (2006), 2, 162; Russian interference post-independence, 7, 162–65; security threats of pro-Western Ukraine, 165–66, 169; Treaty on Friendship and Cooperation (1997), 47, 168; Ukraine's competing orientations to West and Russia, 2, 7, 27, 32, 162–63, 165, 170–71; Ukraine's membership in CES, 164; Ukraine's membership in CIS, 32, 45; Ukraine's policy toward Russia, 32, 47, 168

Schröder, Gerhard, 201
Seviarynetts, Paval, 179
Sharetsky, Siamon, 176
Shcharansky, Anatoly, 99
Shelest, Petro, 24

Shevchenko, Taras, 15
Shushkevich, Stanislau: acting head
    of state in Belarus (1991–94), 63;
    Belarus as "neo-Communist"
    society, 71; opposition to
    Lukashenka, 64, 65, 178; on
    Soviet identity of Belarus, 61
Siumar, Viktoriia, 159
Skoropadsky, Pavlo, 18
Skrebets, Siarhey, 182–83
Skrypnyk, Mykola, 21
Smirnov, Igor, 90, 218
Snegur, Mircea, 83, 84, 87
Solana, Javier, 201–2
Soviet Union: collapse in 1991 and
    CEE independence, 9, 37;
    declarations of independence by
    Ukraine, Belarus, Moldova
    (1991), 27; dissident movement,
    glasnost, and perestroika, 24–26;
    glasnost and dissent in SSRs,
    24–25, 82–84; indigenization
    and ethno-national republics,
    21, 22, 120–22, 130n11; late
    Soviet period in Belarus,
    Moldova, Ukraine, 23–27;
    Molotov-Ribbentrop Pact
    (1939), 22–23, 81–82, 140–41;
    "nationalizing state," 21–23;
    perestroika, 24–26, 82–84;
    security vacuum in former
    states, 37; Ukraine's Soviet state
    identity during Cold War, 35–37
Soviet Union and ethnic
    nationalism: concern about
    "bourgeois nationalism," 23–24;
    declarations of independence by
    Ukraine, Belarus, Moldova
    (1991), 27; dissident
    movements, glasnost, and
    perestroika, 24–26;
    indigenization and ethno-
    national republics, 21, 22,
    120–22, 130n11; nationalist plus
    socialist identity, 120–22;

nurturing of, 6, 27–28, 82,
    140–41; role of intelligentsia, 24,
    57, 59, 122, 124–25
Stakhiv, Yevhen, 100
Stalin, Joseph, 21–23, 25, 57, 59,
    69–70
Statkevich, Mikola, 179
Stăvilă, Ion, 150
Steinmeier, Frank-Walter, 170
Stratan, Andrei, 143
Strategy for European Integration
    (1998, Ukraine), 214
Straw, Jack, 202
Sturza, Ion, 88
Sukharenka, Stsiapan, 177
Supreme Headquarters Allied
    Powers Europe (SHAPE), 40
System Capital Management, 105
Szeged, Jacobovits de, 93, 143, 217

TACIS, 204, 205, 206–7
Taras Shevchenko Ukrainian
    Language Society, 25
Tarasiuk, Borys, 46, 215
Tarlev, Vasile, 88
Technical Assistance and
    Information Exchange (TAIEX),
    205
Tkachenko, Viktor, 102–3
To Stalin Bow, Europe, 69
Transcarpathia, 13, 17, 18, 20, 22
Trans-Dniester Republic. *See*
    Transnistria
Transnistria, 14, 22, 81, 83, 118. *See
    also* Transnistrian Moldovan
    Republic; *entries beginning with*
    Moldova
Transnistrian Moldovan Republic:
    declaration of independence
    (1991), 84, 118; economic
    importance, 129; EU's
    involvement in conflict, 87, 93,
    143, 145, 217–18; negotiations
    on status (2001–present), 90–92,
    93, 94, 143, 145, 217–18;

pan-Romanian sentiment, 118–19; recognition by Voronin (2007), 218; regional identity, not ethnic, 128–29; Russian involvement in conflict, 84, 85, 87, 90–92, 94, 118–19. *See also entries beginning with* Moldova

Treaty of Bucharest (1812), 139

Treaty of the European Union, 133

Treaty on Friendship and Cooperation (1997), 47, 168

Trenin, Dmitrii, 166, 168–69

Trotsky, Leon, 111

Tymoshenko, Yulia, 160–61, 167

Ukraine: 2004 election, 39, 50n12, 158, 164–65; basis for democracy, 2, 158, 160–62; competing East-West orientations, 2, 7, 27, 32, 162–63, 165, 170–71; corruption in government, 159; declaration of independence (1991), 27, 37–38; economic reform post-1994, 159–60; history pre-1939, 11–18, 19–20, 21–22; nationhood, factors leading to, 5, 10, 21, 24–25, 27–28; Orange parties (2004–6), 157–62; Orange parties' pro-Western focus, 2, 27, 41, 165; Orange Revolution, 39, 50n12, 158–62, 164–68; pro-Russian government coalition (2006), 2, 162; prospects for political change, 7, 162; Russia-West relationship, impact on Ukraine, 7, 168; Western diplomatic support, need for, 168–71; Yanukovych (*see* Yanukovych, Viktor); Yushchenko (*see* Yushchenko, Viktor). *See also* Donbas, Ukraine; NATO and Ukraine;

entries beginning with Ukrainian

Ukraine and European Union. *See* European Union and Ukraine

Ukraine and Russia. *See* Russia and Ukraine

Ukraine-Russian Treaty on Friendship and Cooperation, 47, 168

Ukrainian National Democratic Alliance, 20

Ukrainian national identity, 31–33, 35–37, 162. *See also* Ukrainian state identity and European security institutions

Ukrainian nationalism: Chernobyl disaster and, 25; first stage of movement (late eighteenth century), 15, 16–17; Polish assimilation efforts, 19–20; *Rukh* (Popular Movement for Restructuring), 25, 26, 100; during Soviet period, 20–22, 24–26, 100; during WWI, 18

Ukrainian People's Republic (1918), 18

Ukrainian Popular Movement for Perestroika (*Rukh*), 100

Ukrainian Soviet Socialist Republic: annexation of Western Ukraine by Soviets (1939), 22–23; Chernobyl disaster (1986), 25; declaration of sovereignty (1990), 26; dissident movement in 1960s, 24; late Soviet period, 23–27; *Rukh* (Popular Movement for Restructuring), 25, 26; Soviet policy of indigenization interwar, 21–22

Ukrainian state identity and European security institutions: ambiguity of Ukraine's intentions, 46–47, 48–49; CSCE/OSCE and, 36, 38–40; European dimension, 5, 31–33, 35, 46, 47–48; European Union

and (*see* European Union and Ukraine); institutions and state identity, 34–35; Kravchuk's European orientation (1991–94), 45–46; Kuchma's Russian and European orientation (1994–2004), 46–47, 214; NATO and (*see* NATO and Ukraine); post-1991, 31–33, 37–38; Russian dimension, 32, 47; Soviet identity during Cold War, 35–37; Soviet Union's collapse, impact of, 38; "Ukraine fatigue," 47, 48; Yushchenko's "Europe and Russia" policies, 47–48
Ungureanu, Mihai Razvan, 216–17
Uniate Church, 12, 14, 25
Union of Soviet Socialist Republics. *See* Soviet Union
Union Treaty (Belarus-Russia, 1997), 68–69, 185, 190
United Kingdom, 202, 210

Vachudova, Milada Anna, 148
Van Meurs, Wim, 81
Verheugen, Günter, 215
Viachorka, Vintsuk, 176, 187
Volchak, Aleh, 186
Voloshyn, Avhustyn, 20
Voronin, Vladimir: education reforms, 88–89; orientation toward West, 6, 92, 93, 142, 150, 151, 216; recognition of Transnistria (2007), 218; reorientation of Moldovan trade, 85; secret negotiations with Russia, 91, 94
Voytovich, Aliaksandr, 182–83

Wallachia, 13
Warsaw Pact, 35–36
Western Ukraine, 17–18, 22
Western Ukrainian People's Republic (1918), 18
World Trade Organization (WTO), 161, 170, 208
World War I and nationalism, 16, 17–18

Yanukovych, Viktor: 2006 election, 111, 164–65; on EU membership, 170; on NATO membership, 171; popularity in Donbas region, 106, 107–8, 111; prime minister under Kuchma (2002), 106–7, 171; prime minister under Yushchenko, 161–62; Russian support for, 164–65, 167
Yarmoshyna, Lidziia, 184, 188
Yekhanurov, Yurii, 161
Yeltsin, Boris, 64, 197
Yushchenko, Viktor: break-up of Orange coalition, 160–61; Donbas, attitude toward, 105, 106, 107–8; "Europe and Russia" foreign policy, 47–48; gas deal with Russia (2006), 107, 162, 166–67; leadership abilities, 160–62; NATO membership goal, 42, 48, 171, 215; positions pre-Orange Revolution, 105–6; as prime minister, 161–62; pro-EU stance, 170, 215; WTO membership goal, 161, 170

Zakharenka, Yuri, 176
Zhirinovskii, Vladimir, 64
Zviahilskyi, Yukhim, 104

Printed and bound by CPI Group (UK) Ltd, Croydon, CR0 4YY